Slonimsky's Book of
Musical Anecdotes

Slonimsky's
Book of
Musical Anecdotes

By Nicolas Slonimsky
Illustrated by Robert Bonotto

Routledge
New York and London

Published in 2002 by
Routledge
29 West 35th Street
New York, NY 10001

Published in Great Britain by
Routledge
11 New Fetter Lane
London EC4P 4EE

Routledge is an imprint of the Taylor & Francis Group.

Printed in the United States of America on acid-free
paper.

10 9 8 7 6 5 4 3 2 1

Cataloging-in-Publication Data is available from the
Library of Congress.

ISBN 0–415–93938–0

Table of Contents

APOLOGIA

This is a browsing book intended for non-consecutive reading, and it was put together non-consecutively on non-consecutive days.

Much of the raw material for this book has come from newspaper files and old music magazines, from 1784 on, which have yielded a surprising variety of musical perishables that seemed worth preserving, stories on music's great, anecdotes that breathe the air of contemporaneous authenticity and that have eluded the definitive biographies.

Thus, an old Belgian magazine has produced a chapter from unpublished memoirs by a French envoy to Vienna which reveals Beethoven's attitude to Napoleonic France, while a contemporary Panamanian publication supplied first-hand information on the personality of the late Spanish modernist, Manuel de Falla. Soviet magazines contributed fresh items on Prokofiev, Shostakovich and others. Rare musical Americana have been gathered from old music magazines published for more than a century past in New York and Boston.

Nineteenth-century musical journals yielded amusing tales about Rossini, Brahms, Wagner, and Liszt. Further along, there is an explanation of the origin of the German Three B's, the Russian Five, and the French Six. There are also quaint and curious stories of musical animals, and of queer inventions such as a musical bed or a

Victorian hoopskirt with a bird organ attachment. There is the amazing tale of the alleged discovery by a group of spiritualists in London of Schumann's forgotten Violin Concerto, the saga of singing commercials, and the extraordinary case of Stravinsky's involvement with the Boston police over a blue-note harmonization of the *Star-Spangled Banner*. There is a glancing survey of ragtime and jazz. There are assorted poems and limericks about music and musicians climaxing with a piece of verse shaped as a fiddle.

For indispensable help in the gathering of the raw materials for this book, heartfelt gratitude is due to the discriminating Frances Fink, the able Barbara Grund, and the alert Clare Alexander. But the biggest chunk of thanks goes to David Ewen, who has performed the crucial task of arranging the materials of the book in logical sequence, and has tactfully smoothed down some ragged paragraphs here and there.

Nicolas Slonimsky

Boston, February 29, 1948.

Slonimsky's Book of
Musical Anecdotes

I

INCIDENTAL MUSIC

Broadcasting by Telephone

In March 1904, the Boston papers carried a momentous announcement. A company with a reported capital
of two million dollars was incorporated in Massachusetts
for the purpose of piping music into American homes
and public restaurants by telephone wires. The inventor
of the system of telephone broadcasting was Theodore
Cahill, and his invention was called Cahill Telharmonic.
The Boston *Transcript* of March 30, 1904, gave the following description of the Telharmonic:

"The general plan is to establish a central station in every
large city. The best artists only will be employed, and the
music will be varied from Wagner to ragtime, to suit the
tastes and whims of the public. The machine is operated by
making and breaking electric circuits. When the plant is
in working order, one of the dreams of Edward Bellamy
will be realized. By the turning of the switch, the room or
hall or hospital will be filled with the music of the great

[3]

masters. There will be slumber music for the person troubled with insomnia, and there will be waking music to rouse the sleeper for the duties of the day. The service will be on the same plan as the telephone."

There was a feature article in *Harper's* Magazine showing the inventor amidst a bewildering agglomeration of funnel-shaped loud-speakers. There were stories about the new invention in music magazines. Busoni, who was eternally enthusiastic about new ways of spreading musical culture, wrote admiringly about the Telharmonic in his *Essay on New Esthetics in Music*. But despite these manifestations of interest, the whole idea was quietly dropped. Sixteen years after the incorporation of the Cahill Telharmonic, the first commercial broadcasts of musical programs were launched by wireless.

Opera by Cable

The first international opera broadcast was transmitted in 1896 over the cable connecting Calais and Dover. An opera performed at the Paris Grand Opera House was thus heard at the Pelican House in London where an electrophone, or a loud-speaking telephone, was installed. Contemporary reports glowed with excitement about this new achievement of the nineteenth century which one of the enthusiasts described as "the century of enlightenment, electricity, and music."

Gaspipe Radio

Long before Bellamy's prophecy of a central musical station, dreamers, inventors, and visionaries thought of devising a system whereby music could be acoustically piped into homes and public halls. At an exhibition in the Polytechnic of London, experiments were made as early as 1855, with gaspipes transmitting music. *The Builder* published an account of this "Music Laid on Like Gas."

"At the Polytechnic a band playing in a distant apartment is unheard; but connect the different instruments by means of thin rods of wood, each with the sounding board of a harp in the lecture theater, and the music is audible to all as if it were present. The experiments prove what we have often speculated on, that music might be laid onto the houses of a town from a central source, like gas or water."

Machine-made Music

The idea of mechanical music is not new. An instrument named the Componium, invented by M. Winkel of Amsterdam, was exhibited with great success in Paris in the year 1824. The inventor claimed that it could compose variations all by itself. The *Harmonicon* of 1824 reported:

"The astonishment of the hearers was at its height when, after having executed a march with variations by Moscheles, the instrument was left to follow its own inspirations; the applause was loud and unanimous, and some exclaimed that it was altogether miraculous. Still, the more perfect the execution, the stronger the feeling of incredulity became, the result of which was a general and decided opinion that the effects of the Componium could be produced only by some highly finished automaton."

To dispel such suspicions, several scientists were invited by the manufacturers of the Componium to examine the inner mechanism and to certify that no human manipulated the levers inside. The scientists, members of the French Academy, did so and on February 2, 1824 issued a report confirming the claims of the inventor:

"When the instrument has received a varied theme, it decomposes the variations of itself and reproduces their different parts in all the orders of possible permutations. None of the airs which it varies lasts above a minute. Yet through the principle of variability which it possesses, it might without ever resuming precisely the same combination, continue to play not only during years and ages but

[5]

during so immense a series of ages that though figures might be brought to express them, common language could not."

A *Musical Bicycle*

A patent for a musical bicycle was deposited in 1896. A music box is attached to the front forks of a bicycle, and is operated by means of a cord that revolves around a pulley fastened to the spokes. The inventor, an Iowa man, devised the musical bicycle especially for bicycle racing, claiming that the music would encourage the rider to make greater speed.

A *Musical Bed*

A French inventor of the 1880's contrived a musical bed which played a varied repertoire of melodies. The beds were constructed like a chain of music boxes, wound up like a clock and running as long as twelve hours. This enabled the insomniacs to idle away their sleepless hours listening to waltzes, quadrilles, or minuets. The musical bed was a fitting predecessor of the bedside radio set.

The Cylindrichord

Player-pianos seem to be more ancient than commonly believed. In January 1825, a French inventor, one Courcell, presented to the public a contraption which he called the Cylindrichord, and which, according to a credulous contemporary, "is found to be an admirable and efficient substitute for a first-rate performer on the pianoforte." The advantages in using the newly invented instrument are further outlined:

"In small or family parties, where dancing to the music of the pianoforte is practiced, one of the company had always been necessarily engaged at the instrument; that unpleasant necessity became obviated; for by the aid of the Cylindrichord, a person totally unacquainted with music, a child or a servant, may perform in the very best and most correct style quadrilles, waltzes, minuets, country dances, marches, songs, overtures, sonatas, choruses, or indeed any piece of music, however difficult. This instrument is extremely simple and differs altogether from the barrel or self-playing pianoforte: it can be accommodated to the height or dimensions of any pianoforte and, when not in use for that purpose, forms a piece of elegant furniture."

The Nototype

During the last years of life, Haydn was very much aware of his body's weakness. He complained in a letter (which is quoted in the article, *"Die Sonate auf der Schreibmaschine,"* published in the *Hamburger Fremdenblatt* of September 13, 1936):

"The piece on which I am now working would have been already finished if it were not that my hand gets tired of setting the notes on paper. Why doesn't some ingenious person invent a machine which would enable the afflicted composers to write the notes faster and with less fatigue?"

Many attempts to construct an efficient musical typewriter have been made, but composers still write their

[7]

symphonies and sonatas the hard way, putting notes on music paper manually. Yet in the case of the aging and ailing Haydn, a musical typewriter would have been a perfect solution. Another solution is to engage a musical amanuensis. Delius, the English composer of nostalgic mood pieces, was blind and paralyzed in the last years of his life. But his mind was alert and active, and his musical invention needed an outlet. Fortunately for him, a young English musician, Eric Fenby, volunteered to act as his musical secretary. Stretched in his invalid chair, Delius dictated to Fenby his ideas, note by note, correcting and revising as the work progressed until the piece was finished. Delius even managed to dictate a complete orchestral score, entitled *A Song of Summer*. It was performed for the first time by the British Broadcasting Company Orchestra under Sir Henry Wood on September 17, 1931, and the composer had the unique pleasure of hearing a broadcast of that performance in his room in a French village where he spent the last years of his life.

It is conceivable that even a blind man could use a musical typewriter by the touch system, and it is further conceivable that such a typewriter would play back the notes and chords with the aid of some electronic gadget, so that the composer could check on the results.

The most promising musical typewriter was put on the market in Germany in 1937. It was called Nototype. It had a standard keyboard of forty-four keys, with the carriage slightly widened. A special hand lever controlled the vertical line for typing chords. The upper row of the typewriter keys was given to clefs, numerals for time signatures, sharps, flats, and bar lines. The second row was given to notes of the musical staff below the third line, and on the third line itself. The third row carried the notes above the middle line, and the lowest row had stems from a quarter note to a sixty-fourth note.

Rests, dots, and other signs were distributed among the corner keys of all four rows of the typewriter, just as punctuation, quotation marks, and the less frequent letters of the alphabet are tucked away in the corners of the regular typewriter.

Typewritten music is a convenient substitute for engraving, less costly, and more practical for the publication of non-commercial music. Musical typing need not be more difficult than handling a stenotype machine. Each key on a musical typewriter may be assigned a special sound. A musical office, with musical secretaries typing music, may not produce celestial harmony, but the typing polyphony will be both novel and impressive.

Phonographic Typewriter

Every modern music machine had its granddaddy or perhaps its grand uncle. The *Musical World* of February 25, 1871 reports the invention by a Frenchman of a machine for writing music by an electrical contact with the piano keyboard:

"The inventor passes over a metal cylinder, turning regularly by means of a clock movement and communicating with a battery, a band of paper impregnated with a solution that will decompose under the influence of an electric current. The clock movement may be put in motion or stopped at will by an electric or mechanical stop. The band of paper, being placed on the cylinder, the inventor places above it a series of metal wires or plates, isolated from each other in such a way that as they rest at one point on the paper in a parallel direction to the axis of the cylinder, they each communicate, by means of a separate metallic wire, with a contact apparatus placed under each of the keys of the keyboard of the instrument. These contact apparatuses are worked by the motion of the key, either by bringing together two wires or metallic plates, or by plunging one point in a jar of mercury communicating with the battery. The circuit is thus closed for each of the wires only when the key corresponding to it is lowered."

[9]

A Musical Petticoat

The Boston *Musical Times* of September 1860 described an extraordinary invention, a musical petticoat, credited to a Parisian couturier:

"With the aid of scientific mechanism, the crinoline is inflated like a life-preserver. The elegant wearer need only touch a spring arranged to communicate with the pocket of her dress, and the air in the skirt sets in motion a musical attachment, not unlike a bird organ, playing a variety of tunes from the gems of the operas to a nursery lullaby. The inventor declares that the ballroom orchestra may be entirely dispensed with in the future. The ladies wearing his musical petticoats can provide themselves with waltzes, quadrilles, and polkas to their hearts' content."

Modern Ballet A.D. 1883

The modern ballet with characters representing the machines of the modern age was anticipated by the "electrical ballet" presented at the Vienna Electrical Exhibition in 1883. A contemporary accounts reports:

"The chief features were the electromagnets, dynamo machines, telegraph apparatus, and telephones, which were dragged on the stage by fantastic goblins and handled by the graceful danseuses with as much ease as if they were especially trained in the mysteries of electricity."

The Anthropoglossos

On January 5, 1939 a machine looking like a steno-graphic typewriter, named Voder, was exhibited at the Franklin Institute in Philadelphia. It synthetized the primary hisses and buzzes into human song or speech, speaking with the deliberate impersonality of a robot. As often happens in the history of invention, the thing was anticipated many decades before. It was called the Anthropoglossos, and the name undoubtedly impressed the innocents who flocked to watch it perform at St. James's Hall in London during the summer of 1864. The *Musical World* reported:

"The inventor of this extraordinary piece of mechanism is M. Saguish of Constantinople. It represents the head and shoulders of a human being holding in his mouth a trumpet through which issues the sound of the human voice. This extraordinary automaton head sings a variety of songs in so perfect a manner that it is impossible to believe it is produced by mechanism alone. The words of the song are heard quite distinctly, the quality of the voice (a tenor) although somewhat nasal, is exceedingly agreeable, and the inventor altogether one of the most astonishing in this age of miracles. The program consisted of *The Dark Girl Is Dressed in Blue, Polly Perkins, Annie Lisle, A Gypsy's Life Is a Joyous Life, God Bless the Prince of Wales,* and·*God Save the Queen.* The exhibition is to be varied daily. Every curious inquirer will go and hear the Anthropoglossos."

Talking Machine A.D. 1846

Miracle machines and mechanical contraptions always found an admiring public a hundred years ago. Chopin, who was inordinately gullible, was very much impressed with a "talking machine" exhibited in Europe in the 1840's. He wrote to his parents on October 11, 1846:

"Mr. Faber of London, a professor of mathematics and a mechanician, has exhibited a very ingenious automaton which he calls Euphonia, and which pronounces fairly clearly not one or two words, but whole sentences and, still more surprising, sings an air of Haydn and *God Save the Queen*. If opera directors could have many such *androids*, they could do without chorus singers who cost a lot and give a lot of trouble."

Two-headed Nightingale

The sensational success of Jenny Lind, the "Swedish Nightingale" imported by Barnum to America a hundred years ago, inspired envy among other impresarios. Numerous "nightingales" of various nationalities were announced in the theaters. The most spectacular of all was Millie Christine, the "two-headed nightingale" who sang a duet with herself. She was advertised as having "two heads, four arms, and four feet, which in perfect body meet." Whether Millie Christine was really a pair of Siamese twins or simply two little ladies sewn together under a common bodice only the insiders knew.

Four-handed Pianist

The following story published in the *Musical World* of September 6, 1851 makes all comment superfluous.

"Count Orloff has just presented to the Emperor of Russia an extraordinary musical phenomenon in the person of young Frederick Holtz. This man was born with four hands, each having five fingers. He was brought up by a clergyman, who taught him to play on the organ, but the young man made a pianoforte for himself of considerably greater power than that of ordinary instruments. He enjoys excellent health and, with the exception of his hands, presents nothing strange in his person. The arm divides from the elbow into two limbs, each ending in a hand with a double supply of fingers. These additional arms are regularly made, and the only remarkable point observed by medical men is the immense development of the deltoid muscle at the summit of the shoulder. The clergyman, at his death, left Holtz some property, and the young man immediately purchased diamond rings with which he loaded his twenty fingers. Then he performed before the Emperor of Russia, who expressed his surprise at the musical powers of the young man."

Polyvocal Singer

Audiences and music critics of the past century must have been much more gullible than in our modern era. How else explain the appearance of a story in *Indépendence Belge* of 1850 about a polyvocal singer, one Signor Zoni? He was described as "an artist unique of his kind who has contrived, thanks to a special endowment of nature developed by sedulous labor, to make his vocal organ a veritable orchestra." His most successful number was the imitation of a music box, in which he sang, with his naked larynx, so to speak, the imitation of a woodwind ensemble.

Solo Duet and Quartet

In the Victor recording of Bach's D minor Concerto

for two violins and orchestra, the part of the first violin is played by Jascha Heifetz. The part of the second violin is played by—Jascha Heifetz. The trick is easily explained. Heifetz recorded the Concerto playing the first violin part. Then the record was played back. He fitted the second violin part into the music, and the whole thing was rerecorded. The auditory illusion of a live duet is perfect.

A Columbia recording achieves an even greater phonographic miracle: Nelson Eddy is heard singing simultaneously the four voices of four-part hymns.

Music Critic's Burial Money

When an impecunious music critic died in Vienna, his colleagues made a round of local musicians to raise money for the funeral.

"How much is my share?" asked one of them.

"Thirty kronen," was the reply.

"Here's sixty kronen," said the musician. "Bury two music critics."

Bisexual Organist

The Music Committee for London schools advertised for "a candidate as organist and music teacher." One of the replies came in the following letter:

"Gentlemen, I noticed your advertisement for an organist and music teacher, either lady or gentleman. Having been both for several years, I offer you my services."

The Reverse of the Opposite

Among orchestral musicians notorious for their reverse English, a certain radio conductor occupies a special niche of honor. Here are some of his more brilliant malapropisms:

"If you don't know what I'm talking about, write it down."

"Take a pencil and put a cross around it."

"If I would tell you the truth, I would be a hypocrite."

"Play as I tell you, and everything will be topsy-turvy."

"You are playing the reverse of the opposite."

When at a rehearsal he could not get the right tempo, he finally proposed to the orchestra: 'I know what! I will conduct a little slower, you play a little faster, and we'll hit it exactly right." And once he announced to the players that he felt so nervous "they had to give me an epidemic in the arm."

Cannibalistic Flutes

John Constance Davis, Esq., in his book comprehensively entitled *Letters from Paraguay Written by a Gentleman of Liberal Education and Considerable Property Who, Having Been Disappointed in His Hopes for Happiness with a Beloved Female To Relieve the Distress of His Mind Resolved To Travel* relates that in Paraguay he saw a musical instrument "somewhat resembling the pipes of Pan, made out of the bones of one of the missionaries they sacrificed among them some years ago."

That human bones were utilized by South American and Mexican Indians for the manufacture of drums and flutes is certain. The National Museum of Mexico possesses several specimens of notched human femurs which were used to accentuate the rhythm of native songs and dances. In the National Museum in Rio de Janeiro, there is a clarinet with a human skull for a bell. But human bones were not always used by the Indians as impersonal paraphernalia. There is a touching tale of a Peruvian musician who fell in love with a beautiful Indian girl. When she was prematurely struck down by death, he secretly removed the tibia bone from her body and made a flute out of it. As night would fall with equatorial suddenness, he would take out his keepsake flute and play upon it a wistful love song.

The Obstreperous Harmonium

The *Musical World* of August 30, 1862 reports a nightmarish occurrence which sounds like Hoffmann's *Tales*:

"In a small church at a little village near Brighton where the congregation could not afford to pay an organist, they recently bought a self-acting organ, a compact instrument well-suited to the purpose and constructed to play forty different tunes. The sexton had instructions how to set it going and how to stop it; but unfortunately he forgot the latter part of his business. After singing the first four verses of a hymn before the sermon, the organ could not be stopped, and it continued playing two verses more. Then just as the clergyman completed the words, 'Let us pray,' the organ clicked and started a fresh tune. The minister sat it out patiently. When he renewed his introductory words, 'Let us pray,' the organ went off again and started another tune. The sexton and others continued their exertions to find the spring, but no man could put a stop to it. They got four of the stoutest men in the church to shoulder the perverse instrument, and they carried it out down the center aisle of the church, playing away, into the churchyard where it continued clicking and playing until the entire forty tunes were finished."

[16]

Music Criticism — Pleasant and Unpleasant

Some pointed reviews that are as definite as they are brief:

"Mr. X conducted Brahms's First Symphony. Brahms lost."

"Miss Y gave a song recital last night. Why?"

"The orchestra men can play Tchaikovsky's Fifth Symphony in their sleep, and very often do."

There was a review by Irving Kolodin which noted that Korngold's Violin Concerto had more corn than gold; and there was a remark of an anonymous critic that a performance of Chopin's *Minute* Waltz gave the listeners a bad quarter of an hour.

When a baker, who was also an amateur musician, published a song, a waggish music critic described it as a "yeaster-hymn; it begins with *dough*, rises rapidly, but soon falls flat."

Eugène d'Albert, asked to give his opinion of a new piano concerto by a mediocre German composer, Max Vogrich, examined the manuscript carefully and returned it with this comment: "The ink and paper are excellent."

Some pointed reviews are more brief than definite:

Reviewing a Paderewski concert, a music critic waxed enthusiastic about Paderewski's pedaling. "At the hands of Paderewski," he wrote, "the pedal becomes a thing of singular beauty."

Often a misprint combined with a dubious metaphor results in a comic image. A Boston critic opined that Josef Hofmann was a pianist of but a single facet. His review came out this way in print: "Hofmann is an artist of but a single faucet, but what a faucet!"

One critic noted that a certain musician was blowing "his own horn with his tongue in his cheek" — an extraordinary trick for any brass player to perform.

[17]

The pianist Rosenthal once looked over the manuscript of a piano concerto which had been submitted to him by a friend and displayed great agitation. "It is extraordinary," he hept repeating. "Just imagine! The whole first movement hasn't a single solitary theme in it. Nobody has ever achieved so much sound with so little essence."

Paderewski versus Piano

When Paderewski reached New Orleans on his triumphant American tour in 1896, the New Orleans *Item*, which never harbored a music critic, sent a prizefight reporter to review the concert. The following was the result:

"I am here to say that in my opinion he is the best two-handed piano fighter that ever wore hair. He looked like a licked man when he left his corner shuffling his feet across the stage with his fins dangling like a pair of empty stirrups. It looked like a cinch for the piano. Then all of a sudden, he swings his left on the bass end of the keyboard with a smash that rattles the chandeliers. After landing heavily with his left on the stomach of Mr. Piano, he got in a right hand smash or two over the heart that would put any ordinary box of wires out of the business. After some sparring at long range, he commenced fiddling for the head again with the right, running the fingers of his left through his hair.

"Paddy let up a bit in the second round. For an opener, he took on one of those soft, easy things. Anyhow, it gave the piano a chance to get its second wind. The man with the mess of hair saved all his steam for the final round. The air in front of that piano was filled with flying hands and hair. The practiced ear might have picked out of the crash and jumble a concord of sweet sounds, but I was too busy looking to listen. If I were a piano, I wouldn't travel as Paderewski's sparring partner for two-thirds of the gross receipts."

Dangerous Opera

The opera *Charles VI* by Halévy had a strange history. It was banned in Paris after its initial presentation in

[18]

1843 because the spectacle of a weak king going insane resembled too closely the character of the then king of France, Louis Philippe. The opera was revived seven years later during the Second Republic. But by the strangest coincidence, on three successive performances someone in the audience dropped dead after the aria, "God Punish Him and Strike Him Low." In 1858 Napoleon III commanded a revival of the opera. On his way to the theater, revolutionists threw a bomb at the imperial coach. Napoleon and the empress escaped uninjured, but there were many killed in the crowd. The performance of *Charles VI* was canceled on that night, and the opera has long since been dropped from the active repertoire.

Conductorless Orchestras

Among the most prized musical collectors' items is a recording made during one of the orchestral rehearsals under the direction of a world-famous conductor. Visitors are banned at his rehearsals but someone managed to install a hidden microphone and made this recording. The classical strains of great music superbly phrased are here frequently interrupted by outbursts of bilingual abuse and vituperation that is more fascinating than the music itself. Invocations to pagan and Christian dieties alternate with personal advice to some of the players to take up the sewing machine instead of their particular instruments. It is said that the conductor found out about the existence of this recording and tried to suppress it but found the task as impossible as the proverbial attempt of a movie star to destroy every single print of a candid film imprudently made by her in her days of struggle toward film stardom.

Most conductors are autocrats by nature, and orchestral players accept their outbursts as an inevitable evil. But once in a while a cry is heard: "Down with conductors!" Such a cry led to the formation of the first conductorless orchestra of modern times. It was the Persimfans, the abbreviation of *Pervyi Simfonicheskyi Ansambl*, i.e., First Symphonic Ensemble, which was launched in Moscow in February 1922. The idea behind the formation of this conductorless orchestra was in keeping with the revolutionary trends of the first years of the Soviet Republic. Capitalist bosses were liquidated or otherwise removed from social life; why then keep musical bosses?

The First Symphonic Ensemble presented five seasons of concerts featuring classical and modern works. The quality of performance was high. Leading political and artistic personalities of Soviet Russia praised the accomplishments of the new organization. The Chairman of the Council of People's Commissars declared:

"The principle of conductorless performance based on collective creative activity is a revolutionary step in music and is profoundly consonant with our epoch. As a pioneer of symphonic music carried to the factories and Red Army barracks, the First Symphonic Ensemble gives a vivid demonstration of excellent results attained by collective work. This is particularly important at the present stage of the reconstruction of national economy which can be successfully accomplished only with the collective participation of working masses."

The Vice-Chairman of the Council voiced a similar sentiment:

"The idea of collectivism is particularly important in our time, and its realization in the domain of Soviet music should be regarded as a significant accomplishment."

Still another representative of the Soviet government declared:

"The First Symphonic Ensemble has dispensed with the conductor and thus demonstrated that even in such a complex process as the interpretation of a musical composition, the individual will and knowledge brought by a conductor may be replaced by a collective interpretation of musical

[20]

works. The First Symphonic Ensemble is particularly near and dear to every Soviet listener because in its work it has reaffirmed the power of collectivism as a guiding principle in the revolutionary transformation of the social and economic system. My wish is that the First Symphonic Ensemble should be followed by similar ensembles in Russia and abroad, and that its basic idea should embrace not only interpreters but composers of music as well. For in the final analysis, musical composition must adopt a similar principle of the collective creation."

The President of the State Academy of Fine Arts joined the official representatives of the Soviet government in endorsing the conductorless orchestra. He declared:

"The First Symphonic Ensemble is an epoch making organization. It is connected with the idea of collectivism which inspired us all in the first unforgettable days of the Revolution. The romanticism of those days is dead, but the First Symphonic Ensemble is alive, and it carries this idea into life. It has retained its principles in the revolutionary storms, and has forever established itself as a unique artistic organism."

But despite this encouragement on the part of important personalities in the Soviet Union, the First Symphonic Ensemble soon began to show inner contradictions. The first violinist of the orchestra was often referred to as the actual leader, for he gave the tempo at the beginning of the performance and often regulated instrumental balance by signaling with his head and his body. Then suddenly the First Symphonic Ensemble began to disintegrate. Conductors from abroad were invited to lead it in guest appearances. It was found that less time was lost with a competent conductor in settling the tempi and the dynamics than during the conductorless regime. By 1928, the conductorless orchestra was no more.

A conductorless orchestra was organized in New York

[21]

in the 1920's and gave several concerts of competently performed music. But again there were sly references in the music press to the first violinist's being "the conductor of the conductorless orchestra." Economic insolvency soon forced the New York edition of the Persimfans to fold up. Conductors took over once more. They shouted and ranted during rehearsals. They grimaced at the players during concerts. But they delivered highly polished performances. The musicians often wished that one day the conductor would drop dead. They prayed that some other conductor would be engaged to lead the orchestra. But the necessity of having a conductor was admitted by all. The conductorless days were over.

Seduction with Music

In his famous novel, *The Kreutzer Sonata*, Tolstoy blamed Beethoven's music for the adultery committed by the hero and heroine of the story. He thought that the last movement of the *Kreutzer* Sonata undermined the moral sense.

The seductiveness of a musical composition is a matter of conjecture. But when, in 1937, Warner Brothers produced a picture entitled *The Fire Bird*, in which a girl is seduced to the strains of a record playing Stravinsky's ballet music of that name, Stravinsky sued the company for defamation of character and asked for ten thousand dollars' damages. The suit was heard in a Paris court. The judges, steeped in the Gallic tradition, failed to see anything wrong about seduction, with or without ballet music. Stravinsky was awarded only the symbolic sum of one French franc.

Perilous Overtones

Music can kill or maim people and break china. At a concert of "stereophonic" music presented in Carnegie

Hall on April 9, 1940, the sounds varied in acoustical power by as much as ten billion times. According to the tests of the Bell laboratory for acoustics, at the level of 120 decibels (units of loudness composed of the words "deci" for decimal and "bel" for Bell), the sound becomes painful. The New York *Times* ran the headlines for the concert: SOUND WAVES 'ROCK' CARNEGIE HALL. TONES NEAR LIMIT THAT THE HUMAN EAR CAN ENDURE.

Sound waves have never killed a man, but they can kill small animals at short range. Then there is the field of soundless sound, the supersonics, which a human ear cannot hear. In 1942, the United States Navy experimented with these high vibrations as a means of sinking the German submarines.

There have been many stories of singers with voices powerful enough to shatter mirrors and windowpanes. Caruso was credited with playing practical jokes at dinner parties by breaking wine glasses with a high C or making a glass chandelier echo some notes of his arias, though the legend was never substantiated. But Manuel Garcia, the famous vocal teacher, told a friend that the bass, Luigi Lablache, sang a high D into a wine glass, shattering it to smithereens. In the High School for Girls at Herts, England, the school mistress raised her voice in the 1945 Greek class to an an unusually high pitch; much to the amusement of the girls, the sound lifted a glass inkwell on the desk. A reader protested in a letter to the London *Times* of February 2, 1947, that a radio singer's high soprano note in Puccini's *Madama Butterfly* had broken a tumbler on his dining-room table, showering him with glass; he implied that a suit for damages might result from such radio breakage of valuable china. So far, however, no singer has been able to demonstrate before a body of impartial and skeptical observers the capacity of breaking glass by the sheer power of vocal overtones. And there the matter rests.

[23]

Singing in Extremis

Skeptical opera lovers like to point out that the unfortunate heroine of *La Traviata* shows a rather sturdy constitution for a consumptive by singing for a whole act before expiring. But here is a sad report of a young singer's suicide that occurred in New Orleans in 1871 which, from the medical standpoint, is even more extraordinary than the consumptive cadenzas of Violetta. A contemporary journal reports the events:

"The suicide of Amelia Garcia, in New Orleans, has excited unusual sympathy. Deceived by a lover, for whom she had given up society and the profession she loved, she procured some laudanum and so ended her days. The people in the neighborhood of her residence say that about the time that the poison must have commenced its fatal work she seated herself at the piano and played and sang for more than an hour. Her rich, thrilling voice, running to its full compass, reveled in the sweetest music they had ever heard. Strains of passionate grief mingled with the sorrowing cadence of a funeral dirge as the dying cantatrice sang her life away. She was twenty-three years of age, a native of the West Indies. Her father was a Spanish Creole and her mother a German Jewess."

Medicinal Music

Music as a panacea was mentioned as early as 1896 when a "bower" was opened in New York where "fair" patients were cured of their ills: piano, harp, and mandolin played." There was a specific instrument for every ailment, in accordance with the homeopathic principle.

Long-Hair Musicians

A Boston medical journal of 1892 presents the theory that music has a tonic influence on the growth of hair. Twelve percent of composers are bald, which is just about average; but instrumental performers retain their

hair to an old age. Pianists and violinists are particularly distinguished by good heads of hair. On the other hand, the playing of brass instruments is conducive to baldness. Physicians even refer to "trumpet baldness" because so many trumpeters lose their hair. The explanation is that in blowing hard, the blood is drawn to the head, making the hair fall out.

Tarantella and Tarantula

One of the most persistent myths in musicology is that the Italian dance, tarantella, owes its name to the fact that it had curative effect on Italians bitten by the tarantula spider. Of course, the tarantella has nothing to do with the tarantula. It is simply a dance originated in the Italian town of Taranto.

A solemn account by an anonymous writer relates the method of curing spider poisoning:

"In the southern parts of Italy persons are sometimes bitten by a largish sort of spider called tarantula. At certain periods of the year, the person that has been once so bitten feels a pain about the wounded part accompanied with dejection of spirits, sallowness, etc. If sprightly music be played (and a certain jig, called the tarantella, is generally played on such occasions), the patient gets up and begins to dance with irregular gestures; the quickness of his movements generally increases to a certain degree; and the dance continues sometimes for hours without intermission. At last the patient, fatigued and exhausted, throws himself down on the floor or on a chair or a bed to recruit his strength; and the fit is over for that time. The remarkable part is that this exertion cannot be produced without music."

Lord's Prayer, Copyright

The chairman of a women's club wrote in to the publishers of a best-selling song to the words of the Lord's Prayer asking for permission to reprint the text in the club's concert program. The publishers replied, graciously granting the request.

Rimsky, Arranged by Korsakov

An apprentice radio announcer in charge of broadcasting recorded music, announced a Stokowski arrangement of Bach's Toccata as composed by Mr. Bach Stokowski. The music supervisor of the station explained to him that when there are double names, the first is the composer and the second the arranger. The next time when Rimsky-Korsakov's *Flight of the Bumblebee* was broadcast, the announcer introduced it as a piece by Rimsky, arranged by Korsakov.

Half an Octave Down

Studio engineers at radio stations are notoriously lacking in musical knowledge. During a rehearsal of a string ensemble, the radio engineer told the conductor that the violins sounded too high for good transmission.

"Okay," said the conductor, "I'll have them play an octave lower."

"Half an octave will be enough," replied the engineer.

Musical Definitions

The following are actual quotations from school papers:

"Wagner was born in the year 1813, supposedly on his birthday."

"Mandolins are high officials in China."

"The correct way to find the key to a piece of music is to use a pitch fork."

"A sound vibration can only be heard when it makes a noise."

"There are many Russian composers who are radically different only I can't spell their names."

"Sibelius is a nationalist. He is Polish through and through."

"Beethoven's wife and children were always quarreling and made him all the deafer."

"Libretto was an Italian who wrote *Tannhäuser*."

"An interval in music is the distance from one piano to the next."

"Syncopation is emphasis on a note that is not in the piece."

[27]

"Contralto is a low sort of music that only ladies sing."

"Vibrations are osculations to and fro."

"In conducting, only the down beat should be struck downward."

"Beethoven wrote three symphonies: the First, the Fifth, and the Ninth."

"Bach was the master of the fudge, also the feud."

"A bassoon is one-eighth Negro."

"Robinson Caruso was a great singer who lived on an island."

"An oboe is a sort of transient or a tramp."

"The best 'cello players are those with bow legs."

"Folk music is colored people singing what they thought about their parents."

Translations into French

The following phrases for a French primer were suggested by a disillusioned musician of the 1880's:

Does the handsome (*jolie*) daughter of the butcher take music lessons on the voice? No, but the ugly sister of the baker is studying piano.

Has she *(a-t-elle)* any capacity? No, but she has a temperamental music teacher. Who has hurt your sister? Nobody has hurt her: she is singing *Sweet Violets.*

What is the matter with the poor young man? Has he a fit? No, he has not a fit: he is playing a violin solo.

Where are you going? I am going to my hour of musical instruction. I shall return in twenty minutes.

Lord Monday

An English lord who was enamored of the prima donna, Henrietta Sontag, was nicknamed Lord Montag because he followed her with the same inevitability as Monday (*Montag*) follows Sunday (*Sonntag*).

Madame Sontag was also the subject of the worst possible musical joke, published in the *Musical Standard* of 1870:

"We hang on every note Madame Sontag sings —
This proves the lady's great power of execution."

What's in a Name?

The following program would certainly puzzle the most authoritative musicologist:

Overture to "Rienzi" . . . . . . Cartwright
Les Préludes . . . . Flour
Invitation to the Dance . . . . . Weaver
Scherzo . . . . Son-of-Mendel
Largo . . . . Trades
Air on the G string . . . . Stream
Blue Danube . . . . Ostrich
Moldau . . . . Sourmilk
Egmont Overture . . . . . Beet Gardens

Such billing would ensue if the conductor would translate not only the titles of the pieces but the names of composers. Wagner would become Wagoner, or Cartwright. Liszt means flour in Hungarian; Weber is Weaver. Mendelssohn is Mendel's son — hence the double S in the name. Handel, or Händel in German spelling, is the plural of the word *Handel* which means trade or business. Bach is Stream. (German writers speak of Bach as the fountainhead of the mighty stream of music). Strauss means either an ostrich or a bouquet of flowers. Smetana is sour milk. As to Beethoven, whose grandfather was born in Holland, the Beet in the name is identical with the English word Beet, and Hoven is the plural of the Dutch word for garden, similar to the German word *Hof*. Beethoven, consequently, is Beet Gardens. A conscientious biographer ought to investigate whether Beethoven liked beet soup, and whether he ever cultivated a beet patch.

Polytonal Music Lore

George Bernard Shaw is critical of the piano as a musical instrument. As long ago as 1894, he wrote in the *Fortnightly Review* that "time will come when we shall regard the piano as an execrable, jangling, banging, mistuned nuisance."

The celebrated Cardinal Newman cared little for music. In his treatise, *The Idea of a University,* he opined:

"Stuffing birds or playing stringed instruments is an elegant pastime, and a resource to the idle, but it is not education."

Jerome Kern declared in an interview that he got his best melodies from bird calls during his stay at the Austin Ornithological Research Station. The most melodic bird in his estimation is Melospiza Melodia.

The following advertisement appeared in the Fremont, Ohio, *News-Messenger* in 1947: "Help wanted: Base vile player to play with small orchestra."

Wagner did not like the saxophone. He said it "sounds like the word *Reckankreuzungsklankewerkzeuge.*"

Mascagni, who was skeptical about the average intelligence of a tenor, used to say that there are three degrees of comparison in the Italian language, *Stupido, Stupidissimo,* and *Tenore.*

"Brahms — what a pianist! One of ten thumbs!" — Philip Hale.

"Hell is full of musical amateurs. Music is the brandy of the damned."—George Bernard Shaw.

"I love Wagner, but the music I prefer is that of a cat hung up by his tail outside of a window, and trying to stick to the panes of glass with its claws. There is an odd grating on the glass which I find at the same time strange, irritating, and singularly harmonious."— Baudelaire.

"A true music lover is one who on hearing a blonde soprano singing in the bathtub puts his ear to the keyhole."— Anon.

"The opera house is an institution differing from other lunatic asylums only in the fact that its inmates have avoided official certification." — Ernest Newman.

"Jazz will endure as long as people hear it through their feet instead of their brains."— John Philip Sousa.

MELOPIA MELODIA.

"Music is neither secular nor religious. It can at best suggest the beating of the pulse, the rhythm of the blood that accompanies a given order of ideas."— Henry Noel Brailsford.

"Listen to music religiously as if it were the last strain you might hear."— Henry David Thoreau.

"Music is the only divine art we are promised in heaven, and it is certainly the only divine art with which we are tortured on earth." — Mrs. John Lane.

"Music is a kind of counting performed by the mind without knowing that it is counting." — G. W. Leibniz.

"Music helps not the toothache."— George Herbert.

"Music softens, and often rubs out, the cares of the day."— William Feather.

"If one hears bad music, it is one's duty to drown it in conversation."— Oscar Wilde.

"What classic opera needs to succeed in the United States is a hero who can tell the heroine 'I love you' in less than twenty minutes."— Alexander Smallens.

"Beware of the person who says he never goes to concerts because the people, the hall, etc., prevent him from enjoying the music: he is first cousin to the numerous family of those who 'have no time for reading,' the truth being that music bores him — though he dares not say so."— Edward Sackville-West.

"The musician who invented swing ought to."— O. O. McIntyre.

"Musick and women I cannot but give way to, whatever my business is."— Samuel Pepys.

"An old millionaire had waited a long time for his daughters to get ready for a concert. Finally he shouted upstairs: 'What a time you girls take! Look at me —a bit of cotton in each ear, and I'm ready.' "— David Bispham.

"Music is essentially useless, as life is."— George Santayana.

"What I love best about music is the women who listen to it."— Jules de Goncourt.

"Nothing is capable of being well set to music that is not nonsense."— Joseph Addison.

"Of bestial howling and entirely frantic vomiting up of hopelessly damned souls through their still carnal throats, I have heard more than, please God, I will ever endure the hearing of again in one of His summers."— Ruskin (upon hearing a secular cantata).

"Chloroform, they say, will raise the voice and increase the volume of it. The hearer should take it with the singer."— Philip Hale.

"Nothing is wrong when done to music."—Jerome Kern.

"The difference between a good and a bad conductor is that one has the score in his head, and the other has his head in the score."— F. H. Cowen (often misattributed to Hans von Bülow).

"When I was young, I was only the son of Moses Mendelssohn, the philosopher, and now that I am old, I am only the father of Felix Mendelssohn."— Abraham Mendelssohn (first reported in the *Musical World*, March 21, 1839).

"Music is the only noise for which one is obliged to pay."— Attributed to Dumas.

"I know only two tunes: one is *Yankee Doodle*, and other isn't."— U. S. Grant.

"Discords make the sweetest airs."—George Gershwin.

"Music critics are the Tin Ear Brigade."— Jerome Kern.

"A love song is just a caress set to music."— Sigmund Romberg.

"Nightingales sing badly."— Jean Cocteau.

"The skin of all of us is responsive to gypsy songs and military marches."— Jean Cocteau.

"The ear disapproves but tolerates certain musical pieces; transfer them into the domain of our nose, and we will be forced to flee."— Jean Cocteau.

"This birdman, this scarecrow — it's the conductor."— Jean Cocteau.

"What is folklore? I am folklore."— Villa-Lobos.

"A singer is somebody who insists on giving *Silent Night* at the top of his voice."— Boston *Globe* (December 20, 1947).

A Musicologist's Nightmare

The surest way to drive a music scholar daffy is to look up Krakowiak in the *Harvard Dictionary of Music.* It says: "See Cracovienne." You look up Cracovienne. It says: "See Krakowiak."

Boiled Eggs Allegro Moderato

The musical journals of 1882 report the latest hit tune, the *Boiled Eggs Polka,* by one Hardtberg of Berlin, which is useful not only for dancing but also for boiling three-minute eggs with unfailing accuracy. The instructions in the sheet music read:

"Put your eggs into boiling water; then play the Boiled Eggs Polka, allegro moderato; immediately upon finishing the music, take your eggs out of the saucepan, and they will be ready to serve."

Russian Tintinnabulations

Mark Twain's tour de force in translating into English the French translation of one of his short stories has nothing on Rachmaninoff's choral work, *Kolokola,* "Russian poem by K. Balmont, adapted from *The Bells* by E. A. Poe, with an English translation by Fanny S. Copeland." The Russian poem runs like this:

"Slyshish sani mtchatsa, mtchatsa vryad,
  Kolokoltchiki zvenyat
O kak zvonko, zvonko, zvonko
Totchno zvutchny smeh rebyonka."

This is retranslated into English with the following results:

"Listen, hear the silver bells"
  (Poe: Hear the sledges with the bells)
"How they charm our weary senses with a sweetness
      that compels"
  (Poe: What a world of merriment their melody
      foretells).
And further:

"Hear the tolling of the bells,
  Mournful bells!"
    (Poe: Iron bells!)
"Bitter end to fruitless dreaming their stern monody
    foretells!
What a world of desolation in their iron utterance dwells!"
    (Poe: What a world of solemn thought their monody
      compels!)

Outnumbered Piano Tuners

In the summer of 1947 there were sixteen million pianos in the United States and only three thousand piano tuners to keep the pianos tuned up. The American Society of Piano Technicians has disclosed that the average age of piano tuners is fifty-four and that there are few young men willing to take up apprenticeship in

[35]

this highly specialized profession. The Piano Technicians, pointing out that there is only one piano tuner for more than five thousand pianos, view the situation with alarm.

Yaw's High E

The honor of being able to sustain the highest soprano note belonged to the American singer, Ellen Beach Yaw, whose range encompassed the E an octave above the E over high C. "Of course," admitted Miss Yaw, "I cannot give much musical value to a note as high as that. It must be quick and staccato. But the G above the high C, that I can hold."

There are authenticated cases of freak voices that go beyond the range of Miss Yaw's soprano. Henry Cowell, the American composer, possesses the phenomenal capacity of singing deepest bass or the shrillest soprano, practically covering the range of the piano keyboard. In addition, he can sing quarter-tones between the notes of a chromatic scale.

Is the Danube Blue?

An observer watched the Danube for an hour each day during a whole year. He found that on 255 days it was green of various shades, on 60 days it was gray, on 40 days yellow, and on 10 days brown. It never once was blue!

B. Goldberger in a letter to the New York *Times* of September 3, 1945, took exception to this. It seems that the Danube may be gray at Vienna, but is blue upstream. He wrote:

"When we passed the viaduct, we saw the Danube before us, its water a breathtaking glittering blue reflex of the cloudless sky. The blue was like the bluest water in the swimming pools on the Hollywood Technicolor pictures. Since then I have always felt that the waltz, *The Beautiful Blue Danube* is the true expression of the beauty of that river."

[36]

Musical Schizophrenia

When the beauteous heroine in a psychiatric movie goes slightly berserk, there is usually heard from the sound track a weird schizophrenic tone. This sound is produced by the Thereminovox, an electronic instrument invented by the Russian engineer, Leo Theremin. In appearance it is nothing more than a steel rod mounted on a desk. The tone is produced by moving the hand toward the rod or away from it. This movement changes the frequency of vibrations, and the melody goes up or down accordingly. When Theremin came to the United States in 1927, his miraculous gadget was described in newspaper headlines as "ether music." It is, indeed, the nearest approximation to catching music out of thin air. This music can be made unbearably loud or very, very soft. The tone is sustained indefinitely, but the pitch can never be accurate. It is hard enough to play with correct intonation on the violin. On the Thereminovox there are no strings attached, and the hand must grope in the air to find the right notes. But because of this very indefiniteness, the Thereminovox is a perfect medium to express the wanderings of a confused mind. Hence its use for psychiatric movies.

The hand-waving sound production is the most impressive system of constructing electronic instruments. But it is entirely possible to secure the desired pitch by a dial arrangement. In fact, Theremin has constructed several different models of his instrument. By switching an electrical rheostat, the performer can change the register of an electronic instrument at will so that it can play higher than the highest note on the piano and lower than the lowest note on the double bassoon. But these low notes produce such powerful sound waves that they hit you in the pit of the stomach and can actually make you seasick. The very high notes are likely to bring on a headache. For all we know, these super-Theremin waves may be the next secret weapon of a total war. Anyway, they seem to be very effective for killing cockroaches; the exterminators of the future may use an electronic chromatic scale in the low register instead of poison powder.

Modern composers have found electronic music useful for special effects. The most remarkable application of electronic instruments was made by the Russian composer, Nicolas Obouhov, who calls himself Nicolas l'Extasié, because of his religious transcendentalism. He had constructed an ether-wave instrument in the form of a cross and used it in performances of his religious music. Not content with this innovation, Obouhov invented a new system of notation without the benefit of sharps or flats. He wrote his masterwork, *Le Livre de vie,* in this notation. The full score has more than two thousand pages. It has symbolic marks in red representing the blood shed during the Russian Revolution.

Anemic Tunes

During the last war, the British were concerned about anemic music on the air. There was particular criticism of the British Broadcasting Company for including such numbers as *I Threw a Kiss into the Ocean.* The London *Times* wrote:

"The nation is in a Dorian mood; it has in mind to hear something full-throated and vital — something, as Plato said, that 'will fittingly represent the tones and accents of brave men in warlike action or in any hard and dangerous task.' If there is ever a time for a languishing or Lydian mood, it is certainly not the present."

The Devil in Music

During the London blitz of 1940, the London sirens that warned of approaching Nazi aircraft sounded the chromatic scale of the range of a tritone, the interval that was called *Diabolus in Musica* by medieval scholars. But the harmony was in thirds and therefore acceptable to the modern ear. A. Langmead Robinson, writing to the *Musical Times* of November 1940, observed:

"The loudest and most predominant note is D. The B immediately below sounds almost as loud. Much softer, but obviously in evidence, is G. To listen from a distance to a whole chorus of sirens, some on the rising note while others are descending or at their apex, is to experience a thrill which is far from unmusical. Cacophonous as some may think it, the fact that every siren has the G major chord as its foundation gives the whole 'banshee' chorus more claim to definite tonality than much modern music!"

National Anthem or Else

National anthems have been written under the most unusual circumstances, but none more extraordinary than Costa Rica's.

In 1853, the young republic expected the arrival of the envoys of Great Britain and the United States. As a program of suitable festivities was worked out, the authorities suddenly realized that Costa Rica lacked a national anthem. The president, being a man of action, sent out a squad of army men to produce the best musician in the country. In due time one Manuel María Gutiérrez was brought, trembling and fearful, to the presidential mansion. The president congratulated him upon the honor of being selected to write a national anthem.

"But I have never written a tune in my life," pleaded the unfortunate musician. "I play mostly by ear."

The president was infuriated and ordered the man to be thrown in jail until he would deliver the anthem. After several days in a dungeon, poor Manuel María Gutiérrez managed to scribble a march tune. The local bandmaster arranged it for the instruments, and the honor of Costa Rica was saved. The foreign envoys were greeted with the new national anthem. The tune is still the anthem of the republic of Costa Rica.

[39]

Imperialist Music

In the early years of the Russian Revolution, strict materialist dialectic was applied to music as well as to other arts. An Association of Proletarian Musicians was formed to guide Russian composers and performers on the right path. Before it was disbanded by the Soviet government in 1932, the Association produced some extraordinary documents, such as the brochure entitled *Innocent Propaganda of Imperialism* with the word "Innocent" in ironic quotes. It is devoted mainly to the ballet suite, *In a Persian Market* by Albert Ketelby, which was quite popular in Russia in the 1920's. The author of the tract develops his ideas of bourgeois and imperialistic music with iron logic:

"The composer apparently imagines that Persia, and the East generally, is something very primitive and crude. The Eastern nations possess, according to the composer, a limited intelligence capable of reacting only to simple mechanical stimuli. As a result, the music is reduced to an ordinary foxtrot, a little different from such pseudo-national, would-be Negro dances whose cradle is the American cocktail bar. It is obvious that this music has nothing in common with the Persian people, but rather is the manifestation of the devastated, primitive psyche of the bourgeoisie, surfeited with life and hankering after strong sensations in coarse and barbaric emotions. The contemporary East, that is, the colonial and semi-colonial nations living under the double yoke of external imperialism and internal capitalism is nothing like the one painted by the composer. The fact that *In a Persian Market* had its 'immaculate conception' in contemporary imperialistic colonial England intensifies its meaning. The composer's intention is to convince the listener that all is well in the colonies where ripen beautiful girls and exotic fruits, where beggars and rulers live together in peace, where there are no imperialists, no restless proletarians. And if there is unrest, it is the handiwork of malefactors, the result of the agitation of the Comintern."

Anti-Christmas Carols

In those early years of the Revolution, anti-religious propaganda was the accepted policy of the Soviet government. The Central Soviet of the Union of Militant Godless published in 1931 an "anti-Christmas anthology for schools" as a part of a "Library of the Young Godless." There were stories debunking Christianity, Christmas, and Santa Claus. There were instructions for anti-religious games, in which school children were supposed to count numbers and each time they reached the number seven or any number containing the digit seven, they were to say instead "poison." A poster depicting the Pope had an attachable string which, when pulled, caused a swastika, a dollar sign, and two guns to emerge. There was a toy showing a Russian priest and a Jewish rabbi popping from behind a Christmas tree, which, besides having the usual tinsel, was also adorned with a pint of vodka.

In the musical section of the book the Militant Union

of the Godless contributed some anti-Christmas songs. They sounded exactly like Christmas carols, but the words flaunted the precocious atheism of Soviet youngsters:

"We are October's children
From five to eight years old,
We like to beat our toy drums,
We love the color red.

"We never went through baptism,
We do not need the cross,
We never say our prayers,
The priest is not our boss.

"To collectivism
We lead, and not to God.
We are the godless children,
We march to glorious life."

In their heyday, the Union of Militant Godless tried to improve old operas by revising the plots for the purpose of anti-religious propaganda. Perhaps the most hilarious attempt in this direction was the revision of *Faust* in which Mephistopheles was made to appear as the leader of anti-religious forces and a positive character who persuades Marguerite that there is nothing wrong in bearing an illegitimate child and so saves her from moralistic perdition.

The godless movement in Soviet music received its mortal blow unexpectedly from the Soviet government itself. On November 14, 1936, *Pravda* published a decree banning the operatic spectacle, *Bogatiry*, produced by Chamber Theater in Moscow, with text adapted to Borodin's music by Russia's foremost proletarian poet, Demian Bednyi (Demian the Poor). The decree excoriated the production as presenting "a mock version of the Christianization of Russia, which was actually a positive factor in the history of the Russian people, contributing to the establishment of relations with other peoples who possessed a higher degree of culture."

The Union of Militant Godless admitted its ideological error but could never recover after this public denunciation of its methods. It soon went into eclipse, and stopped the publication of its house organ, *The Godless.* With the upsurge of national sentiment during World War II, the Russian Church gained in prestige so markedly, thanks to its role in maintaining the morale of the nation, that the godless movement became practically extinct.

Rock-a-bye Baby

Rock-a-bye Baby, the lullaby that has rocked millions of children to sleep in the past half-century, was written by a young girl, Effie Crockett. She told the story of its composition in a newspaper interview:

"My family had come to Winthrop for a week or two and were visting friends at their cottage. I was sitting on the piazza reading when a lady from Lawrence put her baby in the hammock near by and went away. I went over to the baby, and when it became restless, I remembered the old Mother Goose rhyme and began to hum it. I hummed the words to an impromptu tune, and the child went to sleep. At Christmas, I had a banjo given me and began to take lessons from a teacher in Scollay Square in Boston. One day I strummed the tune for him, and he was so pleased he sent me to C. D. Blake, the Boston publisher. After he heard it, he asked permission to publish it. He did, after I had written three verses to go with the Mother Goose lines. I was afraid my father wouldn't approve, so instead of using my real name, Effie I. Crockett, I used the name of Canning, my grandmother's name. It was not until the song began to sweep the country that I told father I wrote it."

On April 14, 1938, the author of the lullaby, now Mrs. Effie D. Canning Carlton, a married woman of sixty-five, appeared on the radio on the occasion of the fiftieth anniversary of the publication of *Rock-a-bye Baby,* and sang it for the benefit of mothers and children. She died two years later.

Composer of Wines

Michael Kelly, the eighteenth-century Irish composer of theater music and a friend of Mozart (who used to spell his name *all' italiana*, Occhelli), was unsuccessful in his musical career and decided to become a wine merchant. He put up a sign over his wine shop, "Wine merchant and composer of music."

Sheridan, the playwright, who thought that Kelly's wine showed greater taste than his music, advised him to change the sign to read: "Merchant of music and composer of wines."

No Second Fiddles

In pre-Bolshevik times, a Russian Grand Duke was shown the layout of the Imperial Orchestra.

"These are the first violins," explained the conductor, "and these are second violins."

"Second violins in the Imperial orchestra?" exclaimed the Grand Duke. "*All* must be first!"

An Idle Bassoonist

Viennese operettas have a stock character: a Balkan prince who goes to Paris with plenty of kronen, dinars, leva or whatever coins went for money *in partibus infidelium*. These characters are not entirely the figment of operatic imagination. Such a one was the Serbian Prince Milosch, who went to Paris in 1873 and hired an orchestra to play for the reception at his Paris mansion. During an instrumental solo when most players were diligently counting their rests, he singled out a bassoon player and inquired in stentorian tones: "What are you sitting there idle for? You are paid to play. Why don't you play?"

"Highness," stammered out the astounded bassoon player, "I am waiting for the end of the solo."

"Oh, you are waiting, are you?" roared Prince Milosch. "Well, I do not choose to feed idlers. From this day on you are no longer in my service."

Unmusical Dr. Johnson

The great Samuel Johnson was notoriously insensitive to music's charms. Once he heard a violinist perform a highly pyrotechnical piece. Johnson's companion (not Boswell) remarked that it must have been very difficult to play. "Difficult!" exclaimed Dr. Johnson, "I wish to God it had been impossible."

The Navel Bolero

There are names among musicians that look like misprints of better-known names: Schobert for Schubert, Piccinni for Puccini. Thus we read in one reputable music encyclopedia that, during his Paris period, Mozart was influenced by Schubert, an extraordinary occurrence inasmuch as Mozart died several years before Schubert was born. In another compendium, we find an account of the *Puccini*-Gluck rivalry. These slips are usually the result of the supererogatory interference on the part of a proofreader who "corrects" the unfamiliar names.

Felix Borowski once wrote a ballet called *Boudour*. The music dictionaries converted it into "Boudoir." MacDowell's *Norse* Sonata became "Horse" Sonata in Philip Hale's column in the *Musical Record*, circa 1900. But the best musical misprint was the one perpetrated by the typesetter of the New York *Sun* which transformed the Ravel Bolero into the "Navel" Bolero.

Home Sweet Home

The following story was reported in the musical journals of 1885 as an actual occurrence:

When a singer at a prison concert sang *Home, Sweet Home*, the inmates were so deeply moved that seven of them escaped the same night, and were re-arrested in their respective homes the next day.

Violin Solo with Hacksaw Obbligato

It happened at the Del Norte County Jail at Crescent City, California, in July 1947. One of the fourteen inmates of the jail took to playing the fiddle for hours at a stretch. The tone of his violin was strong enough to muffle the sound of a hacksaw which was operated by another prisoner to saw through the iron bars of the jail windows. However, the warden had an ear sensitive enough to perceive the obbligato accompaniment, and the intended jail break was foiled.

This was not the first time that a jail break was attempted behind a musical smoke screen. In 1888 four prisoners sawed off a portion of a window-casing in the Pueblo, Colorado County Jail, and made good their escape while a fiddler made music. The warden explained that he could not tell the difference between the sound of a hacksaw and that of the fiddle.

The idea of incidental string music for jail breaks was used also in a movie, *The Magic Bow*, purporting to be the life of Niccolo Paganini. Paganini plays the violin outside the dungeon windows while a prisoner inside saws the bars in the window opposite. Needless to say, nothing of the sort ever happened to Paganini in real life.

Rimsky-Korsakov Sovsem Sumasoshol

Irreverent musicians often attach doggerel lines to well-known themes of classical music. The first theme of Liszt's E-flat Piano Concerto was sung to the words: "*Sie sind alle ganz verrückt.*" The difficult rhythm in Rimsky-Korsakov's chorus in the opera, *Sadko*, in 11/4 time, was rendered by his students at the St. Petersburg Conservatory to the Russian words: *"Rimsky-Korsakov Sovsem Sumasoshol,"* which means "Rimsky-Korsakov is altogether mad" (eleven syllables in either language). The main theme of Mendelssohn's Violin Concerto, when played lackadaisically by a beginner, was known with the words, "Oh, Moyshe, oh, Moyshe, the business isn't good." The most cynical setting of all is the smoking-room ballad sung to the tune of Dvořák's *Humoresque*: "Passengers will please refrain from flushing toilet while the train is standing in the station, I love you."

Canons with Cannons

The loudest music ever performed was heard during the nineteenth century, reaching its peak about 1850. Bigger and louder instruments were built, and larger and noisier orchestras were assembled. There was an eight-foot double-bass outfitted with a stepladder for the player to reach the upper part of the strings; there were pianos with a range of eight octaves; there were monstrous mechanical organs. The mad conductor, Jullien, presented concerts with the aid of artillery and other sound effects. Even the church was not safe from the penetration of extra-musical noises. The *Gazette musicale de Paris* of 1846 reports a concert of music performed in a Belgian Cathedral:

"When the Mass was performed, an orchestra of four hundred musicians was engaged besides the huge chorus. To illustrate the words, *'Passus et sepultus est,'* musket shots were fired from the loft. One can easily imagine the sensation this formidable instrumental effect must have produced in the congregation. If the conductor intended to produce a realistic effect, it is strange that he should have selected it to illustrate the passing of Christ."

The *Revue de musique réligieuse* commented on the report:

"One is compelled to believe that the degradation of religious music has reached an incredible degree of brutality."

Who Invented Recitals?

The word "recital" for a concert is of relatively recent origin. It was first applied by one F. Beale, the English manager of Liszt, who believed that Liszt's concerts had the quality of a narrative or recitation, and that his music communicated a story to the listeners.

Schubert's Descendants

The following announcement appeared on *Le Guide du Concert* of March 14, 1947:

"Descendants of Franz Schubert live in misery. On the occasion of the 150th anniversary of the composer's birth, the Vienna Philharmonic Orchestra accorded them a life pension."

Schubert's descendants? He was never married.

The Shah and Orchestral Tuning

The story of the Persian Shah and the orchestral tuning, now an integral part of every anthology of musical jokes, originated in the 1890's when the then Persian ruler visited Europe. A concert was given in his honor in Paris. He listened patiently, and at the conclusion, was asked which piece he had liked best.

"The first," was the immediate reply.

The word was passed to the conductor to play again the first piece, the overture to *Tannhäuser*.

"But *that* is not the piece," the Shah protested.

Another work was tried, but the Shah sadly shook his head. Then the orchestra began to tune up for a third try.

"That is it!" exclaimed the Persian ruler as soon as he heard the twanging of the strings. "I like *that* one best of all."

Grand Pianos by Air

When a grand piano becomes air-minded, that's news. A 1,400-pound concert grand piano was flown to Argentina on June 6, 1947, in a Pan-American DC-4 cargo plane from New York, and arrived at its destination on June 8. The flight was made at the request of Artur Rubinstein, the pianist, who was dissatisfied with the grand pianos available in Buenos Aires for his concert there. This was not the first time a piano traveled by air, however. One was flown on a German Zeppelin from Berlin to New York in 1936.

A Musical Comedy of 1822

Composers of musical comedies a hundred years ago liked to anticipate the shape of things to come. In 1822, the Austrian composer, Franz Glaeser, produced an operetta entitled *1722, 1822, and 1922*, in which he gave a picture of the world a century from his time. The lively British magazine, the *Harmonicon*, reported from Vienna:

"A description of what our old mother, the earth, may be a century hence is whimsical enough. Everything is managed by machinery; the plough goes by itself, and the ploughman follows it at his leisure. Balloons supply the place of hackney coaches; every servant girl has a hundred or more a year for wages. The music of Mr. Glaeser is very appropriate: the past represents Handel and Hasse; the present Rossini and Weber, and in a century to come, Mozart is represented as ever new and ever young to our posterity; for the truly beautiful is not swallowed up in the stream of time."

The Digitorium

Quick methods of learning to play the piano have every once in a while sprouted forth in flamboyantly worded advertisements. Here is one from the *Musical Standard* of 1867 describing an instrument called the Digitorium,

[49]

". . . which enables any person to play on the Piano or Organ in an incredibly short time. The position of the hand and stretch of octave is acquired, the wrist is strengthened and the inevitable finger exercises and studies which so soon spoil a piano, are adapted to this remarkable invention."

Musicians for Sale

Wealthy music lovers in old Russia, before the emancipation of serfs, had no trouble in procuring musical entertainment for their homes and palaces. They could purchase musicians outright, the only expenditure being the initial cost of each "soul," as serfs were officially designated. The following advertisements were published in Russian gazettes in the 1780's:

"Musician for sale, age 26, 6 feet 2 inches tall, plays double-bass and clarinet, sings bass; he is a leech, can let blood with lancet, knows barbering, applies clysters."

"A very good clarinetist, 15 years' practice, plays the violin, of exemplary behavior, does not drink spirits. Positively last price, 1500 rubles."

"Two musicians, can read and write; know a little arithmetic, play all kinds of music on the horn, one of them dresses hair and knows cashiering. Also for sale, 2 clarinets, 2 fagotts, 2 flutes, 2 waldhorns."

"Clever player on transverse flute, plays in choirs, knows music, can manage chorus singing, 23 years old, 1,000 rubles."

"Two musicians, very gratifying ability, one of them can be Kapellmeister, plays first violin, clavichord, and other instruments; the other plays on the double-bass, violin, horn, and other wind instruments."

Perhaps the most tempting offer of them all was published in a Moscow newspaper in 1794:

"For sale — a domestic servant, plays the violin, can do secretarial work; also young English pigs and a Danish colt."

Melody of a Single Note

When Josquin des Prés was in the service of Louis

XII of France, he was commanded to write something expressly for the king, who was completely ignorant of music. With the subtle deference of a courtier, Josquin complied and produced a canon with a part marked "Vox Regis." It consisted of a single note sustained throughout. Josquin was richly rewarded by the king for his offering, and responded with a motet, *You Bestowed a Bounty Upon Your Servitor.*

In one of his motets, Mendelssohn wrote a single-note part for his brother-in-law Hensel, who was a painter. Hensel proved "quite unable to catch the note though blown and whispered to him from every side."

A single note may be made diversified and attractive by appropriate changes in harmony. Every note can be used in six different triads, major and minor, in four different dominant-seventh chords, and in a diminished-seventh chord, to mention but the best-known chords. Beethoven, in the second movement of the Seventh Symphony, maintains melodic interest with a single note repeated twelve times before the melody moves upward. Long before Beethoven, Purcell wrote the *Fantasy on One Note.* But a real tour de force was performed by Peter Cornelius, whose song, *Ein Ton,* carries a melody of a single note, B-natural, repeated eighty times. Of course, there are constant modulations so that harmonic changes make up for the monotony. The words, also by Cornelius, speak of "a tone so wondrous rare, like a monotone of church bells."

The Spanish composer, Jaime Pahissa, has written an orchestral score in unison and octaves, appropriately entitled *Monodia.* Despite being entirely composed of unisons, *Monodia* is an exciting composition in a style that Pahissa calls intertonal, which is midway between tonal and atonal. The score abounds in quasi-fugal passages in which the element of imitation is supplied by instrumental tone colors in lieu of the missing polyphony.

[51]

Triple-Threat Oratorio

Musicians trained in the art of counterpoint are supposed to be able to combine several unrelated themes in perfect harmony. Serious composers have amused themselves by writing pieces that can be played upside down as well as right side up. But the most extraordinary composer of combinational music was one Pietro Raimondi, an obscure contemporary of Verdi. His claim to fame is a triple lyric drama which combines three oratorios in one. They can be performed separately under the titles *Potiphar, Joseph,* and *Jacob*. Or else they can be sung together. The score itself is a thing of wonder: It measures 5 x 5 feet. The triple oratorio was actually performed in Rome in August 1852 first separately, then all three

together. For the triple oratorio, there were three conductors, one for each component lyric drama. These conductors were themselves conducted by the composer.
A contemporary account reports:

"The entire house rose spontaneously to its feet uttering
shouts of admiration. Wild gesticulation, enthusiastic cheers,
broke out on all sides while women, leaning out of the
crowded boxes, waved their handkerchiefs."

The Oldest Conservatory

The most ancient conservatory in the world was not
founded in Italy or Germany, but in Korea. At least this
is the claim of the institution known as the Prince Ye
Conservatory of Music founded by the father of Korean
music, Pak Yun, in the year 1418. The first treatise on
Korean music appeared in 1493. The author was Sung
Hyun and the title of the manual was *The Normal Study
of Music.*

The Ye Conservatory of Music maintained eight hundred musicians in the fifteenth century. However, in
1947, the number of musicians was only fifty-eight. And
there is little chance that Korean music will return to its
fifteenth-century prosperity. The descendants of the
Prince Ye, shorn of their royal privileges, find it impossible to cultivate the arts in grand style.

First Female Band

The first orchestra composed entirely of women appeared in Venice in the second part of the eighteenth
century. One William Beckford, writing from Venice in
1780, describes this female band:

"The sight of the orchestra makes me smile. It is entirely
of the feminine gender, and nothing is more strange than
to see a delicate white hand journeying across an enormous
double bass, or a pair of roseate cheeks puffing at a French
horn. Some that are grown old and Amazonian, who have

abandoned their fiddles and their lovers, take vigorously to the kettle-drum; and one poor lady who had been crossed in love now makes an admirable figure on the bassoon."

Unhorsing the Diva's Carriage

The degrees of success at the opera or in concert have long been established in this progression: (1) cordial applause by a small appreciative audience; (2) numerous curtain calls in response to tumultuous applause; (3) deafening, unceasing hand-clapping that ends only when the lights in the hall are turned off. The greatest degree of enthusiasm, before the age of the automobile, was manifested by unhorsing the carriage and drawing it riksha-fashion to the artist's domicile. But there were skeptics even in that age of innocence. The *Musical Courier* of August 29, 1883, reports:

"The few persons who know the facts of the case are always amused when recalling the 'grand ovation' offered to Mme. Patti in Brooklyn last winter. On the occasion of her first appearance of the season, the horses were taken from her carriage after the conclusion of the opera, and the vehicle in which she had taken her seat was drawn to her hotel by 'the enthusiastic populace,' as the newspapers all over the country announced. The 'enthusiastic populace,' however, consisted of a score or so of Brooklyn stablemen who had been hired to perform the laborious service at five dollars a head."

One Sharp

Musicians will have their little jokes. When one of them invited a friend to lunch, he sent a card reading: "The pleasure of your company is requested for luncheon, key of G." The guest interpreted the invitation correctly and came at one sharp.

Piano Marathon Race

The first recorded marathon piano contest was held on

December 13, 1927 at the Ebbing Café in Berlin. A pianist named Eltermann played uninterruptedly for thirty-one hours and ten minutes. J. M. Waterbury of Brockton claimed the record of continuous piano playing: sixty-five hours. While playing, he was shaved and fed several times.

When Ripley announced in his column, "Believe It or Not," that one William Hajek was the champion non-stop player with 336 hours to his credit, he was sued for $605,000 by Eddie Carter, who claimed that Hajek had fraudulently used his identical twin brother as a stand-in. Carter claimed for himself a legitimate record of 238 hours of continuous piano pounding.

The first authenticated speed record of piano playing was established on June 4, 1828 by a Mr. Scarborough of Spalding, England, with a count of 127,512 notes per hour. This record was beaten a century later by Henry Scott whose velocity was 44⅔ notes per second.

Shoestring, Lemonade, and the Opera

There is nothing new in opera seasons financed on a shoestring basis. But it is news when an opera company openly acknowledges this fact. The Shoestring Opera Company, Inc., gave its opening performance, *Tales of Hoffmann*, at Hunter College, New York, on January 19, 1943. The directors announced:

"The name Shoestring has been selected to signify that artistic, dramatic music can be produced solely through the artistic efforts and ingenuity of the members of the corporation; in the vernacular 'on a shoestring' and without the stupendous and prohibitive production cost of 'grand' opera."

In the footsteps of the Shoestring Opera Company, another operatic enterprise with a whimsical name was launched in New York, in 1947. It was named Lemonade Opera Company, after the cooling drink which was served during the intermission. The directors were young men and women; the average age of the members of the staff and of the singers was twenty-five. The Lemonade Opera Company is run on a co-operative basis, with directors and performers contributing twenty-five dollars each and then dividing all profits. Two pianos are used instead of the orchestra. All librettos are in English. After the first few weeks of its informal season, the Lemonade Opera Company actually made a profit.

Drink to Me Only with Thine Eyes

The music of Ben Johnson's celebrated poem, *Drink to Me Only with Thine Eyes,* is usually ascribed to that ubiquitous and versatile fellow, Anon. But there are strong indications that Anon.'s real name this time was Dr. Henry Harrington of Bath (1727-1816). He was the official composer to the Harmonic Society of Bath from 1784 to the time of his death. His claim to the authorship of the song is supported by the fact that his name appears in an edition of the song published in London in 1804 while he was still living. Furthermore, the song is credited to Dr. Harrington in a contemporary album called *A Select Collection of Songs,* which was published in Newcastle-on-Tyne in 1806. The original manuscript has never been discovered, but evidence indicates strongly that Dr. Harrington was indeed the composer of the song.

Musical Larceny

In his autobiography, John Stuart Mill wrote:

"I was seriously tormented by the thought of the exhaustibility of musical combinations. The octave consists of only five tones and two semitones, which can be put together in only a limited number of ways, of which but a small proportion are beautiful: most of these it seemed to me must already have been discovered, and there could not be room for a long succession of Mozarts and Webers to strike out, as these have done, entirely new surpassingly rich veins of musical beauty."

John Stuart Mill lived before the age of chromatic melody, or at any rate he ignored the emergence of the twelve chromatic tones as a new fund of musical resources. But he was right in that the music of seven diatonic degrees has limited potentialities.

There are numerous examples of coincidences, rhythmic and harmonic as well as melodic, among composers of the classical era. Mozart's *Haffner* Symphony in its opening theme is all but identical, in rhythm and melody, with an earlier symphony for double orchestra by Bach's son, John Christian Bach. A theme of Beethoven's *Eroica* Symphony is identical in key and melody with a subject in a little-known Mozart overture. Haydn wrote so many symphonies that in one of them he duplicated note for note the principal theme of an earlier symphony apparently without being aware of it.

The matter of close coincidence of melodies became a deadly earnest affair when composition of melodies grew into big business along Broadway. As long as classical composers, coincidentally or intentionally, wrote similar tunes, only music scholars were interested. But when the composer of a Broadway hit tune helped himself to a previously written ditty, the anterior songster rushed to court. The New York City halls of justice, beginning in 1920, reverberated with the catchy sounds of popular hits, harkened to by solemn and mostly unmusical justices. Music itself had to be given a jurisprudential definition by Justice Holmes as a "rational collocation of sounds, apart from concepts." On January 28, 1921, a a piano, a violin, a trumpet, and a phonograph were employed to prove that *Avalon* was "cribbed" from Cavaradossi's aria in *Tosca*. The hit song was in major; the aria from *Tosca* in minor. The plaintiffs, who owned the copyright on *Tosca*, had a trio play *Avalon* while a gramophone record reproduced the Cavaradossi aria; apart from a flat or two, the result was contrapuntally perfect. The court decided against the defendant.

When the famous pacifist song, *I Didn't Raise My Boy To Be a Soldier*, became a hit (before the entry of the United States into World War I), the composer of an unsuccessful tune, *How Much I Really Cared*, was struck with the similarity of the hit song to his own. He went to court and proved that his song had been performed in the spring of 1914, whereas the hit was admittedly composed not before October of that year. Piantadosi, the composer of *I Didn't Raise My Boy*, was an employee of a music firm and had had access to the earlier song written by the plaintiff, whose name was Cohalin. Both composers were admittedly semi-literate; but it was agreed that Piantadosi was proficient enough to be able to copy a song by someone else. The court heard both songs, found them similar indeed, and ruled in favor of Cohalin.

Sometimes a musical defendant pleaded not guilty by contending that both he and the plaintiff had stolen a successful ditty from somebody else. This was the substance of the defense in the case of a song called *Lady of Love* versus *Without a Word of Warning*. The defendant submitted that both songs were a dead steal from *Die Fledermaus* by Johann Strauss and/or Victor Herbert's *Sweethearts*. The case was thrown out of court before things got too complicated.

One of the most famous cases of this nature was the lawsuit by the publishers of *Dardanella* against Jerome Kern, whose song *Kalua* duplicated the rolling bass of *Dardanella*. This was also the first case where the importance of the bass part was officially recognized by the

[58]

law. The court decided in favor of the plaintiff, ruling that in this case "the bass materially qualifies if it does not dominate the melody." The judgment was unusual. First of all, the bass in *Dardanella* runs in eighth-notes, whereas that in Jerome Kern's tune is in quarter-notes. This type of bass, which became the germ of boogie woogie, can be traced to any number of classical usages. In this case an appeal to a common ancestry of both songs was not sustained by the court.

The most interesting element in the court decisions on musical matters is the dry judicial language employed by often humorous judges in matters concerning popular music. In at least one case a judge constituted himself as a music critic. On May 2, 1908, the Superior Tribunal of Leipzig, Germany, rejected the claims for infringement of copyright by the publishers of Richard Strauss when they objected to the use of thematic materials from Strauss's tone poem, *Ein Heldenleben* by Heinrich Noren in his orchestral suite, *Kaleidoscope*. The court ruled that there was no substance in the complaint on the ground that *Ein Heldenleben* did not have any melody.

The Right To Hiss

On March 20, 1904 at the Colonne Concerts in Paris, Paderewski played a Beethoven Concerto. There was the usual outburst of applause after the end of the first movement. But this applause was mingled with the unexpected sounds of hissing and whistling from three persons named Trotrot, Leprince, and Blétry. They were ejected from the hall and hailed into court. A lawyer delivered a learned plea which was published under the title, "*Le sifflet au concert*." He recounted that:

"On March 20, 1904, a Concerto of Beethoven was performed at Concerts Colonne; that this Concerto was divided into four parts; there was a pause of two minutes between these parts to give the musicians an opportunity to tune up (*réaccorder*) and to the public to manifest their sentiments; that the first part of the Concerto having been finished, considerable applause ensued to which responded several hisses emitted by the three persons now at the dock; that the applause was renewed and that hisses again replied; that threats were proffered against the hissers who had to be protected by the commisar of police; that if the detained persons had applauded instead of hissing, they would not have been reprimanded, for approbation even of the noisiest type never displeases whereas hissing, even light hissing, which is criticism, seems intolerable. If the public has a right to approve, it ought to have a right to express its dissatisfaction. In manifesting their disapprobation in a minuscule form during the interval between the two parts of the Concerto, the detained persons had made legitimate use of their right to disapprove of the work performed. My clients found the frivolity of applause obnoxious, and their youthful wrath expressed itself in plaintive or strident sounds commensurate with the power of their breath or the acuity of their revolving whistles."

Colonne himself, in a brief speech addressed to the public immediately after the disturbance, took an impartial attitude. "It is the defenders of law and order that disturb the performance by their applause in the middle of a composition. As to the possessors of the whistles, let them do as they please if the discordant instrument agrees with them."

The Court adjudged to the defendants ten francs' damages and reimbursement of the cost of the ticket.

Unexpectedly, the fracas led to a general revaluation of a concerto as a musical form. Several eminent musicians were asked whether they thought that symphonic concerts should present concertos at their programs. Vincent d'Indy replied: "It is undeniable that the concerto, a musical form that serves the purpose of virtuosity, is an inferior genre, a degenerate offspring of the noble concerto created by the Italians and raised to its highest degree of power by Bach." Paul Dukas said: "The concerto compared to the symphony is an inferior form because it serves the sole purpose of glorifying the virtuoso and not the music."

Le Petit

An incomparable piano prodigy appeared on the musical horizon of Paris and London in the year 1843. It was Charles Filtsch, a Hungarian boy pianist, known in Paris by the affectionate nickname, "*le petit*." He gave his concerts at the age of thirteen and was a favorite pupil of Chopin. Liszt exclaimed on one occasion: "*Quand ce petit voyagera je fermerai boutique*." But "*le petit*" overexerted himself. He fell ill with consumption and died on May 11, 1845, some two months short of his fifteenth birthday.

Chopin was present when "*le petit*" played at a private gathering in a Paris salon. *Gazette musicale de Paris* reported the event in poetic prose:

"It was at one of such improvised matinees that young Filtsch joined his pleas to ours to hear his master tell us in tones of these delightful études which, when he plays them, resemble improvisations and meditations, penetrated with dreamy wistfulness, a hidden suffering. Chopin spoke to his disciple, to us, and to other artists, his rivals, his friends, his admirers. He spoke to us in this mysterious tongue which is peculiarly his own in which fingers draw designs in playing on the keyboard, signs that form harmonious arabesques, hieroglyphics of which he alone has the secret, a secret so rare which captivates, dominates, and charms by the accomplishment of his art. . . ."

One-Armed Pianists

The foremost one-armed pianist of today is Paul Wittgenstein, an Austrian musician who lost his right arm during World War I. But there was another one-armed pianist before him, Count Géza Zichy, also an Austrian.

Zichy suffered his casualty on September 24, 1863, in a hunting accident at the age of fourteen when a gun was accidentally discharged at close range, shattering his right arm. In his singularly vivid memoirs, Zichy describes the extraordinary scene of the burial and the subsequent exhumation of his arm:

"On the day after the amputation, my servant brought in a little box covered with a white cloth. It contained my amputated arm. We then drove to the cemetary to bury it. I watched my partial interment, certainly a unique experience. Twenty years later my brother had my arm exhumed and placed it in the family mausoleum. There lie my poor bones even now, although not complete, for I had removed the upper joint of my little finger (*phalanx tertia digiti minimi*) and set it in a locket which I presented to my brother as a token of affection."

Zichy was happily married, had several children, and died in 1924 at the ripe age of seventy-five. He counted Liszt among his numerous friends, and his memoirs give a vivid picture of Liszt's informal manners at friendly gatherings when Liszt would sit at the piano and improvise variations on *Chopsticks*. Zichy made an arrangement of Liszt's *Rakóczy* March for three hands, which he played with the composer at a charity concert, taking the bass part with his left hand.

Reading Notes by Gaslight

During the gaslit 1880's, a Boston oculist advertised a "new treatment of the eye" promising to "perform wonders with musical people whose eyes have been too much strained by the constant reading of notes by gaslight in the theater and concert rooms." He also guaranteed a cure for colorblindness, double vision, and other afflictions that might beset his valuable customers. In corroboration of his claims, he volunteered to furnish "references from first-class vocalists."

[62]

Father of the Ocarina

The word "ocarina" literally means a little goose in Italian, but it is known in popular swing bands as a "sweet potato." This bird-shaped, hollow-sounding whistle was invented in 1867 by one Giuseppe Donati of Milan. At least he claimed the honor of the invention against his rival, Luigi Silvestri, who obtained the commercial rights and even got himself nicknamed "papa dell'ocarina." Donati died in 1925 at the age of eighty-eight. Silvestri died at ninety in 1927. Those interested in the claims and counter claims connected with the ocarina will find the pertinent information in the *Gazetta del popolo,* of Turin, April 25, 1927.

The Fearsome Piano

Leopold de Meyer, the piano virtuoso whose success rivaled that of Liszt, tells this barely credible story of his concert at the Sultan's palace in Constantinople:

There was no piano in the palace. De Meyer borrowed one from the Austrian Legation and had it set up in the reception room at the palace. When the Sultan arrived for the concert, he recoiled in horror and angrily demanded an explanation of "that monster" standing there on three legs. Suspecting some evil design, the Sultan ordered the piano legs to be taken off. The body of the instrument was then laid flat on the floor. Squatting cross-legged on a mat, Leopold de Meyer went through his program as best he could. But the Sultan was so delighted at the concert that he paid de Meyer the highest fee the pianist had ever received — five thousand dollars.

Mid-air Opera Seat

This story — utterly incredible — is reported in the *Gazette musicale de Paris* of January 1, 1843. A wealthy Englishman traveling in Italy wanted to hear a new Italian opera. When he tried to purchase a ticket, he found that the house was sold out. Being of whimsical nature and impatient temper, he offered the impresario the sum of one hundred guineas for a seat in the theater. When he could not obtain it he suggested an ingenious plan: to suspend a chair from the skylight in the roof and to be allowed to hover over the audience. The impresario was finally persuaded to agree. When the overture began, the chair with the Englishman seated in it was lowered from the ceiling by means of stout ropes. The public believed at first that the descent of the Englishman was part of the performance. When they realized that he had paid for it in order to get into the jammed theater, they booed and shouted. The performance was interrupted, but the Englishman refused to be dislodged from the aerial chair. The *Gazette* reports that he was finally knocked out, and in his fall hurt several people in the audience. *Se non è vero, è ben trovato.*

A Lady Tenor

Not all tenors are necessarily men. There was a woman tenor who achieved a considerable reputation as a featured singer at the BBC concerts in England. Her name was Ruby Helder. Apart from her tenor voice she was a normal married woman. She died in Hollywood in 1940, at the age of forty-eight.

Flute Players Union, 300 B.C.

Musicians' Unions are over two thousand years old. In the fourth century B.C. the Guild of Flute Players in Rome had a monopoly of all sacrificial games, and also supplied the music at funerals. They were well paid and treated with great respect. They held annual festivals on June 13 when they paraded through the city. When the Roman censors pounced upon them for their inappropriate gaiety at solemn meetings, the Guild of Flute Players protested against this criticism. Then the censors forbade the annual banquet of the Flute Players in the Temple of Jupiter. The Flute Players retaliated by refusing to perform the sacrificial rites. This alarmed the Senate who took up the problem with the censors. The musicians were invited to the Senate and urged to return to their duties. But they stubbornly refused to obey. The censors then played a ruse. Livy tells the rest of the story in Book IX in his *History of Rome*:

"It was a feast day and the musicians were invited to various houses, ostensibly to supply music at the banquets. Like the rest of their class, they were fond of wine, and they were plied with it till they drank themselves into a state of torpor. In this condition they were thrown into wagons and carried off to Rome. They were left in the wagons all night in the Forum and did not recover their senses till daylight surprised them still suffering from the effect of their debauch. The people crowded round them and succeeded in including them to stay, and they were granted the privilege of going about the city for three days every year in their long dresses and masks with singing and mirth, a custom which is still observed. Those members of the guild who played on solemn occasions in the Temple of Jupiter had the right restored to them of holding their banquets there."

Sukhona Boatmen's Songs

The boatmen of the Volga are not the only ones who used to intone their mournful chanteys. Blasius, in his *Travels in European Russia*, describes the songs of Russian boatmen along the Sukhona River in northern Russia, early in the nineteenth century and long before the emancipation of serfs:

[65.]

"The people are not altogether phlegmatic; as soon as they are at their work, they are transformed into new men and pursue their avocations with the voice of melody. This disposition to cheer their labors with songs is most remarkably powerful among the Russians here and rises to a sort of improvisation, of which we had a striking instance among the boatmen of Sukhona. Among our boatmen was a powerful young man with bright eyes and great animation in his aspect who took tenor in several quartets and canons. His father, who seemed to sympathize magically with every tune or thought and feeling in his son, led the bass, while two others filled the harmony. In their canons, they showed such a just feeling for harmony and such science in their figure that we could hardly believe it the production of nature, and yet these men had never left the banks of the Sukhona. Their music was accompanied with ballads and romances which the youth improvised for the occasion with great clearness. His imagination produced romantic stories of kings and princes and fair princesses in splendid palaces where was perpetual feast and glorious array; then he contrived to unite his own feelings with the fiction, told how

he had been invited to the palace and had received encouragement from the princess; but he would prove true to his lowly fisher maiden, in the little black hut by his native river. His companions could not help applauding his poetic success.

The Anglo-French Music War

A hundred years ago the polemical style of musical journals was a robust exercise in which personal insults were freely administered. One of the most extraordinary exchanges of mutual abuse took place across the English Channel between the *Musical World* of London and the *Gazette musicale de Paris,* in the year 1843.

The battle began when the *Gazette musicale* accused the *Musical World* of translating its articles and publishing them in English without crediting the source. To this, the *Musical World* replied:

"The *Gazette musicale,* this exceedingly stupid hebdomadal puff, has the insolence to accuse us of borrowing without acknowledgment from its pages. Considering that the *Gazette* is made up of shreds and patches from the German papers, long meaningless rhapsodies by a hired puffer, M. Henri Blanchard, whose order is to puff in extra-hyperbolical nonsense prose; soporific inflations by one Maurice Gourges; inimitably infamous romances by a certain Paul Smith, and the occasional lucubrations of the sublime proprietor, M. Schlesinger, who knows about as much of music as an orang-outang of mathematics — considering all this, we say, it is somewhat ridiculous for such a charge to come from such a quarter against a journal conducted on the independent principles of the *Musical World.* In the meantime, if we find anything not absolutely soporific in its pages, we shall continue to make use of it, as the *Gazette* does (much more unscrupulously) of our own more interesting and instructive matter."

The French paper snarled angrily back:

"*Le journal anglais, le* Musical World, *continue son système d'emprunts forcés, sans nommer les gens qu'il vole, et il y a de bonnes raisons pour cela. Dans son numéro du 3 de août 1843 il nous prend encore un article et en même temps suivant son habitude, il nous injurie de la manière la plus stupide et la plus grossière. Pour couronner dignement et logiquement ces invectives, il déclare que s'il trouve dans nos pages quelque chose qui ne soit trop ennuyeux* (not absolutely soporific), *il continuera de la prendre sans façon. Décidement le* Musical World *est un plaisant journal."*

It was now the turn of the *Musical World* to strike at the French across the Channel:

"Will it be credited that after the castigation which *La Gazette musicale de Paris* has received at our hands, it has had the temerity to reattack us? Must we carry out our exposé of this silly journal and lay its iniquities bare to the public, which it has for some time so completely and unequivocally gulled? M. Schlesinger, you had better save us the trouble of expounding to the few readers you can boast the manner in which your letters from London (!) are stolen, word for word, without acknowledgment, from the columns of London newspapers. You had better allow us dispensation from the labor of proving that your pretended London correspondent is some poor starving inhabitant of Paris who in a wretched garret concocts the 'original letter' from the pages of London journals a month or two months old. You had better cease to meddle with the *Musical World*."

The last word remained with the French when they compared the *Musical World* with a man who steals your tobacco and then declares that it is rotten:

"Le Musical World *ressemble à un homme qui vous volerait votre tabatière dans votre poche, qui prendrait votre tabac et qui dirait pour toute excuse; 'Votre tabac ne vaut rien.'"*

Music in the Temple of Reason

Musicians prosper during social upheavals, or at least they enjoy national recognition and official honors. During the period of the Terror in France in 1793, there was an upsurge of musical activities. Some interesting documentation on music in Rouen at that time has been published, and it throws a fascinating light on the social psychology of the time. Even the advertisements, with their civic phraseology, are exciting to read:

"There will be celebrated a civic festival at the Temple of Reason on the 20th Frimaire. The orchestra will perform patriotic airs relating to the Revolution and to the reign of Liberty and Equality; hymns and civic songs will be sung. There will be speeches and exhortations to the people. All music amateurs and instrumentalists are invited *au nom de la patrie* to unite in the Temple."

The Temple of Reason was the former Cathedral of Rouen, but it did not remain devoted to the Cult of Reason for long. By the decree of Robespierre of May 7, 1794, the Cult of Reason was abolished in favor of the Cult of Supreme Being, and the Rouen Cathedral became the Temple of the Eternal. The inscription on the portal proclaimed: *"Le peuple français reconnaît l'être suprême et l'immortalité de l'âme."* The Temple of Reason maintained an orchestra of 160 musicians, including many professionals who fled the revolutionary turmoil of Paris. There was a chorus that numbered many singers of the Paris Opéra who were formerly supported by the Royal Court. The organist was an eminent musician of the time, Broche. A typical program began with a chorus, *O Sainte Liberté,* which was followed by a song on the abolition of Negro slavery and a hymn, *Républicains jusqu'à la mort.* Then Broche played his own compositions on the organ including such pieces as *Invocation to the Souls of the Defenders of Fatherland, Ode to Equality,* and *The Battle of Jemmapes.* The latter aroused particular enthusiasm among ardent republicans. As a local newspaper reported:

"He painted in it the clang of arms, the awesome deeds of the battlefield, the clash of the battalions, the din of artillery, the groans of the wounded and the dying, and the

[69]

triumphal chant of the victors. The patriotic fire that inspired the musician was communicated to the listeners. His soul was carried over the organ keys on the torrents of music."

The Committee of Civic Emulation of Rouen expressed the gratification of the citizens and proposed to the Council of the Commune that he should be given an official expression of civic gratitude for his part in maintaining the republican morale. But Broche seemed to be more interested in securing his annual salary of one thousand livres which he drew from the royal authorities, and which was slow in coming after the revolutionary disruption of national finances.

On the 3rd Pluviose of Year II of the Revolution, the mayor delivered a significant speech in which he said:

"Art will no longer serve to provide entertainment for a small number of privileged persons who corrupt it by their gold. Artists will not longer prostitute their talents to satisfy the drunken impulses of depraved souls. They will be enrolled in the service of the Republic. Musicians will sing the victories of the Sans-Culottes, and of Reason, carrying its torch on the ruins of Superstition."

Musicians responded to this speech by pledging that the products of their art would be wholly consecrated to Liberty and Revolution.

The youngest musician of the Commune of Rouen was the sixteen-year-old Mlle. Thiémé. On 10 Floreal of Year II she sang patriotic couplets of her own composition. At that time, the National Agent of the Commune recommended that "having given proof of precocious talent, Mlle. Thiémé should receive felicitations for her civic ardor."

The festivities at the Temple of Reason were extremely successful, so much so that the public often invaded the orchestra pit. The rules had to be established demanding the presentation of a professional musician's card for admission to the enclosure. But soon the civic excitement wore off. The Council of the Commune complained, on 25 Niviose of Year III of the Revolution, that the celebrations at the Temple were unattended and the Temple itself deserted. The concerts continued for another revolutionary year. Then Robespierre fell. The Temple of Reason was returned to the Church, and on May 5, 1796 became once more the Cathedral of Rouen.

The crowds in the Temple of Reason did not always listen to reason. They frequently engaged in mutual vituperation, calling each other Jacobins — the 1793 equivalent of Fascists. Even the performers were not exempt from the atmosphere of mutual suspicion that reigned during the Terror. The famous tenor Garat was arrested in Rouen on suspicion of being sympathetic with the old regime. During his detention in jail he composed an aria entitled *Elegiac Complaint of a Troubadour*. Soon released, he performed his aria with great success on the 26th Fructidor of Year II. He was accompanied on the clavecin by young Boieldieu, the future composer of *La Dame blanche*.

Operatic productions in Rouen showed the influence of the times. There was a spectacle called *L'Inauguration de la république*, with the extraordinary subtitle, "*pièce sans-culottide.*" There was a production entitled *L'Intérieur d'un ménage républicain*. Other presentations included *The Siege of Lille* from an opera by Kreutzer, with the hall decorated to resemble a military redoubt. Announcements of productions bore the imprint of the Revolution in their wording: "*Unité, Indivisibilité de la République Française, Egalité et Fraternité. Aujourd'-hui, spectacle de par et pour le peuple.*" Admission was free of charge, but soon the prosaic necessity of making the opera pay for itself forced the directors to return to the capitalistic procedure of selling tickets. The civic zeal of the early months gave way to a bourgeois desire for entertainment without political connotations. The fate-

[71]

ful month of Thermidor approached, marking the ascendance of Napoleon. Musicians still paid lip service to Liberty, Equality, and Fraternity, but they were seeking favors not from the People's Republic but from a tyrannical autocrat.

Kaiser-hanging Songs

During World War I, the production of war songs was a major industry, and an integral part of this industry were foxtrots and quicksteps threatening the Kaiser with hanging or some other form of execution. There were more than a hundred of these Kaiser-hanging songs. The series was opened on June 7, 1917 with the publication of a song titled *We Are Out for the Scalp of Mister Kaiser Man*. The authors of a song copyrighted on June 11, 1917 were contented with the Kaiser's helmet, *We Want the Kaiser's Helmet Now*. By far the best Kaiser song was one to the tune of *John Brown's Body—We Will Make the Kaiser Wiser*, which was also the first of a long series in which Kaiser was rhymed with wiser. It was copyrighted on August 25, 1917. On September 1 of the same year, a songwriter promised that *The Kaiser Will Be Wiser When Uncle Sam Is Through*, and on September 27 a positive assertion was made, *We'll Put the Kaiser Wiser*.

By the fall of 1917 the songwriters grew really ferocious with the titles, *We're Going To Hang the Kaiser under the Linden Tree* (October 1, 1917); *We're after the Kaiser's Goat* (November 10, 1917); *We're Going To Whip the Kaiser* (November 12, 1917); *We're Truly on our Way To Can the Kaiser* (December 19, 1917).

The song, *We're All Going Calling on the Kaiser*, copyrighted on February 16, 1918, had a flashy title page showing the Kaiser with the familiar handle-bar moustache recoiling before the sight of United States soldiers entering Berlin. On February 25, 1918, an "original jazz foxtrot" was published with the title, *"The Kaiser's Got*

the Blues Since Uncle Sam Stepped In. A boastful title
was *We're Going To Show the Kaiser the Way To Cut Up
Sauerkraut* (March 14, 1918). A "blues" song, *The Kaiser's Goodbye to His Submarines and All His Zeppelins*
was published on March 20, 1918.. In a similar vein were
the songs, *Kaiser Bill Will Laugh No More* (April 3,
1918); and *The Crazy Kaiser* (April 15, 1918).

In March 1918, Russia concluded a separate peace
with Germany. This event inspired the song, *We All
Want a Separate Piece of Kaiser Bill* (April 16, 1918).
Among the other titles of the Kaiser songs before the
Armistice were: *Who's Afraid of the Kaiser* (April 26,
1918); *There'll Be No German Kaiser* (May 8, 1918); *I'd
Like To See the Kaiser with a Lily in His Hand* (May 8,
1918). One more reversion to the Kaiser-wiser rhyme,
Mr Kaiser, You'll Be Wiser, to the tune of *Yankee Doodle,*
appeared on May 15, 1918, on the same day with *We'll
Give the Stars and Stripes to the Kaiser.*

Several songs promised to "kick the hell out of Will-
hell-em" as well as to "kick hell out of Heligoland." Other
variations of the same was a determination to "take the
germ out of Germany." There was a promise in the song,
When the Yanks Yank the Germ out of Germany (July
23, 1918) a definite premonition in *Our Yankee Boys
Have Yanked the Germ out of Germany* (October 7,
1918), and the conclusive *There'll Be No Germ in Germany* which was copyrighted with a slight delay twelve
days after the Armistice.

The streak of ferocity returned in the summer of 1918
with the songs, *Run the Kaiser off the Earth* (May 29);
We Will Can the Kaiser, Submarines and All (July 3);
You Krazy Kaiser (July 3); *I'd Kill the Kaiser for You*
(July 15); *If I Only Had My Razor under the Kaiser's
Chin* (July 20); *Shoot the Kaiser* (August 3); *We'll Yank
the Kaiser's Moustache Down* (August 19); *When We've*

[73]

Taken the Kaiser's Scalp (August 22); *The Kaiser's Pants Afire* (September 14); *We'll Swat the Kaiser* (September 30); *If I Catch that Kaiser in de Chicken Coop* (October 16). In a more serious vein were the songs, *Kaiser Bill, the World's Satanic Foe* (October 1, 1918), and *The Kaiser Is a Devil* (October 15, 1918).

The Armistice caught the songwriters behind schedule. There was a song published November 22, eleven days after the Armistice, which had the licking of the Kaiser still in the future: *When We Lick the Kaiser and His Huns*. Another publisher was more up-to-date. On November 22, he copyrighted a song which put the Kaiser in the past tense: *There Was a Hohenzollern Kid, Wilhelm by Name Was He.*

All was over but the shouting, and the tumult was not voluminous. On November 23, 1918, a song publisher demanded, *Hang the Kaiser to a Sour Apple Tree*. On the same day a songwriter boasted *We've Turned His Moustache Down*. By December 5, 1918, there was almost a feeling of camaraderie in the song published on that day, *We Sure Got That Kaiser We Did, Boys*. And finally as a nostalgic echo of the Kaiser-wiser era, a song was published on December 16, 1918 with the motto, *The Kaiser Now Is Wiser.*

The Kaiser died, unscalped and unhung, still retaining the "hell" in the second syllable of his name; he died not of strangulation, but of a heart attack, in Doorn, Holland, on June 4, 1941 at 11:30 A.M. He lived to witness his successor's greatest victories, and his home was guarded by Hitler's soldiers. The press and the radio hardly noted his passing. The prevailing comment was, if anything, sympathetic.

Raising a Soldier Boy

On January 4, 1915, at the time when pacifism was rampant in America, an obscure music copyist and arranger, Al Piantadosi, published a sentimental tune, *I Didn't Raise My Boy To Be a Soldier,* dedicated "respectfully to every mother everywhere." The title page depicted in flamboyant colors the bombs exploding on the horizon while a kindly-faced, gray-haired American mother protected her darling boy from the horrors of war. The song became an immediate "hit," but as the spirit of the times changed, there were sequels to the song modifying the sentiment: *I Did Not Raise My Boy To Be a Coward* (copyrighted October 18, 1915), and *I Didn't Raise My Boy To Be a Soldier, I'll Send My Girl To Be a Nurse* (January 17, 1917). There was also an irreverent version: *I Didn't Raise My Dog To Be a Sausage* (April 21, 1915).

By February, 1917, pacifism was altogether out of fashion. On February 16 of that year, a song was published, the title page of which pictured the same gray-haired mother (who two years earlier had refused to raise her boy to be a soldier) cheerfully handing over her son to the Army; the title of the song was, *America, Here's My Boy.* Then in quick succession several songs, published during April and May, emphasized the willingness of mothers to raise their boys as soldiers: *I'm Glad I Raised My Boy To Be a Soldier* (April 14, 1917); *I Didn't Raise My Boy To Be a Molly-Coddle* (May 4, 1917). The series continued with *My Boy, He Just Can't Help Being a Soldier* (June 8, 1917); *I Didn't Raise My Boy To Be a Soldier, but He Will Fight for the U. S. A.* (June 13, 1917), and *I Didn't Raise My Boy To Be a Slacker* (July 13, 1917).

Mademoiselle from Armentières

The rowdiest song of World War I was *Mademoiselle from Armentières,* composed by Gitz Rice and Reginald Rowlands of the British Expeditionary Force. When World War II came, the original Mademoiselle turned

[75]

up unexpectedly in a village near Paris. Harold Denny described this momentous joining of time in a dispatch from the front published in the New York *Times* of December 10, 1939:

"Mademoiselle's name is Marie, and she was a buxom young woman of twenty-five when the World War began. She was in love with a *poilu* who had been sent to fight. Later they married and had a daughter. There is now a new soldier song about the daughter of Mademoiselle from Armentières. But the daughter is now married and has a daughter of her own. When we tracked the original Mademoiselle from Armentières to the village where she now lives, we found her sloppily dressed and anything but glamorous, but wearing the same gold earrings she had worn in the Café de la Paix. We invited her into the village café, where she accepted a drink and where her husband, Monsieur Marceau, a truck driver, joined us. Mademoiselle boasts that she speaks English, which she learned 'from British soldiers in Armentières,' and she is quite proud of it. But her English is largely hair-raising profanity that rolls innocently from her lips."

Songs of World War II

In contrast with the First World War when the production of warlike songs was a major industry, the Second World War did not lend itself to singing mobilization. There was general skepticism concerning the potential contribution of Tin Pan Alley to the nation's morale. In its issue of December 29, 1941, *Time* magazine dismissed the warlike ditties of Broadway's songsmiths in a sweeping survey under the caption, "Of Thee I Sing, Baby." It reported that 260 titles were submitted to music publishers in the three days after Pearl Harbor, in which the alliterations "nasty Nazis" and the rhymes "sap" and "Jap" were recurring devices. A typical song was *You're a Sap, Mister Jap,* with a cover in red showing Uncle Sam spanking a midget-like Jap with the butt of his rifle. A song entitled *The Japs Won't Have a China-man's Chance* went into production but was stopped when someone pointed out that the title was disrespectful to the Chinese. The best rhyme among the anti-Jap titles was *To Be Specific, It's Our Pacific.*

The anti-Nazi songs were weak echoes of the bloodthirsty Kaiser-hanging songs of the First World War. There was the half-hearted *Marching to Berlin and to Tokyo* and *When the Yanks Go Marching In.* There was nothing as masculine as the World War I song, *If He Can Fight Like He Can Love, Then Good Night Germany.* Instead, the soldiers preferred sentimental songs such as *White Christmas* (with the inevitable variation, in the South Pacific, "I'm Dreaming of a White Mistress"),

Because of the development of radio broadcasting, World War II witnessed a phenomenon that was highly disturbing to the song industry. Enemy songs were picked up on the radio by Allied soldiers. Such was the case of *Lili Marlene,* a German love song composed by Norbert Schultze to a poem by one Hans Leip. The song was written before the war, in 1938, and was entitled *The Lantern Song.* It was sung in Berlin night clubs by a Swedish singer named Lala Andersen, but attracted little attention. After the Nazi invasion of Yugoslavia, a recording of the song was played repeatedly by the Germans over the Belgrade radio station simply because it happened to be one of the few records available. The broadcast was relayed to Italy and to North Africa, and the song caught on, both with the German and the Allied Armies. Goering's wife sang *Lili Marlene,* and fan mail included a letter from the crew of a German submarine dated "Somewhere off New York Harbor," and stating, "Tonight we tuned in softly in order not to wake up Uncle Sam."

The composer Schultze, encouraged by his sudden leap into popularity, contributed two more songs,

[77]

Bomber auf Engelland and *Panzer rollen in Africa vor.* Unfortunately for him, the bombers were now heard more often over Germany than over England, and the Panzers were rolling in Africa in the wrong direction.

The British took cognizance of the tremendous appeal of *Lili Marlene* in the British Army and produced a film under the title, *The True Story of Lili Marlene.* In it, the original performer of the song was pictured languishing in a concentration camp, and the song was cleverly represented as being anti-Nazi in spirit.

Norbert Schultze turned up safe and sound in the American zone in Berlin in November 1946, working as a gardener on a community vegetable plot. He was also giving piano lessons to musically inclined American soldiers. Shifting his loyalties, he wrote a Military Police march in collaboration with an American lieutenant-colonel. He explained away the composition of his earlier march, *Bombs over England,* as an unfortunate accident. "I just wrote the music for an Air Force documentary film," he told the Americans, "but Goering liked it so much he took it over for propaganda purposes."

The first anti-Hitler song was written in England before the start of official hostilities. It was an innocent ditty entitled *Even Hitler Had a Mother.* The song was scheduled for performance in London, in a musical revue which was to open on April 20, 1939, but the Lord Chamberlain banned the song as an insult to the head of a foreign nation. When it was allowed for public performance in September 1939, the events were too grim for so mild a production, and the song quickly faded away.

Equally ephemeral was another British war song, *We're Gonna Hang Out the Washing on the Siegfried Line if the Siegfried Line's Still There.* It was written on September 11, 1939, by Jimmy Kennedy and Michael Carr and published four days later. So remote seemed the consummation of its promise in the title that the

Nazis sang it in derision in the Paris night clubs after the fall of France. Such was the irony of events that when the Allied Armies did reach the Siegfried Line during the last stages of the war, they did not stop long enough for the laundry to be washed and hung there.

The song that really stirred the hearts of Englishmen during the darkest period of the Battle for Britain was one of general import, *There'll Always Be an England.* It was written in March, 1939, by the thirty-three-year-old Hughie Charles, to the words by Ross Parker. Incidentally, the real name of the lyric writer was Michael Ross. He changed it to Ross Parker in conformity with the rule in the entertainment industry that there should be an "R" in the first and the last names of actors, singers, and musicians.

The only anti-Hitler song produced on this side of the Atlantic that had any popular success was *Der Führer's Face.* It was originally featured in the Walt Disney production, *In Nutsy Land,* in which Donald Duck lampooned the "nutsy" Nazis in heavily Germanized English, in which the letter "v" replaced "w," and "f" was substituted for "v."

The industry was pessimistic about war songs. *Downbeat,* in its issue of February 15, 1942, stated: "Half-baked war songs won't build morale. If we must have war songs let's have good ones." In the February 1, 1943 issue of the same magazine, Glenn Miller, the band leader, wrote: "This war won't produce an *Over There.*" A monthly magazine entitled *Hit-Kit,* the organ of the Special Service Division, Services of Supply, published a number of songs, but the favorites were mostly revivals or such curious song phenomena as *Roll out the Barrel,* a polka written by a Bohemian musician before the war, which somehow captured the imagination of the soldiers and was sung by both the Axis and Allied Armies.

Perhaps the only spontaneously inspired war song of

World War II was *Praise the Lord and Pass the Ammunition,* composed by the soldier-musician Frank Loesser. The slogan was supposed to have been originated by Father Maguire, who was fleet chaplain for the Pacific Fleet on December 7, 1941, during the attack on Pearl Harbor. According to the lyrics of the song, he manned a gun himself after the gunner and then the gunner's mate were killed, shouting, "We got one," as he fired.

Father Maguire heard the song for the first time when he returned to the United States late in 1942. He expressed his great annoyance and stated, in an interview published in *PM* of November 1, 1942: "I did not man a gun on December 7 or at any other time in my career in the Navy. I wish to state unreservedly that the quotation, 'We got one' is false." As for the phrase, "Praise the Lord and pass the ammunition," Father Maguire admitted that he might have said it in the din of the battle. "It may have been heard by an altar-boy. I don't want to disillusion people. But in these circumstances I would probably have been more likely to use the expression, 'God help us' than 'Praise the Lord.'"

Furthermore Father Maguire remarked, "Chaplains with the armed forces are not allowed to fight." It was known that fifty-six Catholic chaplains were prisoners of the Japanese, and Father Maguire expressed his apprehension that they might be subjected to reprisals for his alleged violation of the rules of war. The facts as Father Maguire remembered them were these: He was on a pier at Pearl Harbor waiting to go in a launch to conduct Mass on a battleship, when the first Japanese planes dropped their torpedoes at 7:50 A.M. December 7. He went first to a destroyer and then to a battleship and "tried to do my duty in accord with naval regulations and international law." He heard confessions and assisted the wounded.

The first World War had its *Mademoiselle from Ar-*

mentières with its many ribald versions. The second World War produced *Dirty Gertie from Bizerte*. It is said that the Gertie song was inspired by a mannequin in a department store in Bizerte, which caught the fancy of the American soldiers during the North African campaign. The original mannequin was even photographed in the arms of the soldier who claimed to have composed the song, Sergeant Paul Reif, an experienced Broadway tunesmith. The correspondent who first broke the news about Gertie warned in his dispatch from the Allied Headquarters in North Africa, dated May 29, 1941: "Sorry folks, I can't give you the words — they might burn out the cables and blow out radio tubes. It's enough to say that it will be one of the most popular songs when the boys of this war begin holding legion meetings after it's all over. But until then, you'll just have to wait."

One of the most curious usages of music in war was the scheme of the British Broadcasting Corporation to popularize the slogan "V for Victory" in the Nazi occupied territories. In Morse Code the letter "V" is represented by three dots and a dash. This is also the rhythm of the opening notes of Beethoven's Fifth Symphony. Erika Mann, the daughter of Thomas Mann, wrote in *PM* of July 14, 1940 (and her article was published with the first two measures of the Fifth Symphony inscribed at the top): "This British 'V' Blitz will drive the enemy mad by weapons he is unable to match or even account for. Nazi concentration camps will hammer 'V' rhythm into minds of their slave drivers, and the first notes of Beethoven's Fifth will be sung by children on their way to Nazi schools, whistled in Nazi-dominated factories, played by orchestras tuning their instruments for the Nazi hymn."

In Norway, the "V" sign was often used in triplicate for the words, "ve vil vinne." Performances of Beethoven's Fifth Symphony were greeted with demonstrative applause. Then the Nazis decided to take over the "V" symbol rather than try to suppress it. Their propagandists dug up an old German word *Viktoria* and broadcast the rhythm of Beethoven's Fifth from their radio stations in occupied Europe with an explanation by the announcer that it was "'V' for victory, which Germany is winning on all fronts."

This war of musical themes provided a necessary outlet for the population of occupied Europe. They were enabled to tease the Nazis without fear of reprisals. The songs played their role when the fronts were quiescent. But when the grim business of invasion was begun, there were no new songs to sing. The soldiers sang old Broadway hits that reminded them of home. It is by those songs that World War II is remembered in the hearts of its soldiers.

Mikado and Madame Butterfly

The Gilbert and Sullivan operetta, *The Mikado*, was banned in Japan because of its highly disrespectful treatment of the Emperor. But things have changed, and on July 22, 1946, *The Mikado* was produced in Tokyo with an authentic ballet of Japanese girls. Japanese spectators filled the hall and indulged in plenty of innocent merriment.

With the war's end, another ban was lifted, an unofficial ban on Puccini's opera, *Madame Butterfly*, which had been excluded from the repertory of the Metropolitan Opera and other American opera companies for the duration. Obviously, the spectacle of an American officer seducing a Japanese girl and driving her to hara-kiri could only give aid and comfort to the enemy. As soon as the war ended, the opera was reinstated, and audiences could once more shed tears over the touching melodrama.

Star-Spangled San Min

There are many ways of contributing to international harmony, but the most extraordinary one was demonstrated by Professor Yuen Ren Chao of Harvard University. He discovered that the national anthems of China and the United States could be harmonized and sung or played as a perfect duet, and on July 4, 1943, composed a twin version of the two hymns. He entitled the final product *Star-Spangled San Min*.

II

NOT TO BE FOUND IN
AUTHORIZED BIOGRAPHIES

Periodical Symphonies

What is a Periodical Symphony?

The first Bach's son, Johann Christian — called the "English" Bach because he lived and died in London — has a set of six "Periodical Symphonies" among his works. The title sounds intriguing, conjuring up notions of a symphony with periodically recurring themes. But actually they are nothing of the sort. The title was merely the publisher's way of indicating in his advertisements that he was in the business of publishing symphonies periodically.

For Decayed Musicians

Benefit concerts in eighteenth-century London were outspoken affairs in which the circumstances and need of the beneficiaries were described in the advertisements.

Johann Christian Bach took part in several such benefit concerts. One was given "for the relief of Lady Doro-
thy Dubois, eldest lawful daughter of Richard, the last
Earl of Anglesey," who, as a child of her father's secret
and bigamous marriage, was deprived of her inheritance.
Johann Christian Bach was said, in this advertisement,
to be "as conspicuously endowed with soft compassion
as unequaled in harmony and superiority of genius."

The most intriguing of these benefits was for "decayed
musicians"—though the advertisement failed to specify
whether the "decayed musicians" were living or dead.

Corelli, the Archangel

Arcangelo Corelli, whose historical importance rests
in his having made a virtuoso instrument of the violin
by writing difficult solo pieces and performing them with
brilliancy, was visited in Rome by the German musician
Strunck.

"What instrument do you play?" Corelli asked.

"A little violin and a little harpsichord," replied the other, "and I should be delighted to hear you play."

Corelli acceded to the request and played some of his own music.

"Truly you are an archangel," remarked Strunck, with allusion to Corelli's first name. "But in your technique you are an archdevil."

Trumps in D

Handel was displeased with the new music that he heard in his day in London (circa 1750). He particularly objected to the constant shifting from the tonic to the dominant in the trumpets. When he heard such music he used to laugh and exclaim — using the terms of his favorite card game: "Now D in trumps, now A."

The Murder of Leclair

On October 23, 1764 early in the morning, a Parisian worker passing by the suburban cottage belonging to the sixty-nine-year-old French violinist and composer, Jean-Marie Leclair, noticed that the door was open. At the same time Leclair's gardener was leisurely walking toward the house. They exchanged remarks and soon noticed that the Leclair's hat and wig had been tossed on the ground in the garden. Alarmed, they awakened the neighbors and went into the house. There they found a frightful scene. Jean-Marie Leclair was lying on his back in the vestibule, his jacket and his shirt covered with blood. He had been stabbed three times, in the left shoulder, in the stomach, and in the chest. Next to the body were found several objects that seemed to have been put there intentionally, a book entitled *L'Elite des bons mots,* some manuscript paper, and a hunting knife, which, however, bore no traces of blood.

The police opened an inquest. The obvious suspect was the gardener, who had a prison record. His testimony was confused and contradictory; he declared that he had noticed the open door at six o'clock in the morning, but several neighbors testified that they were awakened by him to come for help at half-past four. The police questioned a woman, admittedly the gardener's mistress. She said that on the night of the murder, the gardener arrived at her house at ten-thirty, while he had maintained he had been there from seven o'clock on. Another woman testified that the gardener had threatened he would take care of her husband in the same way that Leclair had been dispatched.

The motive could not have been robbery; four gold pieces were found in a drawer of Leclair's desk where anyone familiar with the household would have looked. On the other hand, the watch that Leclair was known to possess was not found on the body. The gardener claimed that Leclair had lost it eighteen months before, but the proprietor of a billiard room which Leclair had visited on the night of the assassination testified that he had taken out his watch to look at the time at about a quarter of ten.

Another suspect was Leclair's own nephew, himself a musician. It was known that he had pestered his uncle with demands to recommend him as a household musician to the Duke of Gramont. He was reported as having spoken of his uncle as a miser with no feelings for his family or friends, and as having said that Leclair would some day meet with a violent death. But all this talk was *ex post facto,* and nothing definite could be pinned on the nephew.

The police inspector in charge of the inquest wrote:

"The nephew merits attention; his extraordinary state of agitation and trembling at Leclair's interment noted by my men, whom I had sent to the funeral, and also by others, adds to the circumstantial evidence against him, and makes him highly suspect. I also know that he enjoys the favor of Leclair's widow, which justifies my interest in her part as well. At the same time, I do not abandon my suspicions against the gardener as some information seems to point against him."

Leclair lived alone. He had been estranged from his wife for some years; yet his association with her was not interrupted, for Madame Leclair was not only his wife but his publisher as well. She was a remarkable woman who had learned the art of music engraving, was an expert with the tools of her trade, and seemed to be a person of uncommon energy and physical strength. She continued to print his music even after the separation. Madame Leclair testified that 841 lead plates of the compositions of her late husband were, at the time of his death, in the hands of the printer as a guarantee for the sum of 1,150 livres which the Leclairs owed to the printer. The printer also had in his possession twenty-five copper plates of the engraved map of Paris, also the work of Madame Leclair.

Even the Duke of Gramont was drawn into the inquest despite his rank and position. He made a written statement:

"I visited M. Leclair only twice, and I did not drink nor eat at his house; such company is not for me. For seven or eight years I have not drunk anything but water."

The Leclair's widow enjoyed considerable favor in court circles. She was able to help Leclair to obtain excellent commissions from royal patrons and from the king himself. Her interest in the affairs of Leclair's nephew may have played a role in the ultimate estrangement of the couple. The vague suspicion voiced by the police inspector in regard to the role of Madame Leclair in the murder was not followed up, and the affair was declared closed without the uncovering of the culprit.

The police never made clear that the assassin must have been known to Leclair and received by him at his house at an appointed hour, probably between ten and eleven in the evening, after Leclair had looked at his watch in the billiard room. The three wounds were inflicted in the front part of Leclair's body as he faced his murderer; they might have been caused by a sharp tool used for music engraving — yet there was no examination of these tools in Madame Leclair's apartment in Paris. The correspondence between Leclair and his wife during the period of estrangement was not examined; their business arrangements during that period were not investigated. The meetings between Leclair's widow and his nephew after his death were not watched. Obviously this line of inquiry was not favored by the authorities.

Yet the picture of the assassination should have been clear. Madame Leclair went to see her husband and urged him to help his nephew in obtaining a position with the Duke of Gramont. Leclair, being jealous of his status with his wealthy patrons, refused to do so. He probably accused his wife of showing undue interest in his nephew's welfare. Madame Leclair must have brought with her a chisel or some other tool used in engraving, in anticipation of violent argument, perhaps for self-defense. Being a novice in assassination, she failed to reach Leclair's heart and struck three blows in three parts of his body in order to accomplish fatal results. From all evidence it appears that she spent some time in the room after the murder arranging the objects around his body, removing his hat and wig and leaving them in the garden, all in very amateurish fashion, and at the risk of having been discovered. Only a person intimately acquainted with the victim's mode of life could have gone through these motions. Only a person who knew Leclair's interest in books and music would have placed a book of quotations and music manuscript paper next to his body. Such a person could only have been Madame Leclair, the first woman publisher and music engraver in the annals of music history.

Hail, Farewell Symphony

The story of Haydn's *Farewell* Symphony is a favorite among music commentators. The accepted version is that Haydn wrote this symphony as a gentle hint to his employer, Prince Esterházy, that his musicians deserved a vacation from their labors. The hint was found in the Finale when one player after another departs from the stage until only the first violinist is left.

This story has a strangely unconvincing ring about it. Why should Haydn have employed such a subtle way of asking for a vacation for his men, presumably without pay? Why should the entire orchestra desire a leave-of-absence at the same time? In the semi-feudal environment of the time, any collective action of this kind was extremely unlikely.

A much more plausible version of this episode is found in a half-forgotten book, *Aneddoti piacevole e interessanti,* by an Italian musician, Giacomo Ferrari, published in the Italian language in London in 1830. Ferrari, who knew Haydn personally, tells a story of the *Farewell* Symphony that makes sense.

"At one time, Esterházy became dissatisfied with the musicians of his orchestra and ordered Haydn to dismiss them all, with the exception of the first violin and the harpsichordist. Haydn was compelled to obey, but was distressed by both the necessity of ruining the livelihood of so many people and the personal loss of experienced musicians. He decided to compose an instrumental fugue, and invited Prince Esterházy to hear the performance on a certain Sunday after Mass. The prince complied with his request. After the orchestral section played together, as demanded by the fugue form, the crafty maestro introduced a sort of coda with successive pauses so arranged that one instrument after another ceased to play. The fugue ended with the violin and harpsichord playing one note in unison. Prince Esterházy enjoyed the composer's joke so much that he told him to retain all the players on their jobs."

Quintet — in Four Parts

Haydn biographers have often wondered why he never wrote a string quintet. A partial answer to this is provided by Giacomo Ferrari in his anecdotes. He writes:

"Prince Lobkowitz asked Haydn why he had never written an instrumental quintet. The answer was that he did not wish to have a work of his suffer comparison with the celebrated quintets of Mozart which he regarded perfect. 'Never mind,' said the Prince. 'Write a quintet for me and I will remunerate you handsomely.'

"The famous maestro set to work, and after a short while delivered the manuscript to Prince Lobkowitz. Glancing through the manuscript, Lobkowitz noted that only four staves had been filled, with the fifth left empty.

" 'Dear Haydn,' he said, 'you must have forgotten to put in the fifth part.'

" 'No, Prince. I left it for Your Highness to fill in. I could not compose anything appropriate myself.' "

Lobkowitz must have well understood the subtle irony of Haydn's gesture. He certainly never attempted to fill in the missing part. It is not known whether the four-part quintet eventually became a legitimate string quartet.

Unopened Letters of Mrs. Haydn

Haydn was separated from his termagant wife for a long time. A friend, calling on him, noted with astonishment a pile of unopened letters on the composer's desk.

"Oh, they are from my wife," Haydn explained. "She

writes me monthly, and I answer her monthly. But I do not open her letters, and I am quite sure that she does not open mine."

Haydn and the Dog

While in England, Haydn visited his friend, Venanzio Rauzzini, an Italian musician who had settled in the town of Bath as bandleader and singing teacher. Rauzzini spoke of a recent bereavement: his favorite dog, Turk, had died. Rauzzini had buried the dog in his garden and had inscribed on the tombstone: "Turk was a faithful dog, and not a man." Haydn was so impressed by this story that he composed a "perpetual" canon using for the text Rauzzini's epitaph. The music of the canon is in existence; but the oft-told story that it was engraved on the dog's tombstone is apocryphal. Inquiries at the office of the superintendent registrar of Bath have brought the information that Rauzzini lived at 13 Gay Street, in a house known in his time as Perrymead Villa. But there exists no vestige of the faithful Turk's last resting place. Whether the tombstone was actually put up by Rauzzini must remain an insoluble mystery.

Mozart's Program

Besides being an estimable musician, Mozart's father was also a shrewd business man. When Mozart was a child, his father exploited his public appearances with all the sensationalism of which the eighteenth century was capable. The program which Mozart and his sister presented in Frankfort in 1764 (the text of which was prepared by the father) came to light in 1892.

"My daughter, twelve years old, and my son of seven will execute the concertos of the greatest masters on several kinds of pianos, and my son on the violin likewise. My son will cover the fingerboard of the piano with a cloth and play as if it were uncovered. He will guess, both standing near or at any distance, and name any sound on a piano, on a bell, or any other instrument. In conclusion, he will improvise as long as desired, both on the organ and the piano in all keys, even the most difficult, as anyone may choose."

Mozart's Musical Joke

Mozart possessed a healthy sense of humor. One of his compositions, named *A Musical Joke*, was intended to ridicule inexpert village bands. In it, there is a violin cadenza containing a whole-tone scale; there are parallel fifths in defiance of all established rules. As a climax, the piece ends in several different keys.

Nowadays, these harmonies are no longer funny. The whole-tone scale is part and parcel of French impressionism. Parallel fifths are used by composers writing in the neoclassical idiom. And the simultaneous playing of different keys has acquired the scientific name of polytonality. Mozart, of course, could not in his wildest dreams have imagined that his innocent pranks would a century and a half later become the serious practice of important composers.

Mozart's Long Nose

The following story of Mozart's sense of humor has received wide circulation, even though there is obviously no substantiating evidence.

One day, Mozart taunted Haydn that the latter would never be able to play a piece which Mozart had just written. Haydn sat at the harpsichord, began to play from the manuscript, then stopped abruptly. There was a note in the center of the keyboard while the right hand was playing in high treble and the left hand in low bass.

"Nobody can play this with only two hands," Haydn exclaimed.

"I can," Mozart said quietly. When he reached the

debated portion of his composition, he bent over and struck the central note with his nose.

"With a nose like yours," Haydn conceded, "it becomes easier."

Composition — With Dice

Composers great and small have continually toyed with the idea of composing music by mechanical means.

As a youth, Mozart devised a musical game enabling anyone to put together a passable composition in waltz-time—by playing dice. He wrote out 176 separate bars of music, and made up a table marked from two to twelve, indicating which bars were to be played according to the results of the throw of the dice. Naturally, the first bar in any throw was in the tonic, the second, in the dominant, and so forth according to prearranged harmonic progressions. The melody was more or less in the same register, in the first octave in the treble, so that any bar in the tonic could easily be hinged to any bar in the dominant.

This little game was published in London fifteen years after Mozart's death as "Mozart's Musical Game, fitted in an elegant box, showing by an easy system, how to compose an unlimited number of Rondos, Hornpipes, and Reels."

The Chromatic Mozart

It is difficult to believe today that Mozart was criticized by his contemporaries as an advocate of modern fashions in harmony. The following review from the *Musical Miscellanies* of London (1784) shows that not even Mozart escaped the attacks of carping reactionary music critics.

"Three *Sonatas pour le clavecin ou le forte piano composées par W. A. Mozard (sic),* 7s. 6d.: These sonatas are wrote with spirit; and several of the movements evidence taste and invention in the composer; particularly the Andante of Sonata No. 1 and the Allegro of the Third, which is truly pretty. But there are a number of chromatic passages, grown fashionable indeed, but which hurt the simplicity of the harmony, and have only the appearance of learning. But on the whole there is considerable merit in these lessons, and, what will recommend them to many, these are passages which will well exercise the fingers."

An Individual Named Mozart

When Mozart's opera, *Belmonte und Costanz* (better known under its second title, *Die Entführung aus dem Serail*) was brought out in Vienna in 1782, the following item was published in the Leipzig *Gazette,* signed by Christoph Friedrich Butzner, the author of the original drama:

"An individual named Mozart has taken the liberty of laying hands on my drama, *Belmonte und Constanz,* and turning it into a libretto. I protest solemnly against this violation of my rights, reserving to myself the power of taking ulterior proceedings."

[95]

Musical Skull and Bones

The tribulations of great musicians do not end in the grave; posterity, in a belated desire to render them homage, often disturbs their eternal rest. Thus it has come to pass that the bones of Bach, Mozart, Haydn, Beethoven, and Schubert were at various times exhumed and reassembled before a final interment. Schubert's skull was even photographed.

The dramatic story of the rediscovery and identification of Bach's skeleton is told in vivid detail by George Howard Parker in his book, *The World Expands:*

"I was in Leipzig at the time when the Johannis-Kirche was undergoing extensive repairs. It was known that Bach had been buried in the cemetery connected with this church and next to a. certain wall. When the foundations for this wall were in the process of being rebuilt, the workmen were notified to look with care for an oak coffin with a metal plate on it. Such a coffin was found, though the metal plate on it was so far corroded as to be illegible. The contents of the coffin were carefully transferred to Professor His's anatomical laboratory in the university. The ear bones showed that this elderly man had had good hearing to the end of his life. With the skull as a base, a papier-mâché model of the face was then constructed. All these elements conspired to show that this was the long-lost skeleton of Johann Sebastian Bach. I had been a student in Professor His's lectures on embryology; thinking that I would be interested in such matters, he was good enough to show me Bach's skeleton, now carefully laid out upon a table. I asked Professor His if I might touch the scattered bones of the hand, and he assented. Thus in a way, I have a handshaking acquaintance with this master of great music. As is well known, the remains of Bach after this identification were returned to the Johannis-Kirche and now rest in an identified vault."

It is often asserted that Mozart was buried in a pauper's grave. This is not quite accurate. Mozart was buried in a churchyard in Vienna, and his gravedigger marked the coffin with winding wire. Mozart's widow remarried and left the grave unattended. As a result, ten years after Mozart's death, the coffin was taken to the common grave. His body was placed on the top layer, first on the left. Ten more years passed, and the pit had to be cleared of its contents, in accordance with the rules. The gravedigger, knowing something about Mozart's fame, removed the skull and took it to his home. Before his death, he confessed his deed to Jacob Hyrtl, a professor of anatomy who had business transactions with the cemetery, and offered the skull to Hyrtl, who accepted it. Hyrtl made an inscription on Mozart's brow: "Mozart's Skull: *Musa vetat mori.*" After Hyrtl's death the skull was taken to the Mozarteum in Salzburg.

The story of Haydn's skull is similarly eventful. In 1830 Prince Esterházy decided to place Haydn's remains in the Esterházy family vault, in appreciation of the fact that Haydn had been for many years the family musician. When Haydn's remains were transferred, it was discovered that the skull was missing. How it became detached from the body was told in a confession of one Johann Peter, a governor of the Imperial and Royal Prison in Vienna. The confession stated that after Haydn was buried in 1809, Peter with several friends, one a secretary of Prince Esterházy, bribed a cemetery guard to steal the head of the great musician for the purpose of making a phrenological study. On promise of immunity from prosecution, he and the other participants in the Haydn body-snatching handed the skull over to the police. This, however, is not the end of the story. When the conspirator who actually had held the skull in his possession felt that his dying hour was near, he confessed that the skull he had given to the authorities was not Haydn's. He then produced the real skull of Haydn and willed it to the Vienna Conservatory of Music.

Others claimed possession of Haydn's skull, so that at

one time there were several Haydn skulls in circulation. John Ella tells this story in his *Musical Sketches:*

"On the removal of the body of Haydn to its present abiding place in Vienna, it was found minus the skull. Medical men, it seems, had noticed some ailment of the great master. Without entering into particulars, I shall merely state that during my last visit to Vienna in November 1873, I had the honor of dining with Baron Pokitansky, the chief director of the great hospitals. After dinner the Baron took me into his studio and carefully placed in my hands a well preserved relic — the missing skull of Papa Haydn."

In 1863 the municipality of Vienna decided to undertake the exhumation and reburial of Beethoven and Schubert in view of the poor condition of their graves. The entire operation was completed within twenty-four hours, but in the meantime an opportunity was taken of measuring the principal bones of both skeletons showing that Beethoven was 5'5" high and Schubert only 5'½". Schubert's skull was also photographed, but not Beethoven's.

Strange fate also attended the skull of Donizetti. When he died in Bergamo in 1848, Italy was convulsed by the revolution. During the autopsy of the body, an artillery shell fell near by and the doctors fled. The body was hurriedly interred at a later date. When it was exhumed in 1850, the head was missing. An appeal was made in the public press for the restoration of the skull. It was finally traced to a citizen who somehow had come into its possession and had used it for two years as a holder for blotting sand.

In our own time a great musician lies unburied while two rival political factions dispute the right to his body: Paderewski. When he died in New York in 1941, Poland was occupied by the Germans. At the personal request of President Roosevelt, Paderewski's body was placed in the Arlington National Cemetery until Poland would be once again "free and independent."

At the time of his death Paderewski had been President of the Polish Parliament in Exile. After the liberation of Poland, the Polish government, which was officially recognized by the United States, requested Washington to allow Paderewski's remains to be shipped back to his native country for reburial. Although the postwar regime in Poland was strongly opposed to the political faction represented by Paderewski, it desired to solemnize his memory as a great musician and statesman. This demand was hotly contested by Paderewski's former intimates in the United States. While this diplomatic discussion continues, the body of Paderewski still rests in a plain wooden coffin, unmarked, in a vault at the Arlington National Cemetery.

Toujours Grétry

When Grétry was at the height of his fame, he was introduced to Napoleon.

"What is your name?" the Emperor inquired.

"Grétry," the composer answered.

Sometime later, Grétry was again invited to visit Napoleon. The latter again asked: "What is your name?"

"Alas," replied Grétry with mock dejection. *"Toujours Grétry!"*

The Three B's of Music

Everyone knows that the Three B's of music are Bach, Beethoven, and Brahms. But few realize that the expression began as a German pun. It was perpetrated by Hans von Bülow who wrote: *Mein musikalisches Glaubensbekenntniss steht in Es dur, mit drei B-en in der Vorzeichnung: Bach, Beethoven, und Brahms!"*

In German, 'B" stands for B-flat, or, because a flat resembles a "b," for any flat. Thus von Bülow's remark may be translated as follows: "My musical credo is in the key of E-flat major, with three flats in the key signature: Bach, Beethoven, and Brahms."

To this, a friend of von Bülow rejoined: *"Sie könnten doch bisweilen ein 'H' hinzufügen, um in die Nebentonart zu kommen."*

The German "H" being B-natural, the sense of this second remark is as follows: "You might perhaps add a B-natural in order to modulate into the relative key." B-natural is the leading tone of C minor, and it would provide a handsome passing note from B-flat on top of the E-flat major triad to the tonic of C minor. In this case, "H" may stand for either Handel or Haydn.

Hans von Bülow had toyed with the idea of the three B's for many years. In the 1880's, he wrote in the album of a young lady: "I believe in Bach, the Father, Beethoven, the Son, and Brahms, the Holy Ghost of music." That was after he had ceased to be the perfect Wagnerite (Wagner, after all, had absconded with von Bülow's wife), and had became a Brahmsian. Bülow further bracketed the name of Brahms with that of Beethoven by calling Brahm's First Symphony Beethoven's Tenth. This association of names acquired such popularity that it became a factor in the bitter struggle between the Wagner faction and the Brahms clique.

Wagner himself had proposed a candidate for the position of the third B—Bruckner, a devout Wagnerite who worshiped his master. But Wagner's candidate was never elected by posterity. The Three B's of music are still Bach, Beethoven, and Brahms.

Beethoven as a Child Prodigy

The following advertisement is found in the *Koelnische Zeitung* of March 26, 1778:

"Today, Beethoven [that is, the composer's father], will have the honor of introducing two of his scholars, viz: Mlle.

Averdonc, court alto singer, and his little son of six years, in the Hall of the Academy of Music in the Sterngasse. The former will have the honor of waiting on the public with different beautiful arias, the latter with various fine concertos and trios, in which they flatter themselves that they will give perfect satisfaction to all their high patrons as both have had the honor of performing before the whole Court, to its great pleasure. To begin at five o'clock in the evening. Ladies and Gentlemen not subscribers pay one gulden. The tickets are to be had at the aforesaid hall of the Musical Academy."

A slight correction is necessary to set the chronology straight. Beethoven was eight years old at the time, not six. Beethoven-*père* had doctored the dates for the sake of creating better publicity.

Beethoven's Royal Blood

The worship of royalty was so strong when Europe was monarchial that it was common practice to claim royal blood for all great men. Choron, in his *Dictionnaire historique des musiciens,* claims that Beethoven was an illegitimate son of Frederick II of Prussia. The *Harmonicon* of November 1823 comments as follows on this claim: "That Beethoven is a wonderful man there can be no doubt, but if this prince were really his father, he is the greatest prodigy the world ever saw, for as Frederick II died in 1740, the period of Mme. Beethoven's gestation must have been exactly thirty years."

[101]

But Frederick II died in 1786, not 1740. Chronologically, at least, it was possible for him to have procreated Beethoven. Ries, Beethoven's pupil, quotes the remarks of the *Harmonicon* in his autobiography without correcting the chronology.

Beethoven's Wrong Notes

One evening, soon after the publication of his Sonata in D minor, Op. 31, No. 2, Beethoven was invited to perform in a Viennese home. During the difficult passage of the descending groups of two notes, Beethoven made several mistakes. The Princess Lobkowitz tapped him on the head with her hand and said coquettishly: "If you strike a pupil with one finger for one wrong note, surely it is fair that you receive a blow with the whole hand for playing a handful of wrong notes!"

Beethoven's Tailor

Beethoven's deafness is a boon to Beethoven biographers. In his last years, Beethoven was obliged to converse by means of a notebook in which he set down his questions and received answers. These conversation-books are, even more than his correspondence, the living imprints of his character. The following conversation with a Viennese shopkeeper is recorded in one of these notebooks:

Q. Can you recommend me a tailor? Mine is a fool. This frock-coat fits me like a sack. I look as if I had stolen it.

A. I will send you the tailor who works for me.

Q. Does he call himself an artist in clothes?

A. No. He remains true to the honest old German name for his craft.

Q. My stupid tailor cannot even sew on buttons properly. I have worn this jacket barely half a year, and five are already absent without leave.

The "Brischdower" Sonata

The original dedication of Beethoven's *Kreutzer* Sonata, for violin and piano, Op. 47, was to George Augustus Polgreen Bridgetower (1780-1860), a British mulatto violinist, whose name Beethoven spelled Brischdower. The sonata was performed for the first time by Beethoven and Bridgetower in Vienna on May 24, 1803. Beethoven had barely finished the violin part on the morning of the concert, and he played the piano part from penciled sketches.

Why did he change the dedication? Years later, Bridgetower himself gave the absurd explanation that Beethoven had quarreled with him over a girl and that as a result their relations had become strained. A more plausible explanation, however, is that Kreutzer—whom Beethoven had never met and who never played the *Kreutzer* Sonata in public — had more glamor. Beethoven was sensitive to the attractions of fame — at least the fame of other musicians.

The Title Page of the Eroica

Every music student knows the story of the composition of Beethoven's *Eroica* Symphony. The vivid accounts in all Beethoven's biographies tell us how Beethoven, disappointed in Napoleon's action in proclaiming himself emperor of France, tore up the dedicatory title page of the symphony and would never mention the name of Napoleon again.

This story is told on the authority of Beethoven's biographer and friend, Anton Schindler:

"Beethoven lived in the firm belief that Napoleon entertained no other design than to make France a republic. Hence his respect and enthusiasm for Napoleon. A fair copy of the musical work for the First Consul of the French Republic with the dedication to him, was on the point of being

[103]

dispatched through the French Embassy to Paris when news arrived in Vienna that Napoleon Bonaparte had caused himself to be proclaimed Emperor of the French. The first thing Beethoven did on receiving this intelligence was to tear off the title leaf of this symphony and to fling the work itself — with a torrent of execrations against the new French Emperor, against the new tyrant — upon the floor, from which he would not allow it to be lifted. It was a long time before Beethoven recovered from the shock and permitted this work to be given to the world with the title of *Sinfonia Eroica*."

Schindler's account has a ring of authenticity until one realizes that Schindler was born in 1795, and the *Eroica* Symphony was written in 1804 when Schindler was nine years old. This rules him out as a reliable reporter: all his information must have come second-hand, long after the event. A seemingly more authoritative report is found in the memoirs of Beethoven's pupil, Ferdinand Ries.

"I as well as many others saw this symphony already copied in full score, lying on Beethoven's desk with the word Buonaparte marked on top of the title page, and at the bottom, Luigi van Beethoven. . . . I was the first to break the news to Beethoven that Napoleon had proclaimed himself emperor. Beethoven flew into a rage and exclaimed: 'So he is nothing but an ordinary man! Now he will trample upon all human rights. . . .' Beethoven went to the table, tore up the title page and threw the fragments on the floor. The first page was later rewritten, and the Symphony received the title *Sinfonia Eroica*."

Ries wrote his memoirs more than thirty years after the scene he so vividly described took place. This makes questionable his reliability as a witness. Against the accounts of both Schindler and Ries is the fact that the title page of the *Eroica* has been preserved, showing the dedication to Napoleon carefully inked over, although the word Buonaparte is still visible under the smudged ink. The care with which Beethoven crossed out the

dedication certainly does not testify to the turbulence of spirit such as Ries describes in his memoirs.

Furthermore, there is a letter of Beethoven addressed to his publishers, Breitkopf & Haertel, dated August 26, 1804, in which Beethoven refers to the Symphony as "really entitled Bonaparte." Contrary to Schindler's statement that Beethoven did not permit the Symphony to be published for a long time, Beethoven definitely tried to sell the manuscript to Breitkopf & Haertel; after their refusal to publish it on the ground that it was too difficult to perform, he turned it over to another publisher in Vienna. The score was published in October 1806 with a dedication to Prince Lobkowitz.

What, then, is the real story behind the *Eroica?*

The idea of dedicating a symphony to Napoleon was proposed to Beethoven by the French ambassador in Vienna, Bernadotte, and Beethoven eagerly accepted the suggestion. Beethoven had every right to expect that the First Consul of the French Republic would be no less munificent than a Viennese prince. It is also quite legitimate to surmise that Beethoven must have queried the French Ambassador many times about Napoleon's acceptance of the Symphony. Continuing on the path of surmise, one may imagine the following letter going out from the French Embassy in Vienna to the First Consul of France in April 1804:

Your Excellency: The renowned composer Beethoven, who has acquired great fame among the music lovers of this city through his overtures, sonatas, and other works, has completed the composition of a Grand Symphony which he intends to place in your hands with a suitable dedication extolling your services to humanity and your love of liberty. If I may be bold to offer a suggestion, it would redound to your justly deserved fame as a champion of culture and patron of fine arts to deposit with the French Embassy in this city a purse of money which need not be too high and may be conveyed in local currency at specially reduced rates, this sum of money to constitute a reward for M. Beethoven's labors, the said Beethoven being in difficult financial circumstances despite the greatness of his widely acknowledged genius,

This imaginary missive would have reached Napoleon on the eve of his proclamation as emperor of France. When the news of the coup d'état reached Vienna, Bernadotte must have informed Beethoven that there was no longer any prospect of Napoleon's accepting the dedication. Beethoven was extremely sensitive to disappointments of a financial nature; such disappointment must have intensified Beethoven's undoubted indignation at Napoleon's assumption of imperial power. That Beethoven, as late as two months after the French coup d'état, was undecided as to whether the Symphony might yet remain Napoleon's Symphony is proved by his letter to the publishers quoted above, dated two months after the news of Napoleon's action had reached Vienna.

History willed it that Bernadotte became King of Sweden. Beethoven tried to maintain the old ties with him when, in 1823, he requested him to subscribe to the edition of his *Missa Solemnis*. But the king of Sweden never answered the modest request of his old friend.

As a postscript to the *Eroica*, it is interesting to note: Long after Beethoven and Napoleon were dead, a Dutch musician pointed out in a letter to Ries, that the name of Napoleon in Italian has the same number of letters as the full name of Beethoven in Dutch:

> Lodewyk van Beethoven
> Napoleone Buonaparte

Beethoven Almost Went to Paris

Baron Trémont, Napoleon's diplomatic emissary in Vienna in 1809, met Beethoven and tried to induce him to visit Paris. The Baron's memoirs (excerpts of which were published in *Le Guide musical* in 1892) throw an interesting light on Beethoven's appearance and manners. Particularly intriguing is Trémont's revelation that five years after the *Eroica*, Beethoven was still fascinated with Napoleon's personality.

"The neighbors showed me Beethoven's house. I knocked three times and was about to leave when the door was opened. A very ugly man, who seemed to be in a disagreeable mood, asked what I wished. I said in French, 'Have I the honor to speak to Herr Beethoven?'

" 'Yes, sir,' he replied in German, 'but I must tell you at once that I do not understand French very well.'

" 'I understand German no better,' I answered, 'but my business consists merely of bringing you a letter from M. Reicha of Paris.'

"At this he eyed me critically a moment, took the letter and asked me to enter. His house consisted of two rooms. One of these was an enclosed alcove in which stood his bed, but it was so small and dark that he was obliged to dress and undress in the second room. Here all was untidiness and disorder. Water bottles stood on the floor; music was thrown on a dusty piano, and the little walnut table showed that the contents of the inkwell were often overturned on it; the

[107]

countless pens were crusted with dried ink; on the chairs
stood dishes containing the remnants of meals of past days;
on others hung articles of clothing. Under the bed (I do not
exaggerate anything) *un pot de nuit non vidé*. After he read
the letter he began to ask me what my uniform signified,
my age, my business in Vienna, how long I would remain
in Vienna and whether I was musical. I replied that Reicha's
letter would explain everything better than I could.

" 'No, no,' said he, 'speak; but speak slowly; I then will
understand you although I am hard of hearing.'

"I started to talk with him and after a while we understood
each other, and when I left, he invited me to come again.

"Once, on one of my visits I asked him if he had ever
intended to visit France. 'I often keenly desired it,' he
answered, 'until France gave herself to a master. Still, I
should like greatly to hear in Paris the symphonies of
Mozart, but I am too poor to make such a trip merely to
satisfy curiosity.'

" 'Come with me! I will take you!'

" 'Impossible! I could never consent to your going to
such expense.'

" 'The expense will not be great. My fare is paid and I
have a compartment alone. If in Paris a small room will
suffice, it is at your disposal. Say yes. Paris is worth fourteen
days of your time. You will have the cost only of the fare
home, and that is barely fifty gulden.'

" 'You Parisians will say that I am a bear.'

" 'It is evident you do not know the Parisians. Paris is a
city of freedom. Noted men are treated as it pleases them to
appear and if one, and especially a stranger, is a little eccentric, this is cause for a still greater success.'

"Finally he gave me his hand and said that he would be
willing to go with me. But he never took steps to carry out
his intention.

"Napoleon interested him deeply and he often spoke of
him. I could see that he admired Napoleon because he had
risen so high from beginnings so humble. Beethoven said
to me one day: 'If I go to Paris must I greet your emperor?'
I assured him this would not be necessary unless he was
commanded to do so.

" 'And do you believe he will command me to appear
before him?'

" 'I would have no doubt of it, did he know your worth. But he understands little about music.'

"Our conversation proved to me that Beethoven, despite his protestations, would have felt flattered to be received by Napoleon."

Beethoven as Seen by an Englishman

A vivid picture of Beethoven in life, albeit embellished with romantic frills, is presented in an article signed J. L. and published in the *Musical World* of February 6, 1845, only eighteen years after Beethoven's death.

"Beethoven's features possessed a profound inwardness; they were beaming and refulgent upon us as the full and plenary indication of something grand, majestic, divine. His brow was of an astonishing breadth, being overshadowed by a profusion of well-assorted hair. His eyes were a mass of living and burning phosphorus, majestically yet steadily rolling in their orbits.

"Having gone to Vienna, I, and the gentleman who was with me, alighted fortunately at the Swan Tavern where Beethoven used to take his meals. In the coffee-room our attention was attracted by a gentleman who always entered the room, sat himself in some corner, and communicated with the waiter by signs rather than words. At this period Beethoven's popularity at Vienna was not very great. His *Fidelio* could not be performed at the Court Opera on account of the famous 'Freedom' chorus and the immense stress he laid on that word. His *Egmont* was considered a downright insult to the imperial family by whose immediate ancestor that great man had been slain. Still, the people at the Swan treated Beethoven with marked respect. The landlord told my friend: 'It is strange that when English or American gentlemen arrive at my inn, they never inquire after His Majesty, the Emperor, but many of them wish to see Herr van Beethoven.'

"One summer afternoon, I, in company with a couple of friends, drove from Vienna to Brünn; at a distance of a mile or so, we were overtaken by a tremendous gale of wind, mixed with thunder and rain. Pursuing our way as fast as we could, we espied a person of gentlemanly appearance crossing the way and pacing in all haste across the fields, gesticulating with his right hand. It was *he!* One of our company who knew him hallooed out to him and offered him a seat in our vehicle — but in vain. He nodded and went on. The whole occurrence did not occupy more than a minute, and I had no time to consider then what Beethoven was about. But a hundred times have I since repeated to myself: 'These were his studies after nature; it was the very time, perhaps, when he was writing his *Pastorale.*'"

Beethoven and England

Beethoven shared the fate of all composers who wrote music too modern for contemporary ears. Particularly in his last period was he regarded in musical circles as a mad genius who with approaching deafness lost his musical sensitiveness.

An apparently authentic story tells of Beethoven's meeting with several writers and musicians at the Inn of the Golden Lamb in Vienna. Someone remarked that the English had no talent for music and no appreciation of musical values. Beethoven's opinion on the subject was asked, whereupon he observed with mock seriousness that this dictum was quite correct: "I have received several commissions from England to compose music for their concerts, and they paid me handsomely for my works. This proves beyond peradventure that the English have neither taste nor appreciation for true musical values."

Had Beethoven read the contemporary criticism in England of his last sonatas, he would have known that the English too had fallen into the general line of condemning Beethoven's "third style." The English music publication, *Harmonicon,* wrote as follows in the issue of October 1823:

"Beethoven is not only still numbered amongst the living, but is at a period of life when the mind, if in *corpore sano,* is in its fullest vigor, for he has not yet completed his fifty-second year. Unfortunately, however, he is suffering under a privation that to a musician is intolerable — he is almost totally bereft of the sense of hearing; insomuch that it is said he cannot render the tones of his pianoforte audible to himself. The sonata betrays a violent effort to produce something in the shape of novelty. In it are visible some of those dissonances the harshness of which may have escaped the observation of the composer.... The publishers have deemed it necessary to warn off all pirates by announcing the sonata as copyright. We do not think they are in much danger of having their property invaded."

Beethoven's Life Mask

In his memoirs, the German poet Vogl gives an interesting account of how Beethoven's death mask was taken by a German sculptor who had unsuccessfully attempted to take a cast of Beethoven's features when the composer was still living. This sculptor, named Danhauser, had succeeded in getting Beethoven to his studio in Vienna. He asked Beethoven to remove his coat and open his shirt. "I hope you will not decapitate me," observed Beethoven. Danhauser reassured him, and then proceeded to cover Beethoven's eyebrows with thin slips of paper and his cheeks and chin with oil. The sculptor then applied a quantity of plaster of Paris to Beethoven's face, gave him a quill to put in his mouth for breathing, and asked him to shut his eyes. Beethoven complied, but when the plaster began to thicken, he became horrified at the sensation of the hardening mask.

John Ella in his *Musical Sketches* describes the scene that followed:

"Suddenly jumping up, with hair standing on end, he tried to disengage himself from the plaster and exclaimed: 'Sir, you are a garotter, a bandit, a monster!'

" 'For heaven's sake, my most honored Kapellmeister,' stuttered the confounded artist.

"But Beethoven interrupted him violently, 'A rogue, a cannibal!'

" 'But permit that I —'

" 'Away!' roared Beethoven. Smashing to atoms the chair upon which he had been sitting, he snatched his hat and coat and rushed out of the room, forgetting to put either of his garments on. Danhauser hastened after the raving man and tried to pacify him; but Beethoven, extricating himself from the other's grasp, exclaimed, 'Go back, you cunning assassin. Do not attempt to approach me, or I'll throttle you.' After these words he ran out of Danhauser's house, slamming the door behind him, the face still covered with plaster."

What Danhauser did not succeed in doing with a living Beethoven, he had no difficulty in performing with Beethoven dead. Ella writes:

"Danhauser, having obtained permission to model the deceased, went to the house of the defunct. After having made a portrait in pencil, Danhauser began the necessary preparations for molding. An unforseen obstacle presented itself: the beard of the deceased, which had not been touched during the entire period of his illness, had to be removed. Danhauser sent for a barber, who was willing but demanded a ducat for his services. A ducat was more than the young artist possessed. He therefore had to undertake the operation himself."

Beethoven's Last Hours

Beethoven's biographers agree that two persons were present when Beethoven died on the afternoon of March 26, 1827: his sister-in-law and Anslem Hüttenbrenner. The latter left the most quoted account of Beethoven's last moments. But apparently there was a third witness, the celebrated singer, Luigi Lablache, who was in Vienna at the time of Beethoven's death and served as one of the pallbearers at his funeral. Lablache's account of Beethoven's last day on earth was published in the *Musical Times* of June 1, 1846:

"It was rumored in Vienna that the great Beethoven must die ere the day was spent. Taking shame to myself for remaining in this city so long without having seen the immortal composer, I was soon accompanied to his residence and forthwith found myself in his presence. All was silent save for the sobbing of some privileged friends kneeling at his bedside. Standing apart, I watched the dying Beethoven with breathless anxiety. There he sat, supported by pillows and gazing for a while on vacancy, when, suddenly turning his head, he muttered in faltering accents, 'There, do you hear the bell? Don't you hear it ringing? The curtain must drop. Yes! My curtain is falling?' Gently drooping his head, the mighty master, without uttering another word, now sank into eternal slumber."

Lablache was himself an interesting character. He was reputed to have the greatest range of all bass voices, extending two octaves from E-flat below to E-flat above the bass staff. He possessed enormous physical strength. During a rehearsal, he picked up with one hand a double bass standing in the orchestra pit, held it at arm's length and then gently placed it back in the orchestra. His voice was so powerful that once when he snored at night, his wife, thinking it was the bell of the fire engine near the house, rushed in to wake him up.

No two accounts of Beethoven's last hours agree on particulars. In addition to plausible accounts, fantastic stories were published shortly after Beethoven's death. The *Musical World and New York Musical Times* of July 1854 printed a story that has the quality of romance, and for this reason appeals to those biographers who insist on embellishing upon the known facts in the lives of great men with a complete disregard for historic truth. According to this curious version, Beethoven was in Baden, a suburb of Vienna, when he became indisposed. The report reads:

"Compelled by the necessity of economy, Beethoven accomplished part of the distance between Baden and Vienna on foot. In the evening, he stopped before the gate of a small, mean-looking house and solicited shelter."

It was a farm, and the farmer accepted Beethoven in a spirit of generous hospitality. He noticed that the farmer's wife was performing at the piano. Being deaf, he could not hear the music, but on glancing at the printed music on the piano, he saw that it was the Allegretto from the Seventh Symphony. Then he raised his head and said simply: "I am Beethoven."

Illness compelled him to take to bed at the farm house, according to this account, which continues:

"As he lay upon his bed a man entered. It was Hummel, his old and only friend. Hummel bent toward him, and with the aid of an acoustic instrument enabled Beethoven to hear a few words of his compassion and regret. Beethoven seemed reanimated; his eyes shone; he struggled for utterance, and gasped, 'Is it not true, Hummel, that I have some talent after all?' These were his last words. His eyes grew fixed, his mouth fell open, and his spirit passed away."

Music News 1823

In 1823, subscribers to the London music magazine, the *Harmonicon*, casually read such items as these:

"A musical prodigy has appeared in Vienna in the person of a boy aged only ten years named F. Liszt. This youthful virtuoso excited the highest admiration and astonishment. This prodigy reads any music *a prima vista* and in playing from the score has few equals."

"*Der Freischütz* has been performed above fifty times in Berlin during the past eighteen months. It is said to have produced the managers above thirty thousand dollars [dollars are, of course, thalers]."

"The general complaint against Rossini is that his compositions are light, effeminate, and void of the true philosophy of music. The German journals compare them to a mass of bubbles and to a woman painted up to the eyes, but ill-dressed. They call him the very romance-writer of music [romance-writing was regarded at the time as something extremely cheap and vulgar, and the expression romantic music or literature indicated the highest degree of moral and esthetic disapproval]."

"Beethoven, notwithstanding his deafness, is perfectly well in health and in high spirits; he is now composing an opera."

"Petersburg, Russia: We have been informed that a singular prejudice prevails, both in Petersburg and in Moscow, against the music of Beethoven which has been encouraged by the example of a celebrated Professor R— who is accustomed to speak of the works of Beethoven as the production of a madman and has carried his animosity so far as to refuse to accompany one of his popular songs."

By Reissiger — not Weber

The piano piece known as *La dernière pensée de Weber*, despite its name, was written not by Weber but by Karl Reissiger. The curious misapprehension in titling came about in this manner: Shortly before Weber went to London, where he was to die in 1826, an obscure German composer, Karl Reissiger, gave him one of his waltz manuscripts, published in 1824. Weber carried it with him, and it was found among his effects after his death and subsequently published as *The Last Thought of Weber*.

Authorship of the piece was not cleared up until many years later when someone called the matter to Reissiger's attention, whereupon he produced his album of waltzes published before the discovery of the manuscript and proved beyond dispute that the piece was his own.

Mushrooms and Spiders

Schobert is not a misprint for Schubert. He was an estimable Silesian-born musician who settled in Paris in 1760 and wrote many compositions in the elegant style of the time. Mozart knew his music well and was even influenced by his easy grace in writing piano pieces.

Schobert was also something of a musical scientist. Among his compositions is a page entitled, "A Curious Musical Piece Which Can Be Played on the Piano, on the Violin, and on the Bass, and at that in Different Ways." This page contained five minuets, one of which could be played upside down without any change, one which would result in a new piece when turned upside down, and one which would furnish a continuation upside down. Two could be played on the violin and on the bass by assigning the treble clef right side up and the bass clef upside down.

Schobert's life was uneventful, but death came to him (and to six people with him) in a most extraordinary manner. The story of his end is found in complete detail in the correspondence of Baron Grimm:

"M. Schobert, who is known by music lovers as one of the best harpsichord players in Paris, arranged to go on an outing with his wife, one of his infant children, and several friends among whom was a physician. A group of seven in all, they walked in the woods of St. Germain, where Schobert gathered some mushrooms, of which he was fond. Toward evening the group went to Marly, entered a tavern and asked the proprietor to fix the mushrooms for them. The cook inspected the mushrooms, told Schobert they were bad and in fact refused to cook them. Annoyed by this refusal, the picnickers left the inn and went to another in the Bois de Boulogne where the maître d'hôtel told them the same thing and also refused to fix the mushrooms. A strange obstinacy, fortified by the fact that the physician of the group assured Schobert that the mushrooms were good, caused them to persevere in their intention and led them to their death. They betook themselves back to Paris, to Schobert's own apartment and were served the mushrooms. All of them, including the maidservant who cooked the fatal herbs and the physician who claimed that they were safe to eat, died of poisoning. Because they became ill all at once, they were unable to call for help from eleven o'clock at night until noon of the next day when they were found lying on the floor convulsed with pain. All medical aid was futile. The child died first. Schobert lived from Tuesday to Friday. His wife died on the following Monday. Some of the unfortunates lived another ten days after the accident, but none escaped. Schobert left an infant son who was not yet weaned, and who now remains without help."

Schobert was not the only musician who was victim of his own *gourmandise*. His contemporary, Anton Filz, one of the most important symphonists of the famous Mannheim school, died in 1760 from immoderate indulgence in spiders. Filz insisted that they tasted exactly like strawberries, and he developed his own method of preparing them as a delicacy. But apparently his last meal contained a poisonous variety.

John Field Goes to Russia

The gossipy journal, the *Apollonicon*, published in England in 1832, gives the reason John Field (who originated the form of nocturne before Chopin) decided to leave England:

"John Field, the accomplished English pianist, is about to shake the dust from his feet and depart from his native isle. He may now inhabit Russia without regret.

"Dear Field, do not grieve," said his friend "nor depart
With curses 'gainst England. We have hearts, do not fear!"
"Why, what do I care," answered Field, "for the heart
That spurns native merit — that's dead to the ear."

John Field was indeed happy in Russia, which he visited for the first time in 1823, and where he formed deep attachments. After his last appearance in London in 1832, when he played his Piano Concerto "accompanied by the gentlemen of the Philharmonic" (as the contemporary newspaper phrase had it), he was discouraged by the cool reception. He went on a tour of the continent and indulged more and more in his intemperate habits of drinking. When he reached Naples, a fistula formed in his abdomen. He was found in a pitiful state by a wealthy Russian named Raemanoff who persuaded him to go back to Russia and guaranteed him security from want. Happy to go, he settled in Moscow, where he died in 1837.

Tales of Rossini

When Rossini conducted the première of *The Barber of Seville* in Rome, he was roundly booed. "Never had the theater walls been shaken by such a tumult," wrote a correspondent of the *Musical World* of London. "It was not cries and hisses alone but real howlings. But Rossini continued to conduct imperturbably, and after the Finale of the first act he shouted to the singers, 'Bravo!'"

At the second performance, Rossini decided to relegate the job of conducting to another. When the public realized that Rossini was not present, a messenger was sent to his home to fetch him. Rossini arrived in haste, wearing an extraordinary attire: slippers, swanskin trousers, a long traveling jacket, and a cotton cap such as was worn by butchers. The audience must have liked both his unconventional dress and his music, for he was greeted by thunderous applause and recalled seven times after the final curtain. The theater crowds followed his carriage into the streets after the opera, carrying lanterns and shouting: "*Viva Rossini! Viva il gran maestro!*"

The greatest homage paid to Rossini after the first performance of *The Barber of Seville* in Paris was that of an Italian organ-grinder who serenaded Rossini under the window of his hotel room by playing an air from *The Barber of Seville* on his barrel organ.

This episode recalls another story told at the time. An

organ grinder in Paris played the tunes from *The Barber of Seville* underneath Halévy's window. Halévy called out to him: "I will give you a louis d'or if you go and play an air from one of my operas before Rossini's house."

"I cannot do that," replied the street musician. "Rossini has paid me two louis d'or to play *his* music under *your* windows."

A society fop greeted Rossini at a reception. Noticing that Rossini did not recognize him, he said: "Don't you remember me? I sat next to you when they served a gigantic macaroni pie at a dinner in your honor in Milan."

"Indeed I remember the macaroni very well," replied Rossini, "but I do not remember you."

A group of Rossini's friends conceived the idea of erecting a statue for him while he was still living. Rossini inquired how much it would cost. "About twenty thousand liras," was the reply. Rossini reflected for a moment. "Why don't you give me ten thousand liras, and I will stand on the pedestal myself," he finally said.

Despite Rossini's ready wit, he was left speechless on at least one occasion. One day in 1856 he dropped in at a Paris music store and bumped into Fétis, the celebrated French music scholar. "Must all this be learned, *cher* Fétis?" asked Rossini pointing at the *Treatise on Counterpoint and Fugue* by Fétis which was lying on the counter.

"*Pas du tout*," retorted Fétis, "and you are a living proof to the contrary."

During a rehearsal conducted by Rossini, the horn player hit a bad note which made a squealing noise.

"What's that?" Rossini asked.

"It's I. I . . ." answered the player.

"Ah, is it?" said Rossini. "Then pack up your horn and go home. I'll join you later."

The horn player was Rossini's own father.

When Rossini conducted the première of one of his early operas in Rome, the first clarinet part was played by a barber who habitually shaved Rossini after each rehearsal. Although the barber-clarinetist played numerous wrong notes, Rossini, who was mercilessly severe to other players, never remonstrated with him.

An oboist in a theater orchestra which Rossini conducted played an F-sharp instead of an F. Rossini corrected him and added consolingly: 'In regard to the F-sharp, you needn't be concerned; we shall find some other place to put it."

Rossini habitually marked errors in his pupils' music with crosses. One of his pupils, and by no means the best, was encouraged when Rossini returned his manuscript with only occasional crosses here and there.

"I am so happy there are so few mistakes," exclaimed the young man.

The master looked at him and said: "If I had marked all the errors in the music with crosses, your score would be a cemetery."

Rossini had a poor memory for names — particularly English names. When, on his tour in England, he met Bishop, the composer of *Home, Sweet Home*, Rossini rushed toward him and exclaimed: "Ah! My dear Mr. . . . Mr. . . ." But unable to remember Bishop's name, he began to sing *Home, Sweet Home* instead. Bishop was delighted by this witty tribute to his most celebrated composition, and Rossini was spared an embarrassing situation.

Rossini possessed an enormous appetite, and was a lover of good eating. After a dinner which he particularly enjoyed, the hostess turned to him and said: "Maestro, you have conferred a great honor upon us by accepting our invitation to dine. When will you come to dinner again?" Rossini, smacking his lips over the delicious food, replied: "Right away, Madam!"

When Rossini was scheduled to be present at a performance of one of his operas at La Scala in Milan, he received the following letter: "A lady who wishes to make the acquaintance of the great Maestro will be at the Scala tonight in Box No. 9 to tell you something she cannot put into writing." At the same time, the leading tenor of the opera company informed Rossini that the wife of the French ambassador, famous for her beauty, had arrived in Milan especially to hear Rossini's opera, and that she would occupy Box No. 9. Rossini, greatly excited over the prospect of meeting a beautiful French woman, dressed in his best and arrived at La Scala just as the overture began. He went to Box No. 9—it was empty! The first act of the opera was over, but still the ambassadress failed to appear. When the lights went on, Rossini noticed an envelope on the empty chair next to him. Eagerly he tore it open and read: "My dear Maestro: The ambassadress of France regrets that she cannot come to the theater tonight for one important reason: she is dead — and well decayed. The French ambassador has been a widower for three years. Please accept, Maestro, the compliments of your admirer, 'Primo Aprile.'"

"The first of April!" exclaimed angry Rossini. "Why don't I ever look at the calendar!"

He ran out of the theater and went home without hearing the rest of the performance.

His laziness was proverbial. One morning as he was writing music in bed, a sheet of the manuscript of an operatic duet fell off and floated under the bed. Rossini

tried to reach it without getting up but could not quite make it. With a sigh he took another sheet of manuscript paper and wrote out another duet. Then a friend called on him, and Rossini asked him to retrieve the original manuscript. The two versions of the duet were quite different; the second seemed the better of the two. But since the first wasn't bad, either, Rossini added an extra part and used it as a trio in the same opera.

When a young composer asked Rossini whether it is better to write the overture before or after completing an opera, Rossini described six ways of composing overtures. He said:

1. I composed the overture to *Otello* in a little room in which that most ferocious of all managers, Barbaja, shut me up with a dish of macaroni and told me that he would let me out only after the last note of the overture had been written.
2. I wrote the overture to the *Gazza Ladra,* on the very day of the first performance of the opera, in the wings of the Scala Theater in Milan. The manager had put me under the guard of four stage hands who were ordered to throw down the music pages, sheet by sheet, to copyists seated below. As the manuscript was copied, it was sent page by page to the conductor who then rehearsed the music. If I had failed to keep the production going fast, my guards were instructed to throw me in person to the copyists.
3. I made my task easier in the case of the overture to the *Barber of Seville,* which I left unwritten; instead I made use of the overture to my opera *Elisabetta,* which is a very serious opera, whereas the *Barber of Seville* is a comic opera.
4. I composed the overture to the *Comte Ory* while fishing in the company of a Spanish musician who the whole time talked incessantly about the Spanish political situation.
5. I composed the overture to *William Tell* in the lodgings on the Boulevard Montmartre filled night and day with

a crowd of people smoking, drinking, talking, singing, and bellowing in my ears while I was laboring on the music.

6. I never composed any overture to my opera *Moses*, which is the easiest way of all.

A woman brought her young daughter to Rossini for an audition. After the girl had performed an aria, her mother asked: "Do you think she ought to study voice professionally? If she has not enough talent, I should prefer her to remain an honest woman rather than going on the opera stage."

Rossini paused and then said: "She had better be an honest woman — if possible."

Liszt, as a young man, played his new work for Rossini.
"I prefer the other," Rossini remarked.
"Which other?" asked Liszt.
"The chaos in Haydn's *Creation*."

When a friend called on Rossini in his Paris house, he found a score of Wagner's *Tannhäuser* on the desk of the piano. But the music was placed upside down. When the visitor attempted to put it right side up, Rossini stopped him: "I already played it right side up but could make nothing of it. Then I tried it the other way around, and it sounds much better."

In Paris, Rossini went to a concert given on musical glasses which were partially filled with water to obtain the desired pitch. The program included a set of variations on a Rossini aria from *Moses in Egypt*. After the tenth variation a friend asked him if he wouldn't rather take a walk.

"Not before this gentleman has finished washing Moses," the composer replied.

It was the custom of composers to write at the end of a finished work, "Glory be to God." Rossini did not dare to use this sacrosanct formula at the end of his frivolous operatic creations. When he wrote a Mass, after he reached the Biblical age of three score and ten he extended the formula to an apostrophe: "Good God! Here is my poor Mass. Thou knowest that I was born to write comic operas and that my patrimony consists in a little heart and less science. Be therefore compassionate and leave me enter Paradise."

Extremely superstitious, Rossini believed in omens and malevolent spirits. When he received a gold watch from the king of France, Louis Philippe, a friend to whom he proudly showed it noticed a circular inscription in Arabic engraved on its face. Rossini inquired from learned friends the meaning of the inscription, but no one seemed able to decipher it. Seized with inexpressible fears, Rossini put the watch away; it was found after his death in a secret compartment in his desk.

Significantly eonugh, Rossini died on a Friday, the thirteenth of the month — November 13, 1868.

The Musical Fan

This story is told about Mendelssohn and/or several other composers and pianists.

When Mendelssohn played the the first movement of the *Moonlight* Sonata at a reception in London, a dowager sitting close to him kept opening and closing her fan to the rhythm of the music. Mendelssohn went through the movement without showing any sign of annoyance. But instead of ending the Coda, he kept repeat-

ing the final arpeggios over and over again following the
motion of the lady's fan until she finally caught on and
stopped. Mendelssohn then completed the work.

Mendelssohn in Excelsis

A vivid picture of Mendelssohn improvising is found
in the *Brighton Guardian,* reported by an Englishman
reminiscing as an old man in 1883. The scene described
took place in London in 1844 when Mendelssohn was a
visiting conductor of the London Philharmonic:

"Mme. Sartoris had sung from memory a Scottish ballad
(she was celebrated for her rendition of such music), one
new to Mendelssohn. He was so delighted with her unaf-
fected delivery that he at once expressed a desire to hear
it again and to play an accompaniment on the pianoforte.
Someone longed to hear Mendelssohn extemporize and those
grouped around the piano warmly seconded the request.
At first Mendelssohn hesitated, perhaps not altogether un-
mindful of the many exacting works at that time occupying
his attention. His more intimate friends also knew how great
a mental effort such exhibitions entailed upon him. When,
however, Mme. Sartoris, taking his hand and looking into
his face, pleaded, 'Do,' his resistance gave way, and he took

for his theme the Scottish song his hostess had just sung. At first his harmonies to the melody were simple enough, and the modulations to which he submitted it were equally unstrained. Soon, however, he made it the theme of a fugue elaborately worked out, after which he then dashed off with extraordinary vigor a series of variations baffling description. The intensity of the player's gaze, more particularly as he approached the climax, was painful to witness. His eyes appeared twice their natural size, and his excitement was plainly shown in the expression of his face. He had gone through twenty minutes of the most trying brain work accompanied with a corresponding amount of exhaustion. I can hardly imagine a finer subject for a picture than that splendidly expressive countenance eagerly gazed at by a crowd of attentive listeners."

Mendelssohn and Sausages

During his visit to England in 1846, Mendelssohn and two of his German friends, also visiting in London, walked home together after a Lucullean dinner in Mendelssohn's honor. Their spirits were high, their stomachs full. Suddenly Mendelssohn noticed a butcher's shop with large sausages exhibited in the window display marked "German Sausages, Twopence Each." Mendelssohn himself reports what followed: "Patriotism overcame us; each bought a long sausage; we turned into a quiet street and there consumed our purchases, laughing and singing three-part songs."

— And Pineapples

Handel, who lived in England half his life, could never master English; and Haydn, whose sojourns in London were long and enjoyable, could hardly make himself understood when speaking English. But Mendelssohn, also a frequent visitor in England, wrote and spoke the language all but faultlessly.

On the occasion of the centenary of Mendelssohn's death, the family of the English publisher Novello, who had dealings with Mendelssohn, gave the *Musical Times* of London some unpublished letters of Mendelssohn written in 1837. The letters were damaged by time, but parts that are legible command interest:

"By the bye, my friends tell me they read in the *Examiner* some parts of the letter I wrote to you. . . . O God, I am not a fit person to write English letters for an English public, and pray, why do you allow them to do so and to publish my nonsense about the pineapples?"

The "nonsense" referred to was Mendelssohn's frivolous comments on Queen Victoria's banquet after the coronation:

"And how is music going on in England? Or had you not time to think now of anything else than the Guildhall puddings and pies and two hundred pineapples, which the Queen ate there, as a French paper has it?"

Was Mendelssohn's Hair Black?

In a footnote in his *Dictionary of Music and Musicians,*
Sir George Grove noted that Mendelssohn's hair was
black, crediting this information to J. C. Horsley, the
English musician and portrait painter who was a friend
of Mendelssohn. Grove must have been mistaken. In a
letter which Horsley wrote to Grove on the subject,
which has recently come to light, we read: "Mendelssohn
had dark brown hair and a great deal of it (not that he
wore it unduly long) and it had a natural curl in it."

Eduard Devrient, who knew Mendelssohn as a boy,
describes his hair as brown. "I have seen the boy occasionally; his long brown curls had attracted my notice
as he trudged sturdily through the streets in his big
shoes, holding his father's hand."

Julius Benedict, a pupil of Weber, says Mendelssohn's
hair was auburn colored: "I shall never forget," he writes,

"the impression of that day on beholding that beautiful youth, with his auburn hair clustering in ringlets round his shoulders."

The controversy was finally settled when a lock of Mendelssohn's hair, cut when he was thirty-five, was discovered in London. The color is dark brown.

Mendelssohn himself liked to think that his hair was a strongly individual feature. When he was in Paris in 1832 his friends remarked how much he resembled Meyerbeer, particularly in the waviness of his hair. Mendelssohn was obviously piqued. That very day he went to a barber shop and had his hair cropped short.

How Chopin Played

We know now how Chopin really looked from a recently discovered daguerreotype taken two or three years before his death. It represents a prematurely aged man with facial features showing sickness and exhaustion, with locks of black hair partly covering the forehead.

Unfortunately not even an imperfect phonograph record could have been made of Chopin's piano-playing a hundred years ago. But we have numerous descriptions and music reviews of Chopin's concerts. Those who heard him dwell on the poetry and delicacy of Chopin's interpretations, on the wonderful agility of his finger action. Chopin was never a virtuoso; his piano never thundered, yet according to contemporary accounts he was able to summon sonorities that filled the hall. There was also a mesmeric quality to Chopin's personality that hushed audiences and stifled involuntary coughs and whispers.

The *London and Westminster Review* of April 1839 published a letter from Paris which describes the quality of Chopin's piano-playing at the time when he was in his late twenties:

"Chopin never improvises, as a matter of course, or unless he feels himself thoroughly inspired; but if you have the good fortune of meeting him on one of these happy days — if you follow the play of his animated countenance and the wonderful agility of his fingers, which appear as if they were dislocated — if you hear the anguish of the strings, which still vibrate in your ear after he has ceased — you awaken as if from a dream, and ask if the pale and fragile man you see before you can be the same as he who has so completely subdued you."

Apparently there was no great change in the character of Chopin's piano touch during the last years of his life. Otto Goldschmidt, husband of Jenny Lind, who heard Chopin play in his last concert in Paris on February 16, 1848, reported his impressions:

"Chopin was extremely weak, but still his playing — by reason of that remarkable quality which he possessed of gradation of touch — betrayed none of the impress of weakness which some attributed to his piano-playing, or softness of touch, and he possessed in a greater degree than any other pianist, the faculty of passing upward from *piano* through all gradations of tone."

La Revue et gazette musicale of February 20, 1848, gives a glimpse behind the scenes of this recital, which was to be Chopin's last:

"A concert of the Ariel of pianists is a thing that is too rare to be given with the doors wide open for anyone desiring to enter. A special list was prepared but those whose names were inscribed therein were not at all sure that they could obtain the precious tickets. One had to have influence to be admitted into the inner sanctum, to be allowed to deposit one's offering. This offering was no less than a louis d'or. But who could not find an extra gold piece in his purse when it is a question of hearing Chopin play?

"From all this it naturally followed that the finest flower of feminine aristocracy in the most elegant attire filled the Salle Pleyel. There was also present the aristocracy of artists and music lovers happy to catch this musical sylph on the wing."

Another concert of Chopin was announced for March 10 of the same year, but revolutionary events intervened, and the concert was canceled. Chopin was heard in Paris no more. He lived, lingered, and languished for a year and a half, and then he died.

Chopin and the Skeleton

Friends of great composers often tell imaginative stories about how this or that work has been written, particularly if it concerns a piece of descriptive music. The following story told by a friend of Chopin, the painter Ziem, deserves attention because there are certain specific details in it which lend credibility to an otherwise incredible story.

Ziem was dining with two friends at the house of Paul Chevandier de Valdrome at No. 39 Rue de la Tour d'Auvergne in Paris. The host, somewhat of an eccentric, kept a skeleton in one of his closets and displayed it to Ziem. When the latter met Chopin he told him about the skeleton and Chopin became morbidly impressed with the story. He asked Ziem to let him see the skeleton. A dinner party was arranged at Valdrome's house and during the dessert, Ziem mentioned Chopin's desire. The skeleton was fetched by the servant and placed near the piano in the drawing room.

Ziem describes the scene that followed:

"Chopin, his face pale and his eyes opened to their extent, had enveloped himself in a long winding sheet, and pressed against his throbbing breast he held the ghastly skeleton. The silence of the salon was all at once broken by the sound of music — slow, sad, profound, splendid music, music such as none of us had ever heard before. Immeasurably amazed we were as the beautiful sounds succeeded each other and were gradually fashioned into the world-renowned Funeral March. On to the end played Chopin, still grasping the skeleton, and so spellbound were we that not until the last

[132]

note was struck did we really recover our senses. Then we hastened to congratulate the shroud-robed musician and reached his side just as he was on the point of fainting."

Chopin's Sensory Perception

Chopin possessed an extreme delicacy of senses. He could not tolerate any untidiness or negligence of manners, and he was particularly sensitive in regard to the outward state of his manuscripts. The *Musical World* of March 1876 tells the following story. Chopin lent the manuscript score of his Concerto in E minor to a friend. Knowing how fastidious Chopin was, he handled the pages wearing white gloves so as not to soil the paper. When he returned the score, there was not a stain or spot on it. Chopin carefully opened it, but at once his face was contorted into a horrible grimace. "My dear fellow," he exclaimed, "you were smoking when you went through it."

Hats Off to Chopin!

All music lovers know the story of Schumann's famous salutation to Chopin, "Hats off, gentlemen! A genius!" But few realize that it was not the salute of an established master extended to a novice, but rather a symbolic handshake proffered by a young romantic to a contemporary whom he had never met. As a matter of fact, Chopin was actually older than Schuman, having been born 106 days earlier. Furthermore, Chopin's first publication to arouse Schumann's admiration appeared in print before anything by Schumann.

The facts of the case are these: As a young man of twenty-one, Schumann published an unsigned article in *Allgemeine Musikalische Zeitung* of December 7, 1831. In this article he introduced for the first time the characters of Eusebius and Florestan, members of Schumann's imaginary Society of David. In Schumann's article, Eusebius brings in a newly published piece of music, puts it down on the piano, and exclaims, "Hats off, gentlemen! A genius!" [This is the accepted English translation; the original German has one "hat," in the singular.] Florestan reads the title page, *"La ci darem la mano, varié pour le pianoforte par Frédéric Chopin, œuvre deux. . . .* Chopin —I never heard the name—who can he be?" Impressed by the originality of Chopin's music, Florestan agrees that Chopin is, indeed, a genius. In the same issue of the *Allgemeine Musikalische Zeitung* in which Schumann's story originally appeared, the editor of the paper subjected Chopin's piece to sharp criticism with occasional darts in the direction of young Schumann, who was referred to merely as a pupil of Herr Wieck.

A Schumann Story

A romantic story is told about Clara Schumann. Each time she was asked to play Schumann's works—she survived him by forty years—she would take out his old letters written during the courtship days and reread them to find inspiration for her playing.

This brings to mind the fact that Schumann's penmanship was so bad that in his letters he used to put every twentieth word between two vertical lines, adding a postcript as a sort of lexicon, transcribing each word placed within brackets. One of the illegible words thus clarified was Schumann's signature.

Clara's Semitone

It is little known that, before her marriage, Clara Schumann composed a considerable amount of music, including a piano concerto in the same key of A minor as Schumann's own celebrated concerto. The latter, however, was written much later. The key relationship of the movements in Clara's work was highly unconventional, the middle movement having been written in the remote tonality of A-flat major. A German music critic, reviewing the concerto with a show of ponderous humor, observed: "It would be well if all the daughters of Eve in their domestic and married relations were to confine themselves to slight leaps as these, only a half-tone higher or lower! If such were the case, the sharpest matrimonial difference might always be resolved into pure harmony."

Schumann Via the Ouija Board

In his book, *Les Problèmes psychiques et l'inconnu*, Camille Flammarion, the famous French astronomer who, toward the end of his life, extended his field of exploration to the great beyond, reports experiments performed by one Eugene Nue in 1852, during which complete musical compositions by anonymous dead musicians were sent over, via the ouija board. The titles of the pieces related to astronomy, perhaps as a subtle tribute to Flammarion's interest in spiritualistic science. There was a *Chant de la terre dans l'espace,* a *Chant de Saturne,* and other planetary chants. One of these pieces is reproduced in Flammarion's book showing the distinct influence of Rameau, with certain crudities due probably to garbled transmission.

A new impetus to spiritualistic music was given in our own time when no one less than Schumann himself appeared at séances held in London by Baron Erik Palmstierna, Swedish minister to London; Yelly d'Aranyi, the Hungarian violinist, and others. The appearance of Schumann at the séance should not have come as a great surprise, for he himself while living was sensitive to spiritualistic emanations. Thus on the night of February 17, 1854, he received from Schubert and Mendelssohn a musical theme to which he later wrote a set of variations. The curious thing about the London manifestation was that Schumann spoke in highly ungrammatical German, though he was a master of German in his lifetime. However that may be, Schumann gave a very specific message to Yelly d'Aranyi that she should play his violin concerto. When the astonished violinist replied that she didn't know Schumann had written a violin concerto (it is not listed among Schumann's works in Grove's Dictionary), Schumann said: "Remember what I asked you. Tell Tovey." (The reference was obviously to Sir Donald Tovey, well-known English musicologist.) A letter was dispatched to him by Yelly d'Aranyi; he replied that there was indeed a violin concerto by Schumann which had never been published. Schumann had written it in the last months before his mind collapsed in utter insanity. After Schumann's death Clara Schumann, Brahms, and Joachim decided not to publish the work, as they regarded it as unworthy of Schumann's genius. The manuscript remained in the possession of Joachim, and after the latter's death in 1907, was sold by his family to the State Library of Berlin with the stipulation that it should not be published until a century after Schumann's death; that is, until 1956. (It is interesting to note that in

Brahms's *Schumann Variations,* Op. 23, for four hands, there is a subtitle, *"Geisterthema"* (the spirits' theme), and the theme is that of the slow movement of the violin concerto.

It took nearly four years for Yelly d'Aranyi to get a copy of the concerto. She told Schumann at the next séance how much she liked the music. Schumann was delighted: *"Ich bin so froh dass du mein concerto lieb hast,"* he said, and continued in ungrammatical German: *"Nun die langsame Satz muss sehr warm gespielt sein und mit eine Sehnsucht nach höheren Visionen. Betet für heiliger Einheit der Menschen die sich auf der Erde einander hassen."* In the next sentence Schumann remembered that the word *Satz* is masculine in German, but floundered on the gender of *der Tanz: "Dann kommt Heiterkeit. Man muss heiter sein und den letzten Satz muss du wie ein Tanz aufführen."* Schumann also told Yelly d'Aranyi to make some specific alterations in the violin part. In the summer of 1937 she played the concerto for Tovey. The episode is reported by Erik Palmstierna in his book, *Horizons of Immortality*:

"After the first movement was over, the piano part of which Sir Donald played, he jumped up and said: 'Who did this? It is excellent. It is altogether Schumannesque.' Miss d'Aranyi now told him about the alterations done through messages of instruction from Schumann. Sir Donald asked to be shown the messages and after having studied them said he was convinced they could not have come from Miss d'Aranyi's mind. The messages were characteristically in the composer's language. Sir Donald, a composer himself, said he could see more in them than had Miss d'Aranyi, who was not a composer nor even well versed in harmony or counterpoint."

In the meantime the whole affair had reached the skeptical press, and there were irreverent titters and giggles. To these manifestations Tovey gave an assertive rebuke in a letter to the London *Times* of September 23, 1937:

"To me, as to many others to whom nineteenth-century materialism is as obsolete as the phlogiston theory, it is a mystery how two persons come to understand each other by ordinary human intercourse. And I am not prepared to find anything more mysterious in other means of ascertaining what the minds of Schumann and Joachim have to say to us now. I assert my positive conviction that the spirit of Schumann is inspiring Yelly d'Aranyi's production of Schumann's posthumous violin concerto. The sense in which I make this assertion is my own private affair."

While all this was going on in London, the German music publishing firm, Schott and Company, secured a photostatic copy of the manuscript of the concerto and offered it to the American violinist, Yehudi Menuhin, for performance. Then, like a *deus ex machina*, the Nazi government stepped in, shocked by the possibility that a non-Aryan American violinist might give the world première of an unknown Schumann work, and ordered a performance under strictly Aryan auspices. This performance took place in Berlin on November 26, 1937. Menuhin gave his performance later the same year. As to poor Yelly d'Aranyi, she didn't get her chance at the concerto until February 16, 1938 when she played it with the BBC Orchestra in London. Then the concerto was quietly shelved. There were no more performances. Stranger still, there were no further reactions from Schumann's spirit. Perhaps he decided that, after all, the whole thing was not worth the trouble.

Why Liszt Was Never Ordained

The musical journals of 1886, when he was still living, report an all but incredible story as to why Liszt never became a priest despite his intention. The Paris publication, *L'Opinion* gave the following reason:

"While he was preparing to enter holy orders at Rome, he was asked by the nuns after a service in the Sistine Chapel to play the piano. After Liszt did so, the nuns rushed at him and covered his face with caresses. Pope Pius IX therefore resolved that for the benefit of the clergy, Liszt's religious career should be broken, and ordination was therefore refused him."

Liszt Ate for Two

During one of his tours, Liszt was given a reception by the burgomaster of a small town. When the guests had taken their places at the dinner table, the burgomaster noticed that they were thirteen in number. "Do not be alarmed about that," said the musician. "I eat enough for two."

Liszt's Progeny

When Liszt died, several young men and women appeared in Paris society and claimed rather immodestly that they were Liszt's children out of wedlock. The *Musical Courier* of December 14, 1887 published a letter from Paris which told of an alleged daughter of Liszt but put over it a skeptical caption: LOOKS LIKE AN ADVERTISING DODGE:

"Some interest has been excited by the appearance of a young lady who claims to be a daughter of Liszt. Her mother, she says, was and is a member of one of the reigning families of Europe, indeed one of the most eminent royalties. Her birth was kept a secret, of course, to avoid scandal, and she was brought up in ignorance of her parentage. She was, however, treated almost like a young princess. When Liszt died, she was visited one night secretly by the royal lady in question, who first obtained from her an oath of secrecy and then told her the story of her birth. The young lady still conceals the name of her mother, who is now living, but feels under no obligation to keep the oath so far as her dead father is concerned. She is a handsome girl, with Liszt's cast of features, and her enthusiasm for music is so great that she will give a series of public pianoforte recitals and perhaps make a concert tour of the world."

At least one illegitimate Liszt child is well authenticated, François Servais, a devout Wagnerite and a composer in a Wagnerian manner. In music dictionaries he is set down as a son of the 'cellist, Adrien-François Servais. In reality, he was a son of Liszt and Carolyne Sayn-Wittgenstein. A virtual confirmation of his true parentage is found in a letter from Hans von Bülow to Bechstein. "I have taken a charming young musician into the house," writes von Bülow. "He is the son of the late famous Servais of Brussels, a talented young man who bears a fabulous resemblance to my brother-in-law, and therefore, of course, to Liszt." Servais was thus a half-brother of Cosima, who was at the time Hans von Bülow's wife.

By 1869 Hans von Bülow found that he could no longer continue the pretense of his marriage to Cosima, who had already had a child by Wagner — Isolde, born two months before the first performance of *Tristan und Isolde*, conducted by Hans von Bülow. The mixed emotions must have been unbearable to von Bülow: his admiration for Wagner, his love for Cosima, and his realization of being imposed upon by both. He appealed to Bechstein, the German piano manufacturer and a close friend of von Bülow's, and begged him to find a lawyer who would take care of the divorce proceedings.

With a characteristic *Galgenhumor*, von Bülow wrote to Bechstein: "The best would be for some sympathetic soul to give me the necessary dose of Prussic acid. Is there no accommodating chemist in Berlin? Come, you know so many people there"

In his letter to Cosima, von Bülow took a strangely submissive line: "You have preferred to give your life and the treasures of your mind and affection to one who is my superior. Far from blaming you for it, I approve your action."

The two daughters of Cosima and Hans von Bülow

remained with their mother, and he maintained a continuous correspondence with Cosima about their financial and spiritual welfare. In these letters he addressed his former wife, "dear madame." He continued to conduct Wagner's music but avoided meeting Wagner. However, when Liszt's common-law wife, Princess Wittgenstein, asked von Bülow why he would not make up with Wagner, he replied: "We never broke our relationship."

Hans von Bülow quickly found consolation and comfort. He wrote to Bechstein from Florence: "There is a dancer here with whom I have fallen madly in love. She is not merely a virtuoso but a *toe-poem*." Apparently she pirouetted out of his life as nimbly as she danced into it. Two years later von Bülow was once again in love. He notified Bechstein that he would accept a permanent post in Germany only "if the seventeen-year-old star of my life could be persuaded to become my permanent companion, if I could take this young Italian girl with me to Germany. . . ." This affair was eventually broken up too. Thirteen years after his separation from Cosima, he married a German actress.

Von Bülow's daughters, Liszt's grandchildren, lived long lives and died one after another in the Wagner home at Bayreuth when World War II was already raging. They witnessed the weird obtrusion of Hitler on the Wagnerian surroundings. In fact, Hitler was a frequent visitor at the home of Wagner's daughter-in-law, the widow of Siegfried Wagner for whom the *Siegfried Idyl* was written. There was talk about a romantic attachment when Hitler accompanied Siegfried's widow, arm-in-arm, to the Wagner festivals. He felt close enough to her to write her a note — in the first days of the Nazi regime — proclaiming his intention to commit suicide if things went wrong. One of Wagner's granddaughters — Liszt's great-granddaughter—felt that Hitler's political Wagnerism was bringing chaos and ruin to Germany and skipped to America, denouncing the Nazis. Then bombs began to fall close to Wagnerian shrines. The twilight of the gods had come down on Wagner's household.

A Brahms Potpourri

Brahms always regretted remaining a bachelor. "Lucky man," he used to say to his married friend, Hugo Conrat, when they met on the street. "You are going home [he used the English word home] where you will find your wife and children." But when he was asked whether he was married, his Viennese humor prompted him to retort: "Alas, I am single, thank God!"

Brahms and Conrat were discussing a singer who had a remarkable voice but was very ugly. Conrat maintained that artistry was more important than looks. "For a musician, perhaps," observed Brahms. "But I prefer looks."

Another singer asked him to give her some of his least known songs for her recital. "Take some of my posthumous ones," suggested Brahms. "No one will know them."

Playing a Beethoven 'cello sonata with a friend, Brahms stepped on the pedal a little too energetically. "Softer," pleaded the 'cellist. "I can't hear my 'cello." "You are lucky," said Brahms. "I can."

When a young musician complained that his first opus was delayed in publication, Brahms consoled him: "Patience, young man! You can afford not to be immortal for a few more weeks."

He had a reputation for rude manners, but he usually knew how to mitigate them by a flash of pointed humor.

Once, at a party, when he put on his coat to leave, he said: "If through oversight I neglected to insult anyone among those present, I want to apologize to him."

Brahms was good-naturedly cynical when he spoke of his habits in composition. He said: "The best ideas come to me when I polish my shoes early in the morning."

Brahms was an epicure. When he became seriously ill, his doctor told him that he would have to go on a strict diet.

"But how can I?" exclaimed the master. "I am invited to dine with Strauss, and we are going to have chicken with paprika!"

"That is out of the question," said the doctor. "You cannot eat that."

"Very well, then," declared Brahms, "please consider that I did not come to consult you until tomorrow."

And a Medley of Hans von Bülow

Hans von Bülow was renowned not only as a pianist and conductor, and as the ex-husband of Wagner's wife, but also as a wit. A rash of musical anecdotes and witty sayings attributed to von Bülow broke out in the 1880's. Most of them were communicated by Albert Gutman, the music publisher, who knew von Bülow well.

One aphorism (which has since been attributed to a half-dozen other famous pianists) was credited to von Bülow in 1882: "If I stop practicing one day, I notice the difference. If I stop two days, my friends notice it. If I stop three days, the public notices it."

At a concert in a private home, von Bülow was annoyed by a lady who carried on a whispered conversation during his playing. He stopped in the middle of a piece and said: "Either you stop or I."

A variation of this tale is that the offender was a member of the nobility and that von Bülow stopped playing with the remark: "When Her Highness speaks, all must be quiet."

Still another version is that von Bülow was invited to play for Emperor Napoleon III, who listened for a while, then entered into an animated conversation with one of the guests. Von Bülow finally stopped playing and said: "When His Majesty speaks, all must be silent."

Von Bülow used to conduct wearing white gloves. But when Beethoven's *Eroica* Symphony was programmed, he would remove the white gloves at the end of the first movement and change to black ones in symbolic appreciation of the Funeral March movement that was to follow.

He once appeared at the opera in Berlin in a box close to the orchestra pit, attired in a mourning hat with long black streamers, and a lemon-and-white handkerchief in his hand, according to the German custom at funerals. Naturally his unusual apparel was noticed and correctly interpreted as his silent protest against the staging of a mediocre opera which he felt was unworthy of a public hearing.

When von Bülow conducted in Russia, he changed a certain F-sharp to F-natural in a Glinka score. Musicians of the Imperial Orchestra objected. They insisted that F-sharp was correct, if Glinka, the father of all Russian music, had put it there, no matter how wrong it may have sounded to von Bülow. But the conductor was intransigeant. The musicians, who took their Glinka music most seriously, addressed a petition to the titular head of the orchestra, a Grand Duke of the Imperial family. The Duke, too, believed that Glinka could do no wrong, and dispatched a message to von Bülow earnestly requesting the retention of Glinka's original note. There was no alternative left for von Bülow but to yield. At the next rehearsal he announced loudly: "You shall play F-sharp, by order of His Imperial Highness."

An autocrat of the baton, von Bülow did not believe in free speech at concerts. When some ladies in the audience conversed too audibly, he stopped the music and reprimanded the offenders: "Ladies, remember you are not saving Rome." The reference was obviously to the cackling geese who were supposed to save Rome by sensing the approach of the enemy and raising their warning cries.

An ambitious young composer played his new work for von Bülow.

"How do you like it?" he asked hopefully.

The answer came sharply: "I *always* liked it"—a sly allusion to the many obvious borrowings from the music of the masters.

The reputation for eccentricity pursued von Bülow even beyond the grave. When he died in Cairo in 1894, an autopsy was ordered because his illness was suspected to have been of an epidemic nature. Newspaper reports added these details:

"That the late Hans von Bülow was an irritable and arbitrary personage is still remembered by all. The wonder now is that he was not much more so. In his brain, recently prepared in Egypt for examination, there has been discovered the cicatrix of an internal lesion resulting from an accident in childhood. In the cicatrix the ends of two nerves had got partially pinched. That this would be fatal to any man's equanimity, let alone a musician's, will be readily understood."

Dog Bites Wagner

Wagner was regular in his habits; he liked to maintain a rigid schedule in his work. He was determined to write down the last note of the *Meistersinger* on his fiftieth birthday, May 22, 1863. He told von Bülow so. But on July 26, 1862, as he tried to wash his favorite pet, a bulldog, he was bitten on his right thumb by the unappreciative animal. An infection set in which incapacitated him for ten days, and his schedule was upset. However, the delay in completing the *Meistersinger* cannot be blamed entirely on the dog, for Wagner did not finish the score until October, 1869. But the dog's bite provided him with a jocular excuse.

Wagner at Home

A correspondent of the Boston *Musical Record* in January, 1882, gives a graphic description of Wagner's home during the last weeks of his life.

"Wagner is 'at home' on Thursdays from 8:00 to 11:00 P.M. In the dusk of the evening we strolled through the quiet streets, conscious of being subjected to keen scrutiny by the inhabitants who, seated at their windows, gazed at the distinguished visitors as the latter passed. On approaching the Wahnfried Villa, which stands at the end of the highroad between Rollwenzel and the Hermitage, you feel rather astonished at finding no windows. There is a door however, and a large allegorical painting of a raven, the Greek Muse, and the goddess of music — at least such was the explanation we received of it.

"Madame Wagner, dressed in white silk, with a wreath of roses on her head, receives her guests very gracefully and does all she can to make everyone feel comfortable and at his ease. Is she beautiful? To this question it is difficult to return a precise answer. She is, at any rate, eminently fascinating.

"The company is thoroughly international. In one part of the room Franz Liszt is talking Hungarian to a group of Magyars. Scattered about are various members — male and female — of the aristocracy of Great Britain; French, Austrian, Russian, and Serbian nobles also form an important element in the animated scene which includes, moreover, most of the principal artists engaged in the trilogy.

"Wagner generally comes in late from rehearsal. He is attired in an old German costume. He moves about conversing freely with all. He shakes hands with one artist, compliments another; goes to the piano, sings a verse from some ballad, finishing up as a joke with a few bars of a waltz by Strauss; or sometimes he will show an organ he received as a gift from America, remarking as he exhibits it:

> *Einer geschenkten Orgel*
> *Sieht man nicht in die Gorgel"*

This bit of Wagnerian poetry means, of course, that you don't look into the mouth of a gift organ. (To make the jingle rhyme, Wagner had to change *Gurgel,* "the throat," to *Gorgel,* a nonsense word.)

Wagner's Premonition

That Wagner had a premonition of death is testified by the following episodes. When he conducted his early symphony on Cosima Wagner's birthday, December 23, 1882, he turned to the musicians before taking the baton and said: "This is the last time I shall ever conduct."

"Why?" asked the concertmaster.

"Because I shall soon die," replied Wagner.

On the first day of Lent, in Venice shortly before his death, Wagner hired a gondola and asked the gondolier: "Where is the fashionable place to go today?"

"The Necropolis," replied the Venetian.

Wagner walked long among the mortuary niches.

"Were you pleased?" inquired the gondolier.

"Very much," said Wagner, "particularly since I soon shall have a place of rest myself."

Verdi's Barrel Organs

The *Musical Courier* of September 21, 1887, tells this story. Verdi was staying at an Italian summer resort in a spacious cottage. A friend, calling on him, was received in a small room which seemed to serve as bedroom, drawing room, and work room all at once. "Why don't you use the rest or the house," he asked Verdi. Instead of replying Verdi led him through the rest of the house, which was crowded with barrel organs, ninety-five of them.

"All these organs were playing *Rigoletto, Il Trovatore,* and other operas of mine," explained Verdi. "Obviously I could not work under such circumstances. I decided to hire the organs from their owners. It will cost me about fifteen hundred liras for the summer, but it is not too large a price for a peaceful vacation."

Cavaliere Suppé-Demelli

The most international of all musical composers was undoubtedly Franz von Suppé, the composer of 211 comic operas and other theater music. His real name was Francesco Ezechiele Ermenegildo Cavaliere Suppé-Demelli. He was born in Dalmatia, of Belgian descent, but his career as a composer of light operas was established in Germany. He was the first to set the modern type of German and Austrian operetta in which the main character is the crown prince of an unnamed Balkan country, gallivanting in Paris much to the annoyance of the old man out in the Balkans. The peak of absurdity is reached in the Suppé opera, *Light Cavalry* in which a pompous city mayor providentially named Bums makes love to a Hungarian peasant girl on the bench of a public park while his wife, Apollonia, gets the evidence on him disguised as a marble statue.

[148]

CHASTITY

Stage Fright

Saint-Saëns told Isidor Philipp: "In 1870 I was with the guard on the fortifications of Paris. I heard cannon shots without the slightest emotion. But when after the war I had to play my Second Concerto, my legs trembled so that I could scarcely touch the pedals."

Conservatoriopolis

When Saint-Saëns visited Buenos Aires, he was astonished to find that there was a conservatory of music in nearly every block. In his impressions of his South American trip, Saint-Saëns jokingly refers to Buenos Aires as Conservatoriopolis. Argentine musicians, far from taking offense at the jibe, have picked up the appellation. Buenos Aires has now more conservatories than ever.

Composing Erect

Some composers write music with the piano; others prefer to write their musical thoughts on paper without aural assistance. But the most original method of composing was employed by Saint-Saëns. He wrote music on a high unpainted desk, standing up. He had no piano nor any other musical instrument in his room, and he always wrote out a complete section of a work at a time.

Music Must Be Difficult

Most musicians are trying to make music easy to understand — for economic if for no other reasons. But Saint-Saëns, disgusted with an influx of cocky amateurs flocking to the art, once said to Grovlez: "*Mon cher,* we must make music sufficiently complicated to discourage amateurs." And Busoni said almost the same thing: "Music must become so complex and intricate as to eliminate automatically all dilettantism."

Suite and Low

Arthur Sullivan, stopping in a provincial town, went to a hotel. "What kind of room do you wish?" asked the clerk. Sullivan immediately sang: "*Suite,* and . . . *low!*"

The Last Romantic

Mahler was the Last Mohican of musical romanticism. He died before the advent of an era that may be variously described as utilitarian, pragmatic, or simply realistic. Mahler lived in a world of his own, and believed that his music was an emanation from Heaven — or Hell. When he wrote his *Lied von der Erde,* he was seized with apprehension that this music would do harm to the listeners. "Do you think it is safe to let people sing it?" he remarked once. "Or will they do away with themselves when they hear this music?" He felt a morbid fascination for poetry dealing with death. He composed a cycle of songs, *Kindertotenlieder,* to the words of the German romantic poet Rueckert, poems that are among the most anguished ever written in any language. Rueckert wrote these poems after the death of his two small children. The grief of the poet was transcribed by Mahler into musical sounds with poignant fidelity. Several years after Mahler wrote these songs, his own little daughter died. Mahler believed that somehow her death was connected with the songs and brooded over his imaginary guilt.

His figures of speech abounded in morbid references to to death. After a performance of his Third Symphony which he thought was poorly done, he told a friend who inquired how it had gone, *"Reden Sie mir nicht davon; ich habe mich in meinem Grabe umgedreht."* (Don't speak to me about it; it made me turn in my grave.)

Mahler was most unhappy in his relationship with the New York Philharmonic Orchestra, which he conducted in the last few seasons before his death in 1911. The New York papers were full of gossip about his troubles with the women managers who underwrote the deficit of the orchestra. After Mahler died, his widow spoke bitterly to reporters: "In Vienna, even the Emperor did not dictate to my husband. But in New York, to his amazement, he had ten women ordering him about like a puppet. He hoped, however, by hard work and success to rid himself of his tormentors. Meanwhile he lost health and strength."

Mahler also had a peculiar sense of humor. He once said to the singer who sang the part of Tristan: "Don't forget that before you drink the love potion, you are a baritone; after that, you are a tenor."

Magic in Numbers

As every music student knows, the Mighty Five of Russian music are, in alphabetical order, Balakirev, Borodin, Cui, Mussorgsky, and Rimsky-Korsakov. The interesting thing about the five is that none of them started out as a musician. Balakirev was the son of a wealthy family engaged in business; Borodin was a chemical student and later professor of chemistry; Cui was a specialist in military fortification, and taught military science to the last of the Romanoffs; Mussorgsky was a government clerk in the forestry department; Rimsky-Korsakov was a marine officer. Music for all of them was at first merely an avocation. But they had a new idea. They decided to stop imitating Italian models as did Russian composers before them and to write music in the national Russian style, the kind of music that was still regarded as vulgar by the educated classes in Russia. All five lived in the former Russian capital city, St. Petersburg. Tchaikovsky made his headquarters in Moscow, and that is why he did not get into the circle of the Mighty Five.

The expression, "The Mighty Five," was the invention of the Russian critic, Vladimir Stassov. It all happened when on May 24, 1867 a program of music by composers from the Slavic countries was presented in St. Peters-

burg. Russia was then in the throes of the great Slavo-
phile agitation which eventually led to a Russo-Turkish
war. On the program of the Slavic concert was an overture on Czech themes by Balakirev, a Serbian Fantasy by
Rimsky-Korsakov, and compositions by other Russian
composers. In his review in the *St. Petersburg News,*
Stassov wrote: "Let us hope that our Slavonic friends will
for a long time remember the poetry, the sentiment, the
talent, and the skill that have been revealed by a small
but already mighty company of Russian musicians." The
expression, "The Mighty Company" (*moguchaya kuchka:*
literally, a mighty little heap), was mockingly picked up
by other journalists and eventually received general currency.

In musical quality, the Five are hardly in the same
category. Cui is a minor composer who is remembered
only by a miniature piece called *Orientale.* Balakirev's
name is conspicuously absent from concert programs.
But Rimsky-Korsakov, Mussorgsky, and to a lesser degree, Borodin, have firmly established themselves in the
musical hall of fame.

The naming of the French Six was really due to a *non
sequitur* perpetrated by the French critic, Henri Collet.
On January 16, 1920, he wrote an article in the Paris
paper, *Comœdia,* entitled "The Five Russians and the
Six French." What the connection was between the five
Russians and the six French except that six is the next
number after five, it was difficult to discover. But Collet's
article resulted in the firm bracketing of six names of
French composers: five men and one woman: Georges
Auric, Louis Durey, Arthur Honegger, Darius Milhaud,
Francis Poulenc, and Germaine Tailleferre. Of these, only
two have attained the rank of first-class composers: Honegger and Milhaud. Georges Auric and Francis Poulenc
have devoted themselves mainly to ballet and cinema

[153]

music. Germaine Tailleferre married and vanished from active musical life. Louis Durey turned to the insurance business and never wrote another piece of consequential music since the fateful day when he was nominated to the membership of this group. The patron saint of the group, Henri Collet, emerged as a champion of young musicians of another era when in April 1947 he presented to the Paris public a group of musicians whom he chose to call Sensibilitists. It is doubtful, however, whether his second try at coining slogans will be as successful as his launching of the French Six.

Darius Milhaud gives this account of the birth of The Six, writing in the Vienna musical journal, *Der Anbruch*, in 1922:

"During the intermission, at a performance of the Russian Ballet, a man approached me and said that he was a critic of the French daily *Comœdia*, that he was very much interested in the concerts of our groups and that he would like to obtain the list of our works and our biographical data. It was Henri Collet. Of course, we answered all his inquiries, and a few days later we read in *Comœdia* an article entitled 'Les cinq Russes et les six Français.' From the programs of the concerts of 'Nouveaux jeunes,' Collet selected the names of Auric, Durey, Honegger, Milhaud, Poulenc, and Tailleferre and called them 'The Six;' and this sobriquet remained. Thus the Group of Six was formed without our participation because it had never entered our heads to make a count of our numbers. In the formation of this group we saw the means of coordinating our musical activities, and we began calling our concerts, 'Les Concerts du Groupe des Six.'

"We, The Six, had received different types of musical education, and this contributed to the independence of our individual thinking, taste, and style. We attach great importance to this independence and are proud of it. In view of this, how can we be regarded as slaves of a single code of esthetics, one theory? Auric is influenced by Chabrier; Durey is a disciple of Satie and Ravel; Honegger follows Wagner,

Richard Strauss, and Florent Schmitt; Poulenc writes in the vein of Mozart and Stravinsky; Tailleferre is an impressionist. and I am indebted in a considerable degree to Berlioz and Albéric Magnard."

A Minor God of Russian Music

The name of Vasili Kalinnikov has been retained in the annals of music only due to his early symphony written in a romantically Russian idiom. Kalinnikov died in 1901 at the age of thirty-four from tuberculosis aggravated by poverty and distress. In his student days in Moscow he could never afford a square meal: a glass of Russian tea with lump sugar and a roll was his principal nourishment. He had to leave the Moscow Conservatory because he could not pay his tuition. He toured with an operetta company in Russia as a bassoon player. His first symphony was written at the age of twenty-nine, and a musical friend sent it to Rimsky-Korsakov with a request to recommend its publication. Rimsky-Korsakov's reaction was sympathetic but negative. "If Kalinnikov were not on the point of death," Rimsky-Korsakov replied, "I would have recommended further study. He has some talent but little knowledge, and his harmonic and contrapuntal writing is extremely confused. . . . I cannot accept things like the beginning of the first movement where after a phrase in unison à la russe, there is an irrelevant harmonic progression with all kinds of altered chords or the annoying and feeble syncopation which fills up the entire first movement; or the bad consecutive fifths at the beginning of the Andante; or the melody that follows after that, in which there is no leading tone; or the Trio and the Scherzo, where the leading tone disappears altogether creating a tonality falsely regarded as the Eolian mode but which is a kind of music that Balakirev once described as a barrel organ out of tune; or the Finale with its thematic confusion and a rather inharmonious coda."

[155]

Rimsky-Korsakov's letter dealing with Kalinnikov contains also a characteristic observation about Mussorgsky, who was generally regarded by his friends as a talented but uncultured composer. "Mussorgsky's music is published and performed only in my arrangements, without which it could not possibly be placed on a concert program or published. Since Mussorgsky's days we have made some progress. To compose like Mussorgsky nowadays is disgraceful."

Kalinnikov wrote one more symphony before he died and sold both symphonies to a Moscow publisher for one hundred rubles. In the meantime his health deteriorated, and he went to Yalta in the Crimea, where he joined two other famous tubercular patients, the writers Chekhov and Maxim Gorky. He wrote to Gretchaninov in May 1900: "I have had to remain in the Crimea for another summer. The doctors positively forbid me to go north even in the summer, threatening me with fatal consequences. I had to give in, however reluctantly....My health is very poor. The fever weakens me and does not let me work. I am an invalid, my friend, a complete invalid, and I cannot reconcile myself to it. . . . Rachmaninoff is here. He calls on me and gives me tremendous joy with his playing."

Discordant Alarm

Anton Rubinstein was such a late sleeper that he often missed his appointments in the morning. His wife hit upon a device to rouse him by musical means. The Rubinsteins had a piano upstairs, on which Mme. Rubinstein would play an unresolved chord when it was time for her husband to get up. Rubinstein could not stand unresolved dissonances, and he would run up the stairs in his nightshirt to resolve the chord into a perfect triad. In the meantime Mme. Rubinstein would remove the blankets from the bed, thus preventing his going to sleep again.

Whether true or not, the story at least fits into the known character of Rubinstein.

Polovtzian Dances by Gedeanishvili

Who composed the *Polovtzian Dances?*

The answer is Gedeanishvili! This was Borodin's true paternal name — that of his real father, a Georgian prince. At the age of sixty-two the prince had an affair with the wife of an army doctor, a twenty-four-year-old woman, and the outcome of this liaison was the birth of a great composer. Gedeanishvili was fond of the boy and provided him with all necessities of life. He also gave him

a legal father, Porfiri Borodin, who was one of the prince's serfs. Thus the son of Prince Gedeanishvili became Alexander Porfirievitch (Porfiri's son) Borodin.

In his later life, Borodin was little bothered by his illegitimate origin although modern psychologists would probably find that Borodin's notoriously strange habits were due to a suppressed sense of shame. Once Borodin walked out of his house clothed in full military uniform but with no trousers. At a reception in his house he suddenly put on his overcoat to leave, mumbling that he

lived rather far away and had to get home before night-
fall. However, such incidents were not uncommon among
the Russian intelligentsia who suffered from environ-
mental instability.

Growing Old Musically

Rimsky-Korsakov complained in a letter to his friend,
Kruglikov, that approaching old age was robbing him of
his energy:

"I work badly; I write down wrong notes; I am unable to
arrange correctly a relatively simple rhythmic theme, and
sometimes cannot get the right interval without trying it out
on the piano. Every musical idea that comes into my head
has to be written down right away or else I forget it in fifteen
minutes. In copying, I cannot remember even a couple of
bars correctly and must copy note for note. I find it difficult
to compose even such pages that require no inspiration but
are done through technique and experience — recitatives, for
instance. The result is feeble, the modulations are clumsy.
This increases my revulsion to work still more. I look back
at my former years: the first draft of *The Snow Maiden* was
done during a single summer, and I felt no fatigue except
ordinary and rather pleasant weariness after work, which
passed immediately after a walk, a dinner, or a tea. And now
I feel something that has never happened before, an inca-
pacity to work which I cannot overcome by short periods
of rest. Old age creeps stealthily on. . . . With foreign composers, it comes somewhat later: take for instance Wagner
and Verdi. But I am fifty-eight years old, and for a Russian
it is more than enough."

Love-Hatred for Wagner

In Rimsky-Korsakov's workshop in St. Petersburg, a
portrait of Wagner hung conspicuously on the wall. Rimsky-Korsakov admired Wagner greatly; in the Russian's
later operas, particularly in the religious music drama,
Kitezh, the influence of Wagner is much in evidence. Yet

[158]

Rimsky-Korsakov never missed an opportunity of kicking his idol. In 1901 he wrote to his faithful friend and biographer, Yastrebtzoff:

"I have been ardently reading the score of *Siegfried*. As always after a long interval, Wagner's music repelled me, and I had to get used to it all over again. I am outraged by his various aural aberrations which surpass the limit of the harmonically feasible. Cacophony and nonsense are scattered in *Siegfried* all over the place. I have reached the conclusion that there is considerable similarity between Mussorgsky and Richard. How strange that Mussorgsky could not understand him and refused to recognize him. What terrible harm Wagner did by interspersing his pages of genius with harmonic and modulatory outrages to which both young and old are gradually becoming accustomed and which have procreated d'Indy and Strauss! Can it be that my musical perception is superior to that of Wagner, who composed the music, or that of Nikisch, who tolerated and relished these outrages? Of course not; quite possibly it is inferior to theirs, but I have a musical conscience to which I carefully listen whereas Wagner lost his conscience in his pursuit of fame and novelty."

Color Music

When Scriabin introduced an orchestral part for colored lights in the score of his *Poem of Fire (Prometheus),* there was a great hullabaloo among musical mystics. The part was to be played on a specially constructed organ which produced, or was intended to produce, colored lights that would change according to the harmonies. It seems that Scriabin had a predecessor, one Lewis Bertrand Castel of Montpelier, the author of *Optics of Colors,* published early in the nineteenth century. A contemporary account tells us, somewhat caustically, that the learned man "studied vision and the nature of colors as blended or contrasted with each other till, his imagination getting the better of his understanding, he confounded the eye with the ear and associated the harmony of tints with that of sounds." As a result of his study, Lewis Bertrand Castel invented an ocular harpsichord in which colored tapes were substituted for wires. When the ocular harpsichord was played in semi-darkness, the tapes, made of transparent material, became visible every time the corresponding key was struck. By arranging the scale according to rainbow colors, the inventor brought the melody, rhythm, and harmony into association with the basic colors. His music was for the eye as well as for the ear. What happened to his childishly ingenious invention, no one can tell at this late date.

Scriabin's Absent-Mindedness

Scriabin was exceptionally absent-minded, even for a musician. He could never keep an umbrella, a new pair of gloves or new rubbers for more than two or three days. He would go to a party wearing a pair of new rubbers and come back in two old ones, and even those would not match. He knew his weakness and begged his family not to buy any new articles for him but rather get them second-hand, for he would lose them anyway. His publisher, Belaiev, tried in vain to persuade Scriabin to be more attentive to details in his music, particularly in the use of expression marks, which he rarely put in. In his later works he evaded this difficulty by inserting instead of expression marks, verbal effusions in French, such as *voluptueux, presque avec douleur, avec délice, avec un intense désir, avec émotion et ravissement, avec enthousiasme, limpide, sourd, menaçant, étrange, charmé, avec un effroi contenu, comme un cri, extatique, dans un vertige.*

One day Scriabin received two letters, one from Rimsky-Korsakov and the other from Liadov. Both berated him in an amiably jocular manner for his absent-mindedness in his professional work. Scriabin was very much incensed by these letters and answered them at once with profuse explanations of his weaknesses. Several days later, he received another letter from Liadov, in which was enclosed Scriabin's letter to Rimsky-Korsakov. Scriabin had apparently confused the letters, sending the one for Liadov to Rimsky-Korsakov and the one for Rimsky-Korsakov to Liadov! Rimsky-Korsakov returned his mismailed letter to Scriabin personally, handing the envelope to him silently with a shrug of his shoulders.

Scriabin's Children

Alexander Scriabin died prematurely at the age of forty-three, on April 27, 1915 in Moscow. An abcess of the lip had developed into a gangrenous infection. He left his second wife, Tatiana, with three children: Ariadna, Julian, and Marina. The children were illegitimate, for Scriabin's first wife refused a divorce, and Scriabin's second marriage was only a common-law marriage. However, after Scriabin died, the Russian government, by special dispensation, allowed Tatiana and the three children to assume the name of Scriabin.

Two of these children met with a tragic death. On June 22, 1919, Julian, who was eleven years old, went for a swim in the Dnieper River, in Kiev. With him was a group of children, all of them chaperoned by a woman friend. Julian, shy of the girls in the group, went to swim in a sheltered inlet overhung with willow trees. Toward dusk, the children were all called in, but Julian was not among them. On the next day his body was recovered in a deep spot of the inlet where the bottom had a sudden drop.

Young Julian had inherited his father's genius. At the age of ten he composed piano preludes in a chromatic near-atonal style characteristic of the last compositions of Scriabin himself. He studied in Kiev with Glière and astonished his teacher and other musicians who heard his compositions and improvisations by the extraordinary refinement of his harmonic sense. The manuscripts of Julian's preludes were preserved and published in Moscow in the memorial volume issued in 1940 on the twenty-fifth anniversary of Scriabin's death.

Ariadna Scriabin left Russia and went to Paris where she married the composer, Daniel Lazarus. She lived in France during the occupation by the Nazis and was active in Resistance groups. Her work as a messenger required frequent trips between Paris and southern France. During one of these missions she was arrested and shot.

The only surviving child of Scriabin's second marriage is Marina, who still lives in France. She is an accomplished organist and of late has also begun to compose music. But her style has nothing of the tense chromaticism that was the essence of her father's harmony. Her music is serenely diatonic. There is no ecstacy, no mysticism in the subject matter of her works. The religious spirit is present, but its musical expression is modal and austere.

Composers in Distress

During the entire course of music history, composers of serious music have led a precarious existence mitigated by occasional charity from rich friends or munificent commissions by wealthy patrons. Often these gifts were openly solicited by composers in the guise of loans.

The story of Tchaikovsky and Mme. von Meck, his benefactress, is well known. She was the widow of a wealthy railroad magnate; at the time, Tchaikovsky was a moderately successful composer and a harmony teacher at the Moscow Conservatory. They never met face to face, but during the thirteen years of their epistolary friendship their correspondence was voluminous. When the monthly checks suddenly ceased three years before Tchaikovsky's death — and with it von Meck's correspondence — Tchaikovsky was furious as well as unhappy. He dreamed of moral revenge; he wildly hoped to be able to amass enough money to return every ruble he had ever received from her — tens of thousands of rubles.

Tchaikovsky was genuinely grateful to his benefactress for her help and equally so for her burning interest in his career and in his music. She was not at all averse to meeting Tchaikovsky personally; indeed, she virtually invited him to her house in Florence when both happened to be in that city at the same time. But Tchaikovsky had a mortal fear that the sentiments expressed in her letters on the safe level of intellectual consanguinity would develop into an affectionate romance on her part. He expressed this fear openly in his letters to his brothers, with whom he was quite frank. "The only fly in the ointment," he wrote, "is the proximity of Mme. von Meck. She is a marvelous woman, but I suspect that she is trying to lure me into her house." On another occasion he wrote to one of his brothers: "Received an eight-page letter from Mme. von Meck, full of philosophy, but no check. I cannot understand her. I have only three liras in my pocket."

The stipend which Mme. von Meck was sending Tchaikovsky was agreed upon at the very beginning of their strange relationship; Tchaikovsky did not have to ask for the money or thank her for it every time a check arrived. But even with this generous contribution he never knew how to keep his expenses within his budget. He always had money troubles; he always admitted his lack of planning; he was invariably effusive in his self-flagellation. When he miscalculated his finances on a trip abroad, he wrote to Mme. von Meck from Berlin:

"You will probably be surprised, my beloved friend, to

[163]

know that I am still in Berlin. A circumstance occurred which presents me in a ridiculous light, but nonetheless I will confess it to you. I managed my money in Paris with such wisdom that having paid up all my bills before departure I found myself without enough funds to reach St. Petersburg. So when I arrived in Berlin, I realized that I could not move any further without an additional sum of money. The reason for my mismanagement is principally my sudden mania for high-class clothes, which had never happened to me before. So in the last days in Paris I had the stupidity of acquiring an altogether unnecessary quantity of articles of wearing apparel. I am all the more ashamed to speak to you about it because you know very well that I had plenty of money, which I foolishly squandered away."

Two days later Tchaikovsky dispatched to Mme. von Meck another letter, recapitulating the contents of the first — in case it had gone astray — and further describing his financial difficulties and worries:

"On top of everything, I took a room in a very expensive hotel here. My financial resources are coming to the end, and the uncertainty is beginning to upset and torment me in the utmost degree. In this extremity I decided to telegraph you today and to request you to send me eight hundred francs if possible by a telegraphed draft on a local bank. I am inexpressibly ashamed, not because I ask you for money, but because I give you trouble and reveal myself so grossly in the most disadvantageous light as a person who never could and never can distribute his means wisely."

To these tortured effusions, Mme. von Meck responded in a characteristic fashion. She sent to Tchaikovsky in Berlin a draft for one thousand francs, two hundred more than the sum requested by Tchaikovsky. She also wrote him, in a letter dated at eight o'clock in the morning, reproaching him gently for his hesitations in asking her for more money:

"I am very angry with you, my dear, my precious friend. You promised me, and I cling fast to this promise, that every time you are in need of money you will address yourself to me. Believe me that no one among your friends loves you so ardently and so sincerely as I. Why then forget me in a moment of trouble?"

Even more trying for Tchaikovsky and certainly for Mme. von Meck were the protracted negotiations between Tchaikovsky and his nominal wife, whom he had married in a moment of mad determination to create for himself a false front of respectable normalcy. Tchaikovsky never mentioned her by name in his correspondence with Mme. von Meck, but only, fearfully, as "that certain person." In all sincerity he told Mme. von Meck how he hated the very handwriting of the woman who legally bore his name. When Tchaikovsky hinted in one of his letters that she would divorce him if her financial demands were satisfied, Mme. von Meck reacted with impulsive decisiveness. She wrote:

"I beg you, my dear and precious friend, to do anything to free yourself of her for good. Do not stop at the unpleasant sides of a divorce. It is better to pass once through the sordid and stifling atmosphere and then emerge into the open fresh air than to swallow such miasma periodically all your life.

[165]

Do not stop also before the financial expenditures. Pay her ten, fifteen thousand. You know very well that I would disburse the money cheerfully to secure your happiness. Please take this up energetically. Another thing that I should like to do, but that is something quite different, is to arrange our life *à nous deux* in Brailov. This is very easy to manage, and it depends on your consent. I have a cottage near Brailov. It is a remote and poetic place, and I would be inexpressibly happy if you would consent to live there for a month or even longer when I am in Brailov. Then I would feel every day that you are near, and this thought would give me such a feeling of well-being, joy, calm, and courage that nothing evil could possibly take possession of me. Please think it over, my dear, good, beloved. . . . How wonderful it would be. . . . If you would only consent, my dear, my good friend!"

Tchaikovsky's response to this impassionate offer was contained in a series of daily letters which he finally sent off in a single envelope. The essence of his response, when all the psychological excrescences are eliminated, was that for a variety of reasons he could not accept her invitation at that particular time, although he might have considered it earlier, before he had made his own arrangements for his summer sojourn with his relatives. There is no question that Mme. von Meck understood this veiled rebuke, and in her following letters she somewhat lessened the ardor of her incandescent terms of endearment.

Tchaikovsky never did divorce his wife. In the meantime she had an affair and a child. She died in an insane asylum in 1917. Nothing is known of her child, who bore Tchaikovsky's name.

Mozart also had a friend to whom he turned when in financial distress, a merchant named Michael Puchberg, and a fellow-member with Mozart of the Vienna branch of Freemasons. This gave Mozart an opportunity to address Puchberg as a fraternal soul and thus made his requests far easier to advance. The summer of 1788 was particularly hard for Mozart. On June 17 of that year he moved, with his wife and children, to new lodgings in a Vienna suburb. He had left his previous quarters in Vienna proper under unpleasant conditions, for the landlord had compelled him to pay the back rent before moving out. He liked his new house. It was spacious, and he could always retire to his room to compose in peace, undisturbed by the domestic hubbub. In consequence, he was able to accomplish in ten days an immense amount of work. He completed his thirty-ninth symphony, wrote a fugue for string quartet, a march, and his famous C major Sonata for Piano.

Mozart's finances were extremely low. He wrote to Puchberg requesting a considerable sum as a loan. In a pathetic letter Mozart said that such a loan (five hundred florins were mentioned) would mean happiness for himself and his family. Puchberg, who usually satisfied Mozart's more modest applications (and marked in his notebook: "Sent so much *eadem die*"), balked. Receiving no reply, Mozart sent Puchberg a pair of pawnbroker's tickets, begging him urgently to raise money and keep the tickets as collateral. In each instance Mozart reiterated that the money would be returned in time. Three years later, Mozart was dead, at the age of thirty-five. So far as is known, Puchberg never got back a kreutzer. But he got considerable notice in the index of all Mozart's biographies.

Ferruccio Busoni was a brilliant pianist as well as composer. But he, too, at least in his early years, experienced the agony of financial insecurity. As a youth, still in his twenties, he taught at the Conservatory of Helsingfors and later at the New England Conservatory in Boston. His Boston days were not happy, however, and the Boston *Evening Transcript* complained that Busoni "was shabbily treated, neglected, and obliged to teach young pianists stumbling through exercises."

When his first symphonic poem was performed by Nikisch with the Boston Symphony Orchestra, it was damned by the Boston critics, one of whom compared it to "a full-fledged Dakota cyclone roaring through a wholesale tinware establishment, destroying two or three dynamite factories with wildly explosive results and causing the collapse of a six-story crockery warehouse."

A pleasant oasis was the Gardner Museum, maintained in Boston by Isabella Stewart Gardner. Busoni gave several recitals at that Museum, which was built like an Italian *palazzo* and had a music hall. (Mrs. Julia Ward Howe, who was present at one of Busoni's recitals at which he played Beethoven and Liszt, thought the pianist pounded frightfully.) Busoni's fee was two hundred dollars. But when he departed in 1894 from America's dollar-laden shores and settled in Berlin, he found his finances in an unsatisfactory condition. Recalling the splendor of the Gardner palace, he took pen in hand and addressed to Mrs. Gardner a letter in French, occasionally marred by misplaced accents and Italianate idioms:

"Chère Madame! Il y a longtemps que j'avais l'intention de vous écrire. Mais, pendant l'été des graves occupations m'ont obligé de négliger les devoirs agréables pour les devoirs de stricte necessité.

"Je voudrais pouvoir vous exprimer combien le souvenir de votre maison m'est resté 'incise' dans la mémoire; il y demeure la comme une belle gravure, legère et artistique. Et je voudrais être capable de vous exprimer aussi la reconnaissance et la sympathie que votre aimable et intelligent esprit a sû m'inspirer. Mais mon vocabulaire est bien pauvre en comparaison des mes sentiments."

Busoni then mentioned Mrs. Gardner's expressed intention to visit Italy and added that he himself should have liked to return to his native country for a visit. He then cautiously approached the principal subject of his letter: the request for a loan of one thousand dollars.

"Justement dans ce moment — en attendant le commencement de la saison — je me trouve dans un état de 'crise' très gênante et nuisive à mes travaux. En Europe la carrière d'un artiste coûte sans rien apporter. J'ai quelques bons amis, mais ils sont la plupart de bons artistes et par consequence pauvres. Les bons artistes enrichis ne sont plus mes amis.

"Si vous vouliez me permettre de vous ouvrir mon cœur (et la grande bonté que vous m'avez jadis démontree me donne la confiance et le courage de le faire) j'oserais bien vous appeler en mon aide. J'oserais vous prier de venir en mon secours en me prêtant une somme dont j'ai grande et immédiate nécessité. Vous seule, de toutes les personnes que je connais réunissez la richesse à l'intelligence en faisant de cette heureuse et rare réunion le meilleur usage pour vous même et pour les autres."

Busoni further announced to Mrs. Gardner that his concerts in Berlin were expected to be successful and that this success would probably lead to engagements in London and a re-engagement in America. *"Rien n'est certain, mais beaucoup est vraisemblable."*

The all-important figure in dollars was arrived at in Busoni's letter in an obliquely constructed sentence which must have given the writer some pain to form. He wrote:

"If my projects do not fail. it will be possible for me during the next two years to reimburse to you the sum of one thousand dollars which I imperatively need at this moment. *Voilà mon cœur ouvert et transparent comme du crystal. . . .* This decision has cost me more pain than you can imagine although the realization that I am addressing a person such as you has made it somewhat less oppressive."

Following the tradition of so many benefactors of the past, Mrs. Gardner responded promptly by sending Busoni the requested sum of money. Busoni acknowledged the receipt with gratitude:

"I was touched by your letter which contained the sum of one thousand dollars. The aid which you lend me is of the greatest significance for me. If I confine myself to writing one *merci* which comes from the bottom of my heart, it is because in knowing your great and fine manner of thinking, I am sure that you will interpret this single word as expressive of all that I feel toward you, my dear benefactress. As I was not mistaken in you, I hope that I will never cause you to believe that you have been mistaken in me, either as an artist or as a person capable of gratitude. I hope that you will not disdain to give me the honor of a few lines in reply when circumstances will allow you to do so. At least allow me to write you, and in accepting my letters, grant me the gratifying conviction that you have for me this interest that is dear and precious to me. With my sentiments of deepest esteem and gratitude, I am, Madame, your servitor, Ferruccio Busoni."

But Busoni did not write to Mrs. Gardner for many years after this exchange of letters. There is also no record in the archives of the Gardner Museum of Boston that Busoni ever returned the thousand dollars he had accepted from Mrs. Gardner as a loan. It is doubtful whether Mrs. Gardner ever expected him to return that money. By a curious coincidence, Busoni and Mrs. Gardner died within a few days of each other, in July 1924, he in Berlin, and she in Boston.

Wedding March by Debussy

Mendelssohn's Wedding March, from his music to Shakespeare's *A Midsummer Night's Dream*, was first played as nuptial music at the wedding of the princess royal of England in 1858, and has been a matrimonial favorite ever since, along with the Bridal Chorus from Wagner's *Lohengrin*.

Debussy, too, wrote a wedding march — for the marriage of his good friend, the writer of exquisitely voluptuous poetry, Pierre Louÿs. In 1899 when Louÿs decided to get married, he asked Debussy, in a rather flippant way, to compose a wedding march for the occasion. Louys wrote:

"The marriage will take place in six weeks, at the Saint-Philippe Church. Do you know the organist of that curious edifice? I intend to suggest to him a little Bachian program which would include as an introduction a celebrated unpublished *Hochzeitmarsch* by Debussy! Are you disposed to indite one for two manuals and a pedal in the customary march time in four beats, a piece of festive nature, lascivious and fervent as behooves a nuptial ceremony? It ought to be one of those little masterpieces that one writes at the table in a restaurant between a scotch and a chaser. You cannot refuse an old buddy."

But the old buddy was procrastinating, and Louys wrote again:

"The ceremony is due in eleven days. Do you think you will have the march ready next Saturday? I figure that six days will be enough for the organist who, it seems, is a professor of bassoon playing at the Conservatory."

Debussy apparently came across with a wedding march, for the Paris *Figaro* reporting the event on June 24, 1899, wrote: "*M. Note a chanté la Marche nuptiale de M. Claude Debussy.*" The march turned out to be a a vocal composition. But what happened to the manuscript? The piece was never published and is not mentioned in Debussy's biographies.

General Lavine — Eccentric

Among Debussy's preludes, there is one that bears a rather mystifying subtitle: "General Lavine — Eccentric." The eccentric general of the title was a real person, an American vaudeville entertainer whose act opened at the Marigny Theater in Paris on August 1, 1910. Debussy wrote the piece as a commission for the General's manager.

What happened to General Lavine after his temporary

leap into musical immortality? Alfred Frankenstein, of San Francisco, traced him to his habitation at Twenty-nine Palms in California, where he was living in retirement in 1946.

Debussy's American Friend

The American violinist, Arthur Hartmann, had the rare privilege of knowing Debussy on intimate terms. Debussy was obviously fond of him and felt quite at ease in his company. Hartmann tells of Debussy's sense of humor. When Hartmann arranged Debussy's *Girl with the Flaxen Hair* for violin and piano, Debussy remarked: "I do want to hear her play the violin. I have no doubt that she has considerable talent." Debussy never finished the violin sonata which he promised to write for Hartmann, but he arranged his piano piece, *Minstrels,* for Hartmann. Characteristically he entitled this arrangement, *"Transcription pour piano et Hartmann."*

Debussy had a sharp tongue for his contemporaries. When Hartmann observed that Vincent d'Indy would have made quite a figure if he had lived in the fourteenth century, Debussy retorted: "Yes, a wooden figure." And he pronounced the name Mahler deliberately separating the syllables so that it sounded like Mal-air.

He liked to make fun of things American. He called grapefruit "grappe-fruit," a bunch of fruit. When Hartmann invited him to an American hotel in Paris, Debussy accepted, saying: "I shall immediately have my beard cut off so as to look American."

The incurable cancer that struck Debussy did not deprive him of grim humor. Apologizing to Hartmann for not finishing his violin sonata, Debussy referred to himself as *"un cadavre ambulant."*

Words Without Songs

Erik Satie was a strange figure in the world of modern music. All he ever composed was a number of piano pieces with funny titles. He was uncertain about his own knowledge of the technique of composition and went to study counterpoint at the Schola Cantorum in Paris after he was forty. Yet he exercised a profound influence on his musical betters. He was the master of the Ecole d'Arcueil, a Paris suburb where he lived. It was not, of course, a school in any academic sense of the word, for Satie was a professional anti-academician, an inveterate shocker of the bourgeoisie, a nonconformist by persuasion. But out of this School of Arcueil came the French modernism of the era between the two wars.

What Erik Satie lacked in technique, he made up in the humor of his captions and expression marks. Satie's music must be read, not played. Satie understood this necessity very well, and in his characteristic perverseness, he added a footnote to one of his pieces, *Instantaneous and Centenarian Hours:* "To Whomever It May Concern: I forbid reading the text aloud during the musical performance. Any neglect of this injunction will entail my righteous indignation against the overweening transgressor." Yet without reading the words, the music loses even the illustrative meaning that it may possess. Throughout, expression marks are profuse: "Wait," "Inhale," "Slow down politely," "Go on." In his *Cold Pieces* he warns the player, "Look twice," "From the corner of the hand," or admonishes him as a teacher admonishes a piano pupil: "Once more," "Very good," "Perfect," "Don't go any higher," "Come down," "Obey," "Don't worry," "It's important," "Don't frown," "Suck it in."

The teacher's voice is sometimes amiable and friendly. Satie does not put the conventional slurs over legato passages. Instead he writes in italics: *La basse liée, n'est-ce pas?* He is in his gentlest mood in *Avant-dernières pen-sées*. Even the tempo indications are polite: *"Modéré, je vous prie."*

Satie's most anti-academic composition is the short suite, *Desiccated Embryos*. Here occurs a verbal phrase that has become famous in the annals of musical nonsense, "Like a nightingale having a toothache." In the second of the three *Desiccated Embryos*, Satie inserts the trio from Chopin's Funeral March with the indication, "quotation from the famous Mazurka of Schubert." He, of course, hoped that some careless music critic would chide him for using Schubert for such unpoetic purposes. But even without this provocation, Satie enjoyed insulting the critics. When he sent a particularly scurrilous postcard to a Paris music critic, the latter called in the police and had Satie spend a few hours in jail.

Even in his religious compositions such as *Messe des pauvres*, Satie could not resist using irreverent expression marks while pretending piety, *"Très chrétiennement."* If Satie believed in after-life, he intended to make sure that he would not land in Paradise.

A Musical Offering

After a performance of Schubert's *Trout* Quintet (so nicknamed because the fourth movement of the Quintet consists of variations on Schubert's song, *The Trout*) Max Reger, who played the piano part, received a basketful of trout from an enthusiastic admirer. Reger wrote the sender a letter of thanks and added significantly that at the next concert he was going to perform the "Minuet of the Ox" by Haydn.

Pomp and Circumstance

Elgar's march, *Pomp and Circumstance*, stands next to *God Save the King* in rank and importance at official functions in England. The title is from Shakespeare in *Othello*, when the Moor recounts "the pomp and circumstance of glorious war." Elgar's other music is rarely played in America, but in England Elgar is a modern Beethoven. George Bernard Shaw said of Elgar that he could put out a shingle saying, "Beethoven's business transacted here." Shaw also said that Elgar's music "wrote itself on the skies for him," and that his range was Handelian, from symphonies to popular marches.

MacDowell in Darkness

On November 15, 1906, a remarkable document was published in the newspapers in New York, Boston, and elsewhere. It was an appeal for funds to maintain MacDowell in comfort during his last years of life. Among the signatories were musicians Horatio Parker, Victor Herbert, Arthur Foote, George Chadwick, and Frederick Converse. There were also the signatures of Andrew Carnegie, J. Pierpont Morgan, and the ex-president of the United States, Grover Cleveland. With such names signed to the appeal, it is difficult to understand why it was necessary to go to the public for funds. Surely J. Pierpont Morgan and Andrew Carnegie could have raised the necessary money by personal subscriptions.

The text of the appeal, not reproduced in biographies of MacDowell, sheds an interesting sidelight on the conditions under which American musicians, even of MacDowell's stature, had to live.

"In Edward MacDowell, America was just beginning to find a new voice in music — noble and virile music, neither academic, nor crude and barbarous, but full of that freedom which comes from true knowledge and that mystical poetry which hides in the heart of a strong, resolute nature. Trained in the best schools of Europe, master of the old-world tradition, he came home to his native country in the flower of his youth and for eighteen years devoted his genius and

[175]

his vigor to the service of his great art. Symphonies and sonatas, concertos and idyls, songs and studies, in which the old poetic traditions that belong to all humanity are treated with the new lyrical breadth and intensity of passion, and novel original themes are woven together in forms of beautiful and coherent art. MacDowell's work in music, like Hawthorne's was in literature, is distinctly and unmistakably American. It is an honor to a country to produce such an artist. America was proud of MacDowell and paid him abundantly — but not much in money. Serious and lofty works like his are rarely if ever profitable in music, at least in the present day. It would have been easy for him, in all probability, to take his talent into the market place and give himself to the production of light, frivolous, perishable stuff which would have brought in plenty of money. But this he would not do because he wanted to do better. So he gave himself to the hard, honorable, tiresome task of teaching for his living; and he did it well, with infinite eagerness and zeal, strenuous, faithful, persistent, until — the fatal, secret flash of lightning struck in the dark! Something snapped in his overwrought, overburdened brain. The fountain of pure music sank suddenly and forever out of sight. The lights went out in the palace of poetic dreams and all the garden of genius was desolate. He still lives, this devoted artist, and is likely to live for years. But art and work have become impossible for him. What a life is that! At the age of forty-five that mind which teemed with splendid thoughts and images has become like the mind of a little child, feeble, innocent, helpless, pleased with a plaything, infinitely pathetic in the peaceful ruin and quiet, slow decay. So he must live until the end comes, unable to do anything for those who are dependent upon him and needing constant care. How long will it be, this silent, hopeless waiting for the inevitable, no one can tell. But it will be strange indeed if those who love music do not provide for the comfort of this noble musician while his natural life continues, and for a fitting memorial to his name when he passes into the brightness of our country's history."

III

THIS MODERN STUFF

Definition

The most outspoken definition of modern music is found in *Key to Musicianship* by Christine Trotin, published in New York in 1927:

"Modern music seems to be the product of a revolt undertaken by a certain group of musicians against any rule whatsoever and reflects the trend of thought in the present generation. It is supposed to be based on what is called the 'whole-tone scale,' which explains the frequency of the discords, which, at times, follow each other in the most distressing manner."

Pietro Mascagni once wrote: "Modern music is as dangerous as cocaine."

The Hearing Aid Gag

An elderly woman wearing a hearing-aid apparatus listens attentively to a concert of modern music. Gradually an expression of dismay comes over her face. She takes off the hearing gadget, shakes it violently, puts it on again and goes through the same agonizing experience as the modern harmonies relentlessly beat through the membrane. Now convinced that the thing is out of order, she leaves her seat and walks out of the concert hall, presumably on the way to the store where she bought it.

The story is told with several locales and dramatis personæ, about Stravinsky in Geneva, Aaron Copland in Boston, and Schoenberg anywhere. Its latest appearance is in the autobiography of George Antheil, *Bad Boy of Music*, in which he says the ubiquitous lady with a hearing aid showed up at one of his recitals in Europe.

Wrong Euphony

Rehearsing an orchestral piece by an ultramodern composer, the conductor suddenly stopped and said: "Wait a minute! Something must be wrong — it sounds too good."

Ah, Hindemith!

It is common practice among café musicians in seaboard localities where semilegal characters congregate, to warn the entering acquaintances of any danger by playing discordant notes. But modern music being what it is, this method no longer seems effective. The *New Yorker* of October 26, 1946 observed melancholically: "Under such circumstances, the outlaws only say, 'Ah, Hindemith,' and sit there placidly enjoying the music until the cops come in."

The Beautiful Noises

In an orchestral score by Musard, a contemporary of Chopin, there is found an indication, *Chaise*, which meant that the player should seize his chair and bring it down on the floor with a loud thump. The inclusion of noises and even animal cries is not exceptional in orchestral music, and certainly not in modern music. There is a thunder machine in Strauss's *Alpine* Symphony, a factory whistle in the Second Symphony by Shostakovich, and a steel sheet in the score of *Iron Foundry* by Mossolov. Werner Janssen's score, *New Year's Eve in New York*, calls for a klaxon, a siren, and automobile horns. In the section marked New Year's Celebration, the score bears this indication: "All those not occupied with wind instruments shout, *ad libitum*, Happy New Year and cheer." In the meantime the trombones play *Auld Lang Syne*.

In a performance of Walter Piston's ballet, *The Incredible Flutist*, the recorded sound of a barking dog was included in the section which represents a circus show. In another score by a contemporary composer, toy balloons are exploded with the aid of hairpins at the climax.

Henry Cowell has achieved a modicum of percussive immortality by his invention of tone-clusters, which are played on the piano with fists and forearms. When he gave the first and last performance of his fist-and-forearm concerto in Havana, Cuba — where Latin tempers are likely to reach the boiling point at the slightest provocation — the conductor of the orchestra asked for police protection. Cowell was told to run for the nearest exit in case of a riot, but the sight of the Cuban constabulary was enough to secure tranquility. As a matter of fact, there was applause, and praise in the newspapers.

The American composer, John Cage, has put musical noises on a commercial basis by conducting concerts of percussion music, including such esoteric contrivances as tin pans, buzzers, water gongs, rice bowls, Korean dragons' mouths, Japanese temple gongs, anvils, and Indian rattles. He has also perfected the so-called "prepared" piano, which one might describe as a tampered-with clavichord. Another American, Harold G. Davidson, went Cage one better in his *Auto Accident*. In the score there is an instrumental part described as follows: "Two

[179]

glass plates, each resting on a wash bowl or crock, with a hammer or mallet in readiness to smash them. On page nine, measure four, these plates are to be shattered with the hammer, one on the second count, and the other on the second half of the third count. In the next measure, the bowls containing the broken glass are to be emptied on a hard surface, table, or floor."

George Antheil, the American composer who began his career as a musical noisemaker and went to Hollywood where he blossomed forth as a columnist for the lovelorn, achieved a spectacular sensation with his *Ballet mécanique,* which was to expound "the esthetic of an automobile built for speed, yet mechanically beautiful." When it was performed in Carnegie Hall in 1927, an airplane propeller was put up in front of an orchestra of multiple pianos. The *New Yorker* said after the performance: "The notes we carefully took on our program were blown away by George Antheil's wind machine." But Antheil confessed afterward that the propeller was merely a stage prop, and that there was not enough atmospheric turbulence to agitate a feather. The skeptics said that some of the audience reactions—such as a man's hoisting a white handkerchief attached to his cane as a sign of surrender — may have been stage-managed. A pun was circulated: "Don't make a mountain out of an Antheil." To make things sound more shocking than they were, Antheil was quoted as having replied to the question, "What is your opinion of Beethoven?": "I love him but I do not respect him."

The reviewers had a field day of wit and invectives. Lawrence Gilman wrote:

"The *Ballet mécanique* is unconscionably boring, artless, and naive. Throughout its stupefying length, it never once speaks vividly, creatively. Its rhythms are infantile, its dynamic effects are unresourceful and unexpressive."

[180]

The true apostles and martyrs of noise music were the Italian futurists who flourished, if it can be called flourishing, shortly before World War I. The leader, Luigi Russolo, published a book entitled *The Art of Noises,* now a collectors' item, in which he outlined the basic theory of noise music. "We derive much greater pleasure," he wrote, from ideally combining the noises of streetcars, internal combustion engines, automobiles, and busy crowds than from rehearing the *Eroica* or the *Pastorale.*" In place of the classical orchestra, he suggested a noise ensemble with such effects as thunderclaps, crashes, splashes, roars, whistles, hisses, snorts, whispers, murmurs, mutterings, screams, screeches, rustlings, buzzes, shouts, shrieks, groans, howls, laughs, wheezes, and sobs.

Before giving a concert of futurist music in Paris, in April 1914, Russolo and his comrades-in-arms wisely took a training course in boxing, which stood them in good stead. For during the performance of a *Fourth Network of Noise,* the audience advanced menacingly on the performers. The futurists, always ready, divided their forces so that some of them continued to manipulate their thunderclaps and screechers while others repelled the attacking audience so efficaciously that eleven persons had to be hospitalized while the futurists got off with minor bruises.

Atomic Music

When the atomic bomb was being hatched at Oak Ridge, one of the music-loving scientists there discovered the recording of a composition called *Ionization* by the French-American ultramodernist, Edgard Varèse.

Ionization, of course, is the chipping off, the spallation of electrons which become ionized as a result of intraatomic action.

Varèse wrote the piece in 1931, long before the atomic bomb, thus performing a unique feat of musical prophecy. The score is indeed atomic in its instrumentation. There are gongs and drums, Chinese blocks and slapstick, suspended cymbals and sleigh bells, anvils and a parchment-covered bucket with a rosin cord, called lion's roar. There are also two sirens, which sing their ominous crescendos in air-raid-like counterpoint. There are no instruments of definite pitch, only knocks, pecks, pokes, bangs, and shakes. They can coo as gently as any symphonic dove, and they can also roar with deafening force. In short, *Ionization* is a perfect picture of atomic activity, from a one-watt pile to the mushroom of the bomb.

When *Ionization* was performed at the Hollywood Bowl, an anonymous listener sent in a postcard offering his own work, written for the kitchen sink with accompaniment of broken crockery. But that was long ago, when they also laughed at Einstein.

Star-Spangled Stravinsky

Few musicians realize that according to law they can be arrested for playing sour notes in *The Star-Spangled Banner*. Stravinsky found that out, much to his discomfiture, when he conducted his own arrangement of the national anthem in a concert with the Boston Symphony Orchestra in January 1944. His arrangement adheres generally to the established tonality, but there are some contrapuntal countersubjects and toward the end a modulatory digression into the subdominant is introduced by means of a passing seventh, commonly known as a blue note. Stravinsky declared: "Searching about for a vehicle through which I might best express my gratitude at becoming an American citizen, I chose to harmonize and orchestrate as a national chorale the beautiful sacred anthem, *The Star-Spangled Banner*. It is a desire to do my bit in these grievous times toward fostering and preserving the spirit of patriotism in this country that inspires me to tender this, my humble work, to the American people."

The American people, however, seemed little appreciative. After the first rendition of the embellished anthem, at least one person among those present made a telephone call to the Boston police. The constables, at first perplexed by the necessity of appearing as a jury on musical matters, dug up a statute in the law books which clearly states:

"Whoever plays, sings, or renders *The Star-Spangled Banner* in any public place, theater, motion picture hall, restaurant or café, or at any public entertainment other than as a whole and separate composition or number, without embellishment or addition in the way of national or other melodies, or whoever plays, sings, or renders *The Star-Spangled Banner* or any part thereof as dance music, as an exit march, or as a part of a medley of any kind shall be punished by a fine of not more than one hundred dollars."

On the night of the second concert, with Stravinsky conducting, a squad of twelve policemen, including a captain and a sergeant, joined the symphony audience, all set to arrest Stravinsky in case of any infringement on the statutory harmonies. Before the concert got under way, the captain remarked: "Let him change it just once, and we'll grab him." Fortunately Stravinsky was fore-warned, and when he launched into *The Star-Spangled Banner*, the harmonies were all serene. The police did not stay to hear the rest of the program.

Stravinsky — Ninety Million Years Off

In his Technicolor masterpiece, *Fantasia*, Walt Disney made use of Stravinsky's score of *Le Sacre du printemps* as incidental music for the earthly events in ancient geo-logical eras. There were erupting volcanoes, primeval forests, gigantic monsters, and other fauna and flora of the time when the earth was young. The setting was ex-tremely effective, but a curator of Carnegie Museum who attended the picture noted a paleontological discrepancy. In the picture a giant Tyrannosaurus Rex of the Cretace-ous period was shown fighting with a Stegosaurus of the Jurassic period. The trouble is that the Cretaceous and the Jurassic periods were some ninety million years apart and their denizens couldn't have both been present at the same time, Stravinsky or no Stravinsky.

The Prizeless Ravel

One of the greatest scandals of musical Paris early in the century was Ravel's failure after three attempts to obtain the coveted Prix de Rome. Like most prizes, the Prix de Rome was not always awarded to the most tal-ented, but more often to the most acceptable and con-formist composers. Nevertheless, in the course of the nearly 150 years of its existence, the Prix de Rome was awarded to a number of excellent composers, particu-larly if they wrote operas. The names of Gounod, Bizet, Massenet, Pierné, Charpentier, Rabaud, Laparra, and even Debussy, are found on the list of recipients of the Grand Prix de Rome since its establishment for musicians in 1803.

Ravel, who was in need of material help when a young man, applied for the Prix de Rome three times. On his third attempt, in 1905, he ran into heavy opposition and failed to pass even the preliminaries. In the selection of candidates in that year. Lenepveu, a member of the jury and a respectable though untalented conservatory professor, managed to get six of his pupils on the list of candidates. Lenepveu himself was a veteran of the Grand Prix de Rome and knew well how to pull strings in the committee. In 1905, two first prizes were to be awarded because of the ineligibility of the 1904 prize-winner through marriage (celibacy was one of the conditions for the Prix de Rome). When both the first prizes and four second prizes went to pupils of Lenepveu, even the conservative circles in the musical world of Paris stirred uncomfortably. The musical press went into action with considerable violence. Pierre Lalo wrote in *Le Temps*:

"The competition for the Prix de Rome is preceded by a preparatory test which serves to eliminate students insufficiently prepared. The jury for this test is formed by the music section of the Académie des Beaux-Arts, which includes several composers who are not members of the Academy. Teachers of competing students may not be members of the jury unless they are members of the Institut de France as well, in which case they are jury members by virtue of their status. There are three professors of composition. One is Fauré, who has in the meantime become director of the Conservatory and who is one of the most original and finest artists of our time. The second is Widor, admirable organist and learned composer. Neither of the two is a member of the Institut. The third is a poor musician, author of a few worthless compositions; but he is a member of the Institut. It is unnecessary to mention him by name. Each of these three professors presented their best pupils for the preliminary test. The first two, not being members of the jury, could not defend the interests of their students, but the third protected his pupils well, and was amply justified by the outcome. As if by coincidence, his pupils were the only ones to be admitted at the final competition, from which it naturally follows that they divided all the prizes, and that their class would get all the honors of the competition and their professor would derive a great luster from it. Inasmuch as the poor musician in question was scheming at the time to obtain the directorship of the Conservatory, he counted on this glory so acquired for his designation as the choice of the administration, a profound calculation which was upset by the events. This story is in itself rather extraordinary; but certain details make it scandalous. Among students who were not passed in the preliminaries there was Ravel, pupil of Fauré, and Mlle. Fleury, pupil of Widor, who not only were admitted to the finals in previous years but who were each awarded a second Grand Prix. But this is not all. Mlle. Fleury's adventure is painful; but Ravel's is even more so. Mlle. Fleury can compete again in the future; but Ravel will not be able to do so for he has reached the age limit this year. Then, whatever are the qualities of Mlle. Fleury, she has not heretofore disclosed exceptional talents, while Ravel, through a singular and deplorable coincidence for the Institut, is one of the two or three young men on whom French music can rightfully put her highest hopes."

Much more vehement was the article by Jean Marnold, *"Le Scandale du Prix de Rome,"* published in the June 1905 issue of *Mercure de France.* He went so far as to use unprintable invectives: *"Pissenlits ou chardons rougiraient de se voir incarner par les membres du jury,"* he fulminated. "It is not forbidden by law to be an idiot, because it is a congenital malady. But when one is afflicted by it, he is given suitable therapeutic treatment, in which considerable progress has been made, thanks to brain surgery and the thyroid serum."

One of the repercussions of the Ravel incident was the change of directorship of the Paris Conservatory. Théodore Dubois, who had been director since 1896, submitted his resignation in the spring of 1905. His resignation was possibly precipitated by his tolerance toward Lenepveu, the successful professor of six Frix de Rome winners. The necessity of injecting new blood was evident to everyone. Gabriel Fauré, the eminent musician and composer, was elected director. The reign of mediocrity was broken at the Paris Conservatory, and this change influenced the interlocking committees governing the affairs of the Prix de Rome. Ravel had to be sacrificed for this revolution to succeed, but a revolution did take place.

The Bolero

For many years Ravel was a great composer without money. His music was highly regarded by cultured audiences all over the world, but he had failed to establish contact with the masses. Then in 1928 he wrote a dance piece in Spanish 3/4 time called *Bolero*. The remarkable feature of this work was that it went on for seventeen minutes in the same rhythm, with the same tune and in the same key of C major, outside of a brief digression into E major toward the very end. It was little noticed in Paris when Ida Rubinstein danced to it on November 22, 1928, but in repeated performances as a concert piece, the popularity of *Bolero* spread like wildfire. The crowning success came when it was arranged for a jazz band. It was the first piece of serious music that penetrated the lower regions of musical culture. Ravel himself was as much bewildered by this sudden leap into popular glory as anybody else. He was eager that his purpose in writing *Bolero* should not be misconstrued. In a letter to the English music critic, Calvocoressi, Ravel wrote:

"I am particularly desirous that there should be no misunderstanding as to my *Bolero*. It is an experiment in a very special and limited direction and should not be suspected of aiming at achieving anything different from, or anything more than that which it actually does achieve. Before the first performance, I issued a warning to the effect that what I had written was a piece lasting seventeen minutes and consisting wholly of orchestral tissue without music — of one long, very gradual crescendo. There are no contrasts, and there is practically no invention except in the plan and manner of execution. The themes are impersonal — folk tunes of the usual Spanish-Arabian kind. Whatever may have been said to the contrary, the orchestral treatment is simple and straightforward throughout without the slightest attempt at virtuosity. . . . I have done exactly what I set out to do, and it is for listeners to take it or leave it."

There is an instrumental effect in the score of *Bolero* that is unique. It is a forced change of tone color in the solo instrument, the French horn, by bolstering up the natural overtones through their doubling by two piccolos. One piccolo takes the third partial tone and the other the fifth partial. In fact, the piccolo parts are written in G major and E major, while the theme is in C. The effect is not that of consecutive major chords in open harmony, but the enhancement of the corresponding partials in the tone of the French horn. Ravel marks *pianissimo* for the piccolo playing in E, and *mezzo piano* for the one in G, to imitate the relative strength of natural overtones, while the horn solo is to be played *mezzo forte*. If performed correctly, the tone color of the solo horn will suffer a change that must be a surprise to the player himself. Unfortunately, the dynamics indicated by Ravel are rarely observed, and the piccolos are permitted to play loud, thus killing the intended effect.

Composers Anonymous

In the first decade of the twentieth century, Paris was the musical battleground between the modernists (represented by Debussy and Ravel) and the clique of the Paris Conservatory which hoped to turn the musical tide back to Gounod. The daredevils of the musical vanguard hit upon a scheme to confuse the Philistines by giving a concert of anonymous compositions. This took place on May 9, 1911, when a *"Concert des auteurs anonymes"* was presented by the Independent Music Society of Paris. The program included, among other works, the first performance of Ravel's *Valses nobles et sentimentales.* In his autobiographical note, Ravel wrote:

"The title, *Valses nobles et sentimentales,* was a sufficient indication that my intention was to compose a set of waltzes in the manner of Schubert. They were performed amidst protests and booing at the concert without the names of composers. The listeners voted for the authorship of each piece. The paternity of the *Valses* was attributed to me by a weak majority."

Emile Vuillermoz reported his impressions of the concert:

"The professional critics cautiously abstained from voting, and on the next day failed to publish a single word about the concert. As to the rest, they naively attributed compositions in which the personality of our modernists was clearly reflected, to Mozart, Schumann, Chopin, Gounod, Wagner, or Mendelssohn. Ravel himself was seated in a loge in the midst of a group of society dilettantes who habitually swooned when they heard the sounds of Ravel's music. Heroically faithful to his oath as a conspirator, the composer of *Valses nobles et sentimentales* had not warned them that his work was included in the program. When they heard it, they began to jeer in the hope of pleasing Ravel by assailing this composition which they believed to be by someone else. Ravel accepted these manifestations in silence."

Schoenberg Blesses His Enemies

No contemporary composer has been abused in print so much as Arnold Schoenberg, the creator of the twelve-tone technique in which an entire work is based on a single motive of twelve different tones, appearing also in retrograde motion, melodic inversion, and retrograde inversion. What most music critics heard was a jumble of noises and said so repeatedly and insistently. Here are sample quotations of critical response to Schoenberg's music over a period of nearly half a century:

"Schoenberg's opus is not merely filled with wrong notes, but is itself a fifty-minute long protracted wrong note."

"Schoenberg's music is the reproduction of the sounds of nature in their crudest form."

"The endless discords, the constant succession of unnatural sounds, baffle description."

"Schoenberg's music is the last word in cacophony and musical anarchy, the most ear-splitting combination of tones that ever desecrated the walls of a music hall."

"The Schoenberg piece combines the best sound effects of a hen yard at feeding time, a brisk morning in Chinatown, and practice hour at a busy conservatory."

"New exquisitely horrible sounds . . . the very ecstasy of the hideous. . . . The aura of Arnold Schoenberg is the aura of original depravity, of subtle ugliness, of basest egoism, of hatred and contempt, of cruelty and of the mystic grandiose."

Instead of retaliating by similar invective directed against his detractors, Schoenberg chose to bless his enemies. In a letter accepting of the 1947 Award of Merit for Distinguished Achievement bestowed upon him by the National Institute of Arts and Letters, Schoenberg gives full credit for his achievement to his critics. With subtle irony, Schoenberg seeks to exculpate them from their ignorant offense:

"I do not contend it was envy — of what was there to be envious?

"I doubt also that it was absence of good will — or worse — presence of ill wishing.

"It might have been their desire to get rid of this nightmare, of this unharmonious torture, of these unintelligible ideas, of this methodical madness — and I must admit: these were not bad men who felt this way — though, of course, I never understood what I had done to them to make them as malicious, as furious, as cursing, as aggressive — I am still certain that I had never taken away from them something they owned; I had never interfered with their rights; with their prerogatives; I never did trespass their property; I even did not know where it was located, which were the boundaries of their lots, and who had given them title to these possessions.

"Maybe I did not care enough about such problems; maybe I myself failed to understand their viewpoints, was not considerate enough, was rough when I should have been soft, was impatient when they were worried by time and pressure, ridiculing them when indulgence was advisable, laughed when they were distressed.

"But I have one excuse: I had fallen into an ocean, into an ocean of overheated water and it burned not only my skin, it burned also internally.

"And I could not swim.

"At least I could not swim with the tide. All I could do was to swim against the tide — whether it saved me or not.

"Maybe something has been achieved, but it was not I who deserve the credit for that.

"The credit must be given to my opponents.

"They were the ones who really helped me."

New Musical Notation

Schoenberg once suggested that the notes of the twelve-tone scale should be named after the first syllables of the names of modern composers. The chromatic scale might then run like this: Deb, Rav, Strav, Schoen, Bart, Hon, Shost, Prok, Cop, Har, Pist, and Hind.

A Russian-born musician, Herman Darewski, invented a method of teaching children the piano by giving each note the name of an animal. He taught this method to Princess Elizabeth of England. Many other attempts to rename musical notes have been made in the past thousand years, but the system of Guido d'Arezzo, our familiar do-re-mi-fa-sol notation, still persists.

The Kafka of Modern Music

Anton von Webern was one of the most esoteric musicians who ever lived. He was the Kafka of modern music, a creative interpreter of the subtlest musical emotions. With two other Viennese, Schoenberg and Alban Berg, he explored the regions of musical expression where thought and sound come together. His music was therefore difficult if not impossible to comprehend without sympathetic study. Besides, the technical complexity of his style is a stumbling block for most performers. It is like living in the ionosphere: all musical atoms are electrified, and every tone possesses an individual importance transcending by far the ordinary particle's role in the fortuitous motion described by Lucretius.

No wonder then that under the impact of this music, the weaker minds crack up. Thus it happened that during the performance of a trio by Anton von Webern in London, the 'cello player suddenly went berserk and, jumping from his seat, exclaimed: "I can't stand it any longer." The incident precipitated a heated discussion

in the press as to the rights of a performer to censor the music.

Schoenberg established the principle of melody building on twelve different tones. Anton von Webern extended this principle to postulate the diversity of twelve instrumental colors as well. In his Sinfonietta, each instrument of the orchestra is allowed to play only one note at a time, and this self-imposed limitation created a weird impression on those who heard the work in its first and last performance at the 1931 International Festival of Contemporary Music.

Berg died before World War II. Schoenberg emigrated to America. Anton von Webern lived through the Anschluss, though his music naturally was not allowed to be performed. After the war, von Webern went to visit his daughter and son-in-law at a small Austrian town. Toward evening, September 15, 1945, he stepped out of the house to smoke. He advanced a few steps when he heard a voice warning him to stop. It was a military police officer of the American occupying force. Von Webern, thinking the officer wanted to speak to him, advanced still further. A shot rang out, and the composer of expressionistic Viennese music fell dead.

The Strange Case of Béla Bartók

The tales of poverty, suffering, and cautious but payless recognition are the substance of musical biography. The hope entertained by musicians that these historic precedents need not be followed in modern times is apparently futile. Some composers, whose names are familiar to all music lovers, are too proud to admit their economic insecurity, in which cases society has the excuse of convenient agnosticism. Not so with Béla Bartók, the greatest composer of modern Hungary, who came to America in 1940 after the seizure of his native land by the Nazis. Columbia University gave him an honorary degree as "a distinguished teacher and master performer of the piano; internationally recognized authority on the folk music of Hungary, Slovakia, Rumania, and Arabia; creator through his composition of a musical style universally acknowledged to be one of the great contributions to the twentieth-century literature of music; a truly outstanding artist who has brought high distinction to the spiritual life of his country." However Bartók's music, complex and difficult to perform, was still prudently avoided by the leading symphony orchestras and chamber music organizations. His appearances as pianist in programs devoid of mass appeal brought him little material returns. Amazingly enough, he was never offered a position at any music school or college. At first his impecuniousness remained his private affair, but soon it developed into a matter of common knowledge. A newspaper article entitled "The Strange Case of Béla Bartók" was published, and as a result, the American Society of Composers and Publishers came forward with some help. But it was too late. The little great man (he never weighed more than 116 pounds and sometimes as little as ninety) was stricken with the dread leukemia, in addition to his old illnesses, asthma, skin trouble, stomach ulcers, and fever, In September 1945 the white cells in his blood multiplied rapidly, and the vital forces collapsed within his frail body. He died on September 23, 1945 shortly before noon. His funeral expenses were paid by ASCAP.

Rachmaninoff — of Russia and the World

Rachmaninoff died half a world away from his native Russia — in Beverly Hills, California, on the night of March 28, 1943. In his last moments of consciousness he kept asking: "Who is playing there all the time?" When assured that no one was playing, he added sadly: "Then it must be in my head."

This reminded Chaliapin's son, one of Rachmaninoff's intimate friends, of a conversation he had had with the composer long before this. He had asked Rachmaninoff: "How do you compose music? What is your process of composition? Do you hear it clearly before you put it down on paper?" And the composer had answered: "Yes I *do* hear it — in my head."

When the musicologist, Joseph Yasser, tried to trace the theme of Rachmaninoff's Third Piano Concerto to Russian church motives or folk songs, Rachmaninoff wrote him:

"The first theme of my Third Concerto is *not* taken from any folk-song forms or from church sources. It wrote itself. You will probably explain it by 'subconscious' derivation. But if I had any plans when composing this theme, they were purely melodic. I intended to 'sing' a melody on the piano as singers do, and to find a suitable accompaniment which would not drown out the theme. That is all there is to it."

It was because of this demand for songfulness in music that Rachmaninoff often remarked that he did not understand and could never appreciate so-called modern music. But he was always willing to listen to new works in the hope of finding something interesting. Chaliapin's son, writing in an anthology published to honor the memory of Rachmaninoff, describes the composer-pianist listening to the Toscanini broadcast of Shostakovich's Seventh Symphony:

"In the summer of 1942, the Rachmaninoffs lived in California, near Hollywood. On the day of the broadcast of Shostakovich's Seventh Symphony, I went to Rachmaninoff not only to hear the symphony but to learn Rachmaninoff's opinion of the work. As the first strains of the symphony were heard, Rachmaninoff was sitting at his table, smoking his customary cut-off cigarette butt (he always cut a cigarette into three parts), and looking somewhere below. From time to time, I glanced at him, trying to catch on his face his reaction to the music; but his face was immobile. His eyes were focused on a single point in space. The symphony was over. I finally asked Rachmaninoff what he thought of it. Instead of replying, he got up, smiled and said: 'Well, let us have some tea.' I could never find out whether he liked the symphony or not."

But in his youth, Rachmaninoff was not at all averse to experimenting with modernistic devices. When he met Rebikov — the Russian composer famous for his early modernism, and the first one to write a piece entirely based on the whole-tone scale, *Les Démons s'amusent* — Rachmaninoff played for him from memory a Rebikov waltz. Suddenly, he began performing the same piece in the whole-tone scale, half seriously, half in jest.

Rachmaninoff had a sense of personal dignity from childhood on. When his teacher Zverev berated him for insisting on having a second piano in the house and, during the argument, raised his hand against him, Rachmaninoff (then sixteen years old) left, and refused to study with him any longer. They were reconciled after Rachmaninoff played his first opera, *Aleko,* on the piano for the jury of the Moscow Conservatory. Zverev embraced him, took out his gold watch and put it in Rachmaninoff's pocket. This watch the composer kept as one of his priceless possessions for the rest of his life.

Rachmaninoff never revisited Russia after 1917, but things Russian always were close to his heart. He cried when he heard a recording of Red Army songs. Bertenson, his Russian-American friend, writes in the memorial volume:

"I recall as we listened to the solemn and triumphant finale of *The Firebird* Rachmaninoff's eyes filled with tears, and he exclaimed: 'Great God! What a work of genius this is! This is true Russia!' And when he was told that Stravinsky liked honey, he bought a large jar and personally took it in his car to Stravinsky's house."

Rachmaninoff owned a large Cadillac and drove it himself. He was inordinately proud of his ability to drive and often volunteered to chauffeur his guests home.

Despite his proverbial undemonstrativeness, Rachmaninoff possessed a streak of sentimentality which affected him at times profoundly. Michael Chekhov, a Hollywood character actor and nephew of the great playwright, called on Rachmaninoff in Beverly Hills and, obeying a sudden impulse, fell to his knees and bowed to the ground in Russian fashion. When Chekhov, overcoming his embarrassment, lifted his head, he saw that Rachmaninoff, too, was on his knees, bowing to the ground. Some deep-seated instinct made Rachmaninoff imitate Chekhov's gesture, perhaps in reverence to their common heritage, in a Dostoyevskian reassertion of Russian-soul democracy.

The Ugly Duckling of Russian Music

When Prokofiev's ballad, *The Ugly Duckling* (after the tale of Hans Andersen) was performed for the first time, Maxim Gorky exclaimed: "He must have written this about himself." Prokofiev was indeed the Ugly Duckling of Russian music. His piano pieces, full of youthful vigor and uncommon poetry, shocked the academic circles of St. Petersburg in the years before World War I. Prokofiev was the first composer to write frankly in two different keys at once. At the Conservatory, Prokofiev wrote a piece which described falling snow by descending passages of unresolved seconds. When he came to the composition class presided over by Liadov, the composer of the celebrated *Music Box*, Liadov asked him: "Is it true that you have written a piece in which there are nothing but seconds?" and he illustrated these seconds by closing his index and middle fingers and waving his hand in the air.

In his young days, Prokofiev rather enjoyed shocking the academicians. He arranged one of his piano pieces for a bassoon quartet. When the four bassoonists filed onto the stage, armed with their forbidding-looking instruments and proceeded to bark out Prokofiev's incisive rhythms, a member of the audience rose and remarked: "Let's leave before they start shooting."

Prokofiev received first prize in composition when he was graduated from the St. Petersburg Conservatory, despite the fact that the venerable Glazunov walked out of the hall when Prokofiev performed his discordant piano concerto. Prokofiev tells the story of his concerto in his autobiography:

"In the spring of 1914 at the age of 23, I was graduated from the St. Petersburg Conservatory in the classes of piano and conducting. I felt an overwhelming ambition and was determined to be the first in the piano competition. The

[198]

sporting desire played a very great role, for the best student was to receive the Rubinstein prize, a grand piano. For the competition I selected not a classical concerto but my own. I did not hope to outplay my competitors in the classics, but my own concerto might have struck the imagination of the examiners by the novelty of its technique; perhaps, I thought, they would not be able to figure out how I managed this technique. Besides, the piano score of my concerto was published just before the examination. I bought twenty copies and distributed them among the examiners. When I appeared on the podium, I saw the scores of my concerto open on twenty knees, an unforgettable spectacle for an author who was just beginning to publish his works. . . . The first prize was adjudged to me after a long and stormy session. Apparently, a group of young and progressively inclined instructors voted for me while the old professors, headed by Director Glazunov, voted against. Glazunov was quite beside himself with rage and refused to announce the results which, according to his opinion, promoted a harmful tendency."

The critics pounced on Prokofiev the moment he exhibited his music in public. When Prokofiev played his Second Piano Concerto at a summer concert in 1913, the St. Petersburg *Gazette* described the scene in the following dispatch:

"A youngster appears on the podium. It is Serge Prokofiev. He sits at the piano, and begins to dust the keys, trying to find out which key sounds higher and which lower. The audience is puzzled. Some are indignant. The young composer's concerto concludes with a mercilessly dissonant combination of brass instruments. There is a regular riot. The majority hisses. Prokofiev is recalled to the stage, bows, and plays an encore. From all sides one hears: 'To hell with this futurist music!' But a group of progressive critics is enthusiastic. 'A genius! What freshness! What temperament, what personality!' "

One Moscow critic, Leonid Sabaneiev, was so incautious as to review a Prokofiev concert *in absentia*. Prokofiev was scheduled to conduct his orchestral work on the subject of pagan Russia, the *Scythian Suite*. But at the last moment, the piece was taken off the program because of the difficulty in getting extra musicians for the enlarged orchestra required — it was during World War I, and many musicians were mobilized. Sabaneiev went right ahead and wrote a devastating review of the Prokofiev piece that was never performed. Prokofiev struck back in a letter to the editor explaining that the whole thing was the product of the critic's imagination and that the critic could not even have seen the music because the score was unpublished, and the only manuscript copy was in Prokofiev's own hands.

After the Revolution, Prokofiev went around the world via the Orient and the United States. He gave a concert in New York with the Russian Symphony Orchestra, conducting his *Classical* Symphony, a very gentle work composed in imitation of eighteenth-century symphonic writing. The New York critics, like their Russian colleagues, found in Prokofiev's music nothing but noise. Wrote *Musical America*:

"In these days when peace is heralded and the world is turning from dissonance to harmony, it comes as a shock to listen to such a program as that given by the Russian Symphony Orchestra. Apparently there were many present who incline to musical Bolshevism, for the applause which Mr. Prokofiev received was most enthusiastic. But those who do not believe that genius is evident in superabundance of noise looked in vain for a new musical message in Mr. Prokofiev's work or for evidences of worth in its thematic content. Nor in the *Classical* Symphony, which the composer conducted, was there any cessation from the orgy of discordant sounds. As an exposition of the unhappy state of chaos from which Russia suffers, Mr. Prokofiev's music is interesting, but one hopes fervently that the future may hold better things both for Russia and listeners to Russian music."

It took Prokofiev only ten or fifteen years to transform himself from a musical Bolshevik into a modern classic.

Or rather, it was the musical world that gradually adjusted itself to Prokofiev's music. Then in 1936 Prokofiev wrote his symphonic fairy tale, *Peter and the Wolf*. He composed the whole thing in a couple of weeks for a performance at the Children's Theater in Moscow. The story was of his own invention. This simple little musical tale became Prokofiev's greatest success all over the world. Yet musically speaking, there are discords and unapproved harmonic progressions that would have shocked old Glazunov, who died just a month before *Peter and the Wolf* was composed.

Prokofiev became more and more respectable as time went by. In fact, he found himself outdistanced in musical aggressiveness by young Shostakovich. Prokofiev's Fifth Symphony, very Russian in character, was welcomed as a modern masterpiece. His cantata, *Alexander Nevsky*, which glorified the exploits of a medieval Russian prince who defeated the Teutons seven centuries ago, was praised to the skies by critics in Russia, in western Europe, and in America. The Ugly Duckling of Russian music turned out to be a mighty figure among modern immortals.

Shostakovich Up and Down

Shostakovich is a barometer of political currents in Soviet music. Whenever the line changes, Shostakovich is made the prime target of either praise or vehement denunciation. But although he has had many ups and downs, he is never down and out. Like one of those Russian toys that are weighted at the base and can never be toppled, Shostakovich jumps up after every assault and cries, "Here I am!"

Shostakovich has written nine symphonies. The First, composed as a graduation piece at the Leningrad Conservatory when Shostakovich was nineteen years old, became a favorite all over the world. The Second and Third, written on Soviet subjects, were soon dropped from the active repertory. The Fourth is an enigma, for it was never performed. Shostakovich put it in rehearsal with the Leningrad Symphony, but the attitude of the musicians was so negative that he decided not to have it played. The Fifth Symphony brought to Shostakovich his first glory. Soviet newspapers, from *Pravda* down, hailed it as a great achievement of modern Russian symphonism. The Sixth Symphony rated less well. But it was the Seventh Symphony that carried Shostakovich to exalted heights, the extraordinary *Leningrad* Symphony written during the siege of Leningrad and performed during the darkest hours of Russia's retreat. In this symphony, Shostakovich predicted the ultimate victory, in blazing C major. In Russia, in England, and in America the *Leningrad* Symphony was an international event. As one American writer put it, it was almost an act of treason not to like the *Leningrad* Symphony. The Eighth Symphony was the longest, taking more than an hour to play; so great was the glamor of Shostakovich's name that the United States Rubber Company, which sponsored the New York Philharmonic Symphony concert broadcasts, paid the record sum of ten thousand dollars for the rights to its first performance in America. Then came the Ninth Symphony. It was severely attacked in the Soviet press for the lack of socialist optimism. It seemed that Shostakovich's star was dimming.

But Shostakovich has survived greater assaults than that. In 1936 his opera, *The Lady Macbeth of the District of Mzensk*, was assailed in an unsigned, and for that reason all the more important, article in the all-powerful *Pravda*, which accused Shostakovich of harmful anti-Soviet tendencies, and actually implied that he was catering to decadent bourgeois tastes. The *Pravda* writer was particularly incensed over a bedroom scene in which the lovers retreat behind a curtained alcove, while the orchestra plays extremely suggestive music featuring a trombone glissando. After that, Shostakovich forswore the opera form and turned his attention exclusively to symphonies and chamber music. However, in 1947 it was announced in the Soviet press that Shostakovich was writing an opera on the subject of Fadeyev's novel, *The Young Guard*, dealing with the Nazi invasion of Russia. But in the meantime Fadeyev himself was attacked for some weaknesses in his novel, and Shostakovich's projected opera became once more a problematic undertaking.

Throughout all these trials and tribulations, Shostakovich has maintained an energetic mode of life. *Moscow News* of April 11, 1947 gives a vivid picture of Shostakovich as a composer, pedagogue, and family man.

"We were sitting in the study of Shostakovich's new apartment on the Mozhaisk Highway. Two Steinway grand pianos were the chief furnishings of the room. Noticing the faint lines of weariness around the composer's eyes and mouth, I remembered that he had recently been laid up with a severe case of diphtheria. He admitted that he had not properly rested after his illness.

" 'But I simply couldn't desert my pupils any longer with the examinations only a few weeks away,' he said.

"Typical of Shostakovich, incidentally, is his devotion to his pedagogical duties. Besides his composition class at the Moscow Conservatory he is at present supervising the studies of a group of students at Leningrad's Conservatory as well. 'On his deathbed, Maximilian Steinberg, who was my teacher, asked me to take over his class and see it through until graduation. I could not refuse such a request.'

"And so Shostakovich makes a special trip to Leningrad once a month for six budding composers bequeathed to him by his old tutor. After verifying their progress, he leaves them in the care of an assistant.

"Shostakovich is a hard worker. His day begins at 7:30

A.M. when he and his two children — Galina, aged eleven, and Maxim, aged nine — do their physical jerks together to the accompaniment of the radio. The composer, by the way, is quite a sports fan. Football is his passion.

"Until noon he works at home, answering his mail, of which he receives a goodly amount. On the days when he is not due at the Conservatory he usually listens to music by composers who submit their work to the Stalin Prize committee, of which he is a member. A good deal of Shostakovich's time is spent working in his capacity as musical adviser to the Ministry of Cinematography and the Committee on Arts. The arts councils of these two organizations, which include the country's leading actors, composers, and artists, meet regularly to review new films and theatrical productions, discuss the work of the different theaters and troupes and give advice and guidance.

"While we were talking, a huge dog came loping into the room, barking and whining. 'Tomka's upset because the children are going off to the rest home,' Shostakovich explained. 'You know,' he added earnestly, 'I have a theory that dogs live such short lives because they take everything so much to heart.'

"We went into the living room where Galina and Maxim were noisily preparing for the journey, aided by their mother. Nina Shostakovich, the composer's wife, is a physicist; cosmic rays is her field.

"Both of the Shostakovich children are quite talented. Galina, whose French is as good as her Russian, loves music and has already begun to compose. Maxim, the 'spitting' image of his father, is musical too, but he has a bent for drawing besides, and it is hard to say at this juncture which of his two gifts is the more pronounced. Shostakovich gives their natural bent absolutely free rein — he never praises Galina for her compositions, or Maxim for his drawings."

In the Shadow of Sibelius

In the minds of music lovers, Finland is concentrated into a single image, the granite figure of great Sibelius. For the past quarter of a century, Sibelius steadfastly refused to accept invitations to visit England and America, the countries where his music is especially prized. He preferred to remain at his family estate near Helsingfors. He stayed there through the first World War and through the devastating two wars with Russia in the 1940's. He has composed no music since his Seventh Symphony of 1924. He was given extraordinary honors by his country on his eightieth birthday in 1945 when, as a unique distinction, postage stamps bearing his features were issued by the government of Finland.

But Sibelius does not comprise in his single towering person the entire treasure of Finnish music. There are per capita more composers in Finland than in any other country. Operas, symphonies, and chamber music are produced by Finnish composers other than Sibelius in quantities that are disproportionately large in a country with less than four million inhabitants. What is more, these productions, including full symphony scores, are published. A volume of 762 pages in the Finnish language. *Suomen Säveltäjiä* was published in 1945 containing illustrated biographies of ninety Finnish composers.

Who outside Finland knows Leevi Madetoja? A 160-page monograph on him has been published in Finland, as well as the complete scores of his symphonies and other works. Most of these secondary Finnish composers have a faint aura of Sibelius in their musical expression. Or perhaps it is the common musical heritage of the northern country, curiously unemotional in its philosophical imperturbability, but burningly intense in its national self-assertion.

The Character of Manuel de Falla

Manuel de Falla personifies the spirit of twentieth-century Spain. His music is as colorful as the trademark, "Made in Spain" would require, and at the same time it is modern in harmony and rhythm, marking it off from that of his immediate predecessors, Granados and Albeniz.

After the Civil War in Spain, Falla went to Argentina where he died. Another Spanish composer, Jaime Pahissa, who knew him both in Spain and in Argentina, gives a vivid portrait of Manuel de Falla as a man. Here are a few striking details:

"Five hours a day, which later were extended to six, were required to take care of his physical self. He used to get up very late, and he spent much time in washing and dressing; when he was through with these chores, it was already half past three or four o'clock; and only then he would have his breakfast. After that he rested and at seven-thirty had some tea. Then he would start to compose until midnight, at which time he would have his dinner. This schedule might appear fantastic, but it was not disordered. It was merely a delayed schedule. Falla always intended to answer his correspondents. Letters accumulated in a pile on his desk. When I gave him the sad news of the death of the painter Zuloaga, Falla exclaimed: 'What a pity! He died before I answered his letter which he sent me five years ago!' "

During the last years of his life, Falla was ailing and had to absorb a considerable quantity of medicine. Often, preoccupied with the conversation, he would not remember whether he had taken his medicine. He would suddenly interrupt the interlocutor to ask: "Did you see whether I had taken my pills?"

Manuel de Falla had a horror of draughts. He also believed that the full moon was harmful to him and that the equinoctial seasons were bad for his health. For this reason he avoided seeing visitors during the period of full moon or in March and September.

Falla had an aversion to ostentatious display of his name or public honors. When friends wanted to donate to him a country house in Spain, he refused to accept it, saying: "I don't feel like a property owner." When he received an advantageous offer from the United States, he declined, giving as his reason that he was offered too much money.

Bach in the Jungle

The universality of Bach's music spreads as far as the Brazilian jungle. Villa-Lobos, the unique composer of jungle-inspired Brazilian music, has created a new form of composition which he calls *Bachianas Brasileiras*. The title indicates the inspiration from both Bach and Brazil. Indeed, while the melody is Brazilian, the counterpoint is Bachian. In a chorale from one of these Brazilian *Bachianas*, a persistent high B-flat is used in the music. This B-flat, however, is not a mere inverted pedal point. It is, according to Villa-Lobos, the literal imitation of the cry of a Brazilian jungle bird, Araponga. Other jungle birds and beasts make appearances in the music of Villa-Lobos.

Prophet of Music to Come

Music historians like their composers to fit into a definite category, classical, romantic, modern, ultramodern. But Charles E. Ives does not fit into any rubric. He never participated in any collective musical movement, seldom went to performances of modern music; and never studied scores by contemporary composers. Strictly speaking, music was not his profession at all, and he never made one cent by any musical activities. He earned his livelihood in the insurance business.

In 1922 he published a volume of 114 songs, with the following characteristic notation:

"As far as the music is concerned, anyone (if he be so inclined) is free to use it, copy it, transpose or arrange it for other instruments. This book is privately printed and is not to be sold or put on the market. Complimentary copies will be sent to anyone as long as the supply lasts."

The album is now a collector's item. The 114 songs are written in 114 styles, from the simple church hymn type to the ultramodern harmonies. The first song, *Ma-*

jority, contains chords of fourteen white keys and chords of ten black keys to be played with the aid of a ruler. There are also chords to be played with fists. Many texts of the songs are written by the composer. Sometimes humorous footnotes are added, such as: "Though there is little danger of it, it is hoped that this song will not be taken seriously or sung, at least, in public."

Or again, "This song is inserted for association's sake on the ground that that will excuse anything; also to help clear up a long-disputed point, namely, which is worse, the music or the words?"

One song is marked: "Not sung by Caruso, Jenny Lind, John McCormack, Harry Lauder, or the Village Nightingale." In the same song an alternate chord with a "blue" note, a B-flat in C major, is inserted with a notation: "Use Saturday night." Another song has a "Kazoo chorus." In a postscript to *A Song for Anything,* written in 1892, the composer states:

"An Amen was tacked onto the end of this song; a relative of the composer remarked at the time that it was about as appropriate to this kind of tune as a benediction would be after an exhibition of the Circassian Beauty at the Danbury Fair."

There are other characteristic postscripts:

"Men with high, liquid notes, and lady sopranos may sing an octave higher than written. The voice part of this Aria, however, may be omitted with good effect. To make a deeper impression, a violin may play the right-hand tune, and may be omitted — for the same reason."

"Some twenty years ago an eminent and sure-minded critic of music in New York told a young man that X was one of our great composers; what he meant by 'our' is not recorded, nor is it remembered that this profound statement was qualified by the word 'living' — probably not, as this arbiter of tears and emotions is quite enthusiastic over his enthusiasms. The above collection of notes and heartbeats would show, but does so very inadequately, the influence on the youthful mind of the master in question."

Ives, who is an idealist of the most uncompromising sort, actually preaching the establishment of international and social good will and mutual love by force of self-evident argument, was greatly perturbed when Harding was elected in 1920 and the League of Nations was voted down. He wrote a song entitled *November 2, 1920,* with words unique in song literature:

"Some men and women got tired of a big job; but over there our men did not quit. They fought and died that better things might be! Perhaps some who stayed at home are beginning to forget and to quit. The pocketbook and certain little things talked loud and noble and got in the way. Too many readers go by the headlines; party men will muddle up the facts. So a good many citizens voted as grandpa always did, or thought a change for the sake of change seemed natural enough. 'It's raining; let's throw out the weather man. Kick him out! Kick him out! Kick him out! Kick him

out! Kick him!' Prejudice and politics and the stand-patters came in strong and yelled, 'Slide — back! Now you're safe, that's the easy way!' Then the timid smiled and looked relieved. 'We've got enough to eat, to hell with ideals!' All the old women, male and female, had their day today and the hog-heart came out of his hole; But he won't stay out long; God always drives him back!"

Concurrently with the 114 songs, Ives published privately his *Concord* Sonata, now also a collector's item. Instead of the usual subdivision into four movements with Italian titles indicating the tempo, Ives utilized movements named after the Concord writers, Emerson, Hawthorne, The Alcotts, and Thoreau. The Sonata is probably the most difficult piece ever written for piano, and one of the longest. To go with the music, Ives published a book, *Essays before a Sonata*, with a typical dedication:

"These prefatory essays were written by the composer for those who can't stand his music — and the music for those who can't stand his essays; to those who can't stand either, the whole is respectfully dedicated."

The orchestral scores of Ives are the most complicated pieces of music ever written by any composer anywhere. In the bassoon part of one of them is a notation: "From here on, the bassoon may play anything at all." In one movement of his *Three Places in New England*, the music depicts the clashing sounds of two village bands marching toward town and playing in different tempos. This is to be conducted with the right hand beating march time, while the left hand conducts the second half of the orchestra at a faster tempo, so that three-quarter notes of the right hand equal a whole bar of the left hand. The downbeats do not coincide except for every fourth bar of the left hand and third bar of the right hand.

Counterpoint of the Financial Page

One of the most titillating shockers in the repertoire of the late great musical theorist, Joseph Schillinger, was to play on the piano a polyphonic composition and then ask the audience to name the composer. The guesses ranged from Palestrina to Bach. With a triumphant chuckle, Schillinger would announce that the music was the projection of the business curve in the financial section of *The New York Times* showing the fluctuations in wholesale prices of agricultural produce. By tracing the ups and downs of the price curve on graph paper and then assigning proportionate values in musical intervals for every unit of the graph, Schillinger wrote out a melody corresponding to a given curve. Combining the melody of the Chicago grain market with that of Nebraska corn and Georgia sugar cane, Schillinger created an impressive musical composition in three-part counterpoint.

Schillinger had other tricks up his inventive sleeve. He would multiply the intervals in a Bach fugue by two. As a result, all semitones would become whole tones and the whole-tone scale being the basis of much of Debussy's music, the effect of such multiplication was Bach's counterpoint in a French impressionistic idiom.

Schillinger taunted professional musicians by such

provocative statements as these: "Many pianist-composers of the past, such as Chopin and Schumann, had very chaotic styles of piano writing, from both the acoustical and the harmonic standpoints. This is due to the fact that their compositions emerged from piano improvising." Schillinger mocked at the Italian opera composers: "One has a humorous or a pitying reaction toward the 1900 horseless carriage. We have exactly the same picture in melodies composed by a Verdi or a Bellini; the mechanical efficiency is so low that it makes us smile." He declared in an interview that the proof positive of Beethoven's deficiency as a composer lies in the fact that he erased or smudged over so many passages in his works before arriving at the final version. If he knew what he intended to do, reasoned Schillinger, he would have written out his music in fair copy without preliminary trials.

To remedy this situation, Schillinger prepared a formidable system of musical composition which analyzed all possibilities in melody, rhythm, harmony, orchestration and form in all styles from plain chant to the most complicated types of ultramodern music. The most amazing thing about the Schillinger System is the fact that when it was published in two huge volumes after his death and marketed for $30, it proved a commercial success. Special Schillinger schools were formed in Boston, New York, Philadelphia, Los Angeles, and other cities, with Schillinger's disciples as authorized exegesists of the System. Despite the tremendous difficulty of Schillinger's theory, hundreds of students patiently work at it hoping to achieve the promised perfection of musical technique.

Two Bits for Fifty Cents

When Henry Cowell, the American composer, sent his little piece for flute and piano entitled *A Bit* to his publisher, the latter replied that the piece was too short. Would Cowell compose a companion number? Cowell complied, but specified that the product, now entitled *Two Bits*, should sell for fifty cents. The pieces were published accordingly, with the title page proclaiming: *Two Bits for Flute and Piano*, Price 50 cents.

The Gershwin Saga

The apocryphal story has it that Gershwin wrote to Stravinsky in Paris asking him how much he charged for private lessons, to which Stravinsky cabled back: "How much is your annual income?" To this Gershwin replied: "About $100,000." Stravinsky then sent another cable: "Am coming to America. How much do you charge for private lessons?"

When Gershwin died in Hollywood, his estate was far short of the reputed million dollars. It comprised exactly $341,089, which went to his mother. Gershwin died three and a half years after the publication of an article in the *Boston Herald* which commented on the fact that Gershwin wrote his *Rhapsody in Blue* in three weeks at the age of twenty-five. "When Gershwin shall be three times twenty-five years," said the article, "this piece is likely to be his best-known and best-loved composition. 'This piece,' says Gershwin, 'seemed to sweep through my mind. It was the heart of America, the feverishness of life, the musical welter of races, of peoples, their joys and their passions, their dissipations and their exaltations.'"

As often happens with famous musical works, Gershwin's *Rhapsody* produced but an indifferent impression on music critics. And Lawrence Gilman made an extraordinarily bad guess when he wrote: "How trite and feeble and conventional the tunes are, how sentimental and vapid the harmonic treatment under its disguise of

fussy and futile counterpoint! . . . Weep over the lifeless-
ness of the melody and harmony, so derivative, so stale,
so inexpressive."

The *New York Times* of December 27, 1931 gives a
first-hand account of the *modus operandi* of the Gershwin brothers composing a musical comedy:

"George Gershwin and his brother Ira are a harmonious
team. They play a happy duet in composition, although
George plays his part on the piano and Ira performs his on
the typewriter. Between shows the two write but little. Once
they receive the outline of a plot, they really get down to
work. They go over this carefully and decide which situa-
tions are best suited for tunes, and what type of tune. George
Gershwin has no regular routine. Sometimes he is at the
piano early in the afternoon, sometimes at three o'clock in
the morning. When he gets eight bars that he likes, he can
finish a chorus in a few minutes. He has been known to write
four songs in a single afternoon. He composes very fluently.
Once when returning from the tryout tour of *Funny Face,*
he discovered that he had left two notebooks containing at
least forty tunes at Wilmington, Delaware. When the hotel
there informed him that the books could not be located, he
neither raved nor stormed. He simply sat down and wrote
forty more.

"When George has completed the melody of a song, he gives it to Ira, who fits the lyrics to it. He works from the title. When he has decided on one, he skips to the last line, where he tries to work in the title again, with a novel twist if possible. Every time he writes a line he tries it on his own voice to see how it sings. Ira never uses a 'lead sheet' in writing his lines for the sufficient reason that he cannot read music. He can play the piano by ear after a fashion, tapping out the tunes with one finger."

Composer-Sniper

In the early days of World War I, when the Germans approached the Marne and occupied the village of Baron, a civilian sniper fired several shots, killed a German soldier and wounded another. This sniper was Albéric Magnard, the French composer of emotional and grandiloquent music, including four symphonies. The Germans threatened to burn down the village unless the sniper was found. At 11:40 A.M. on September 3, 1914, a detachment of German soldiers, acting on information received, went to Magnard's villa and shouted: *"Komm heraus! Einmal, zweimal, dreimal!"* The rest of the story is told by Magnard's son-in-law:

"I swear to tell the truth. On September 3 I was going back home when I noticed a detachment of German soldiers near the house. At that moment my father-in-law fired two shots through the blinds of the window on the first floor. Two Germans fell. Then the soldiers fired broadside on the house. A superior officer appeared and ordered the house set on fire by means of hand grenades. While the house burned, I heard a shot inside, and my impression was that my father-in-law had killed himself. He had told me before that he had five bullets in his revolver, four for the enemy and one for himself."

His body was not recovered until a month later. Magnard's widow wrote:

"On October 4, 1914, I went to the village and attempted

[215]

to find the remains of my poor husband in the ruins of our house, of which only a pile of rubble remained. The position in which I found the body enables me to state that he was standing behind a window when he died. I am convinced therefore that he was killed by German bullets. I also found near him the blackened and burnt pages of his unfinished opera, *Bérénice*."

Composer-Hero

On June 20, 1940, a French motorcyclist patrolled a road near Saumur during the last days of French military resistance. Approaching a curve, he heard the tread of heavy boots. Without hesitation, he threw his machine into the field, grabbed his carbine and faced the Germans. He killed sixteen before he was finally shot down. The Germans buried him with military honors. His name was Jehan Alain. He was twenty-nine years old when he died, and he was one of the most talented composers of young France. During his brief span of life he wrote 127 opus numbers. He was an organist of great gifts, and most of his works are written for the organ. The value of these pieces is confirmed by repeated performances all over the world.

Music A.D. 6938

What kind of music will our descendants wish to hear five thousand years hence? This question had to be answered by the ingenuous group of people who packed up a lot of memorabilia of our century and buried them in a Time Capsule at the New York World's Fair, September 23, 1938 with instructions that the capsule be opened on September 23, 6938. The musical selections for the Time Capsule were the gramophone recordings of *Finlandia* by Sibelius, Sousa's march, *Stars and Stripes Forever*, and the swing number, *Flat Foot Floogie*.

[216]

IV

MUSICIANS ARE LIKE THAT

Figured Bass

Composer Ferrari, a contemporary of Beethoven and
Rossini, tells this improbable story in his memoirs. On a
cold December night a naked man was seen standing
in front of the open window of his house. A neighbor
shouted to him: "For God's sake, what are you doing
there without a stitch of clothes on?"

"I am catching a cold," the man shouted back. "I have
to sing bass tomorrow in church."

When this story appeared in the Boston *Musical
Gazette* of February 1847 it was characteristically toned
down, as follows: "A man who sat on a bridge with his
feet in the water was asked why he did so, and replied:
'I am to sing bass tomorrow and am now endeavoring
to take cold to prepare my voice.'"

Dragonetti Salute

Dragonetti was called the Paganini of the double bass, and he was the first to give concerts on that instrument. He was also a man of considerable wit and worldly wisdom. He often showed his reactions to music in curious ways. At the first rehearsal of Verdi's opera, *Alzira*, in Naples in 1845, Dragonetti, who had been invited as a specially honored guest, raised his Neapolitan bonnet after several arias in the opera. Verdi, puzzled by this action, asked why he did so.

"Each time," said Dragonetti, "that I meet an old acquaintance, I raise my hat in salute."

It is fair to add that the same story has been told about a dozen other musicians. But Dragonetti seems to have a priority. The *Musical World* of May 21, 1881 carries the story for the first time, from a report by an eye witness.

Caruso's Spaghetti

Caruso was famous for his unique tenor voice but also for his love of foods. He particularly appreciated spaghetti and was amazingly adept at rolling it onto a fork and dispatching it into his mouth without losing a particle. He favored the product of the Atlantic Spaghetti Company, using it at home and on tour. Crates of the goods were shipped to him at the various cities where he performed. He was so enthusiastic about the product that in 1917 he allowed the company to use his name on the package. On March 30, 1917, he wrote from New York: "A thousand thanks for the packages of spaghetti sent to me and which the company is desirous of packaging with my name. I have no objections provided they will always be good." The company promptly cashed in on this permission and renamed itself Caruso Foods Inc., with all food items bearing the name of Caruso, his photograph, and a facsimile of his signature.

Baritone Stinco

A name most unlikely to contribute to commercial success is that of an Italian baritone who was a shining opera star two generations ago. He never got to first base with American concert managers, for his name was Enrico Stinco-Palmerini. The word Stinco is respectable in the Italian language, meaning a shinbone.

The Murderous Bass

It happened in Mexico in 1945. Ignacio Ruffino, the basso of the National Opera of Mexico, was preparing to sing the Commandant in a production of *Don Giovanni* conducted by Sir Thomas Beecham. Ruffino got away early one day from rehearsal and went to the movies. There he found his wife, a plump and beautiful matron, enjoying the same picture in the company of his best friend. With Latin impetuousity, Ruffino took out his revolver and shot the man. He was arrested but later released on bail. The sympathy of Mexican society was entirely on his side and as of late 1947, Ruffino had not been tried. He continues to be a regular member of the National Opera of Mexico. Among his roles since the murder was that of one of the conspirators in *Un Ballo in Maschera* and that of Capulet in *Romeo and Juliet*. He is reconciled with his wife, and she wears an angelic smile when they appear together.

Ross Parmenter of the New York *Times* adds this to his account of the case: "Apparently they are perfectly happy together, and she does not hold her husband's impetuosity against him. It sounds like a story by Somerset Maugham."

The Opera Bug

It happened on a summer night in 1947. The tenor of the Memphis open-air theater, with the magnificent name of Romolo de Spirito, reached for a high note which was in the best register of his mellow voice when he suddenly gasped, gurgled, and choked. The golden note was cut short. A little green aphid had done a tailspin and landed on the tenor's tonsils. De Spirito tried to recapture the aria but had to give up. He stood shaking his head in dismay. The audience was sympathetic and kept up the singer's spirits with encouraging bravos and applause. He finally coughed up the bug, and after a brief pause went on with the performance.

The Case of a Beardless Baritone

On October 28, 1914 an operetta called *The Lilac Domino* opened in New York at the 44th Street Theater. The two romantic leads were Wilfrid Douthitt and Eleanor Painter. The New York *Times* said on the following morning that the two singers had scored tremendous hits. It described Wilfrid Douthitt as "a splendid baritone voice of great range." The show ran for 109 performances.

Chapter II of the story began in the fall of 1915 when a dashing young singer arrived in New York from Europe. He gave his name as Louis Graveure and said he was a Belgian. He wore a Van Dyke beard, but his facial features were remarkably similar to those of Wilfrid Douthitt. On May 2, 1916 Graveure married Eleanor Painter, Douthitt's leading lady. Confronted with the remarkable parallelisms in his career and that of Douthitt, Graveure shrugged off the whole thing as a coincidence.

Meanwhile Graveure gave several recitals in New York during the 1915-1916 season. Like Douthitt he had a pleasant baritone voice. One critic said that "the effect of his singing is hypnotic; he seizes his listeners in an instant, holds them breathless, hanging on his lips until the last note is finished." Graveure continued his concert career in Europe and America as a baritone; then, without warning, he announced a concert in New York on February 5, 1928 as a tenor. The New York *Herald Tribune* wrote cautiously that he was "well able to negotiate the top notes of his arias although there was a slight hardness in the quality of tone."

His domestic affairs had in the meantime deteriorated. Eleanor Painter claimed desertion and started proceedings for divorce in June 1930. She obtained her divorce and on October 23, 1931 married Charles Henry Strong, a millionaire businessman. When she died in November 1947, the obituary mentioned her first marriage to the mystery man, Louis Graveure, who, the papers said again, may or may not have been Douthitt.

The next chapter finds Graveure in Germany where he became active in films. The German *Wer Ist Wer* of the 1930's lists him as a permanent resident, but in lieu of the customary birth date and birthplace, the entry on Graveure said merely "Engl." It is noteworthy that his claim of Belgian origin was not supported in the official German directory.

During the Nazi regime, Graveure remained in Germany almost up to the outbreak of World War II. At the time of the French armistice of June 1940, Graveure was on a French boat leaving for America. But the British consul in Bordeaux advised him to get off, and he was later evacuated to England, now admittedly as a British subject.

He arrived in America again in June 1947 with his second wife, whom he had married in England. Again he was asked by newspaper men whether he was Douthitt. To that he replied that the story of his origin was worth tens of thousands of dollars of publicity to him and that he had no intention of giving it out for nothing. When he was asked when and where he was born, he replied, "I don't know myself." He told Ross Parmenter of the New York *Times* that he could not locate the registry of his birth although the records had been searched within ten years of the probable date.

He could not have searched very far. A certified copy of the birth of Wilfrid Douthitt can be obtained by anyone from the General Register Office in London, for the sum of two shillings and sixpence. From this birth certificate it appears that Wilfrid Douthitt was born in the District of Belgravia in London at 26 Little Chester Street, on March 18, 1888, the son of John Read Douthitt, a master builder. The document also establishes with finality that Douthitt is Graveure. For the maiden name of Wilfred Douthitt's mother is set down in his birth registry as Charlotte Maria Cordelia Graveur. Douthitt merely added an "e" to his mother's maiden name and became Graveure. His mother may have been Belgian, to judge by her surname. If so, Douthitt's original claim as a Belgian contains one-half truth.

The Infinite Cadenza

When Joachim appeared as a soloist with a provincial orchestra in Germany, the conductor was deferential to the point of complete subservience. The cadenza that

Joachim played in the concerto ended on a long trill, during which the orchestra was supposed to come in with the theme. The conductor was so overwhelmed with the soloist's virtuosity that he hesitated to abbreviate Joachim's trilling. Joachim was greatly amused by this show of respect. Finally he whispered to the conductor: "When you have had enough, you may tell the orchestra to come in."

Audience Near Zero

When Wieniawski played in Boston, only a handful of people attended.

"You must come here again," urged a friend.

"Oh, no," retorted Wieniawski, "I'll get out of the habit of playing in public."

Twins and Violins

Walter Winchell reports in his column of December 17, 1947:

"Leopold Godowsky (son of the late pianist-composer) asked his sister to drive his three-year-old twins to their Westport home. 'By the way,' said Leopold, 'please drive carefully as I have two violins worth fifty thousand dollars in the luggage compartment.'

" 'Which,' inquired his sister, 'should I watch first, the twins or the fiddles?'

" 'The twins, of course, of course!' said Godowsky. 'The violins are insured.' "

Einstein's Rhythm

On the authority of Walter Winchell (in his column of November 22, 1945), great mathematicians are not necessarily rhythmical:

"Albert Einstein, the top mathematician and atomic bomb authority, likes to relax with a violin. Recently he invited the renowned pianist, Artur Schnabel, to his home for a musical week-end. They were running through a rather involved Mozart sonata, and Einstein was having some trouble playing. Finally, after several explanations, Schnabel became irritated. He banged his hands down on the keyboard and groaned: "No, no, Albert. For heaven's sake, can't you count? One, two, three, four. . . ."

Batonless First

A hundred years ago conductors used to lead the orchestra with white gloves and an incrustated scepter-like baton. The gloves were discarded toward the end of the nineteenth century, and now the baton itself is in danger of disappearing. One conductor after another abandons this symbol of authority in favor of conducting with his bare hands.

The first modern conductor to dispense with the baton was Vassily Safonov. Strangely enough, this innovation was due to a political murder. How? Thereby hangs a tale, told by Leopold Godowsky. He was scheduled to rehearse the Beethoven *Emperor* Concerto with the Moscow Symphony Orchestra, Safonov conducting. It was on the morning of February 4, 1905. Russia was losing in the Japanese War, and the Revolution was brewing on all sides. Godowsky was in the dining room of his hotel, when suddenly a tremendous explosion took place outside. Grand Duke Sergei had just been assassinated by a bomb thrown at his carriage, and his remains were strewn all over the street. The news of the murder plunged all Moscow into a state of turmoil. All concerts and theater performances were canceled, Godowsky's concert included.

After a few days, things in Moscow reverted to normal, though some nervous tension persisted. When Safonov came to rehearsal for the postponed Godowsky concert, he looked for his baton. It was nowhere to be found.

"Do you mind if I lead without the stick?" asked Safonov.

[224]

"I don't mind if you do not use the baton even at the concert," replied Godowsky.

"A great idea!" exclaimed Safonov.

At the concert, he stepped onto the stage, his baton conspicuously absent. The performance went off exceptionally well — musicians seemed to be exhilarated by the batonless conducting. The newspapers commented favorably. The ice was broken. Safonov conducted without a baton during his visit in New York in 1906, also exciting considerable favorable comment.

The Stamping Conductor

In the Gay Nineties, orchestral conductors presented a robust appearance and directed their musicians with gestures that were vigorous and rustic. But when Emil Paur, who conducted the Boston Symphony Orchestra from 1893 to 1898, stamped his foot at the orchestra, the proper-mannered and witty Philip Hale objected:

"Our new conductor, Mr. Paur, is a man of action. He cuts with his arms all manner of figures in the air; he is a series of living diagrams; he is an animated conductorial chart. With his fingers he picks effects off the players. And ah! his foot! You remember perhaps in your earlier days the church choir in the country, where the most earnest man had the loudest voice and the heaviest foot.

"Well, Mr. Paur is so in earnest that he cannot control his foot. It beats with his arm. As a result the sitters near the stage, just as they are ready to enjoy the proper emotion

> Hear a foot begin to stump
> Thump! lump!
> Lump! thump!
> Like the specter in *Don Giovanni.* . . .

"Why should not Mr. Paur be presented with a pair of thick fur boots with felt soles? There might be a subscription list, with the motto, 'Suaviter in modo.' "

Musician Showman

In the annals of musical showmanship, the bushiest laurels belong undoubtedly to Louis Jullien, French-born conductor and composer who captured the imagination of both continents with his spectacular exhibitions. The first half of the nineteenth century, in which he flourished, was the era of bigness, in the arts as well as in industry. "Monster concerts" were the rage of the time, and Jullien was the chief apostle of musical monstrousness.

An article published in the British magazine *Belgravia* in 1880 gives a vivid picture of Jullien's personality:

"In the year 1847 the management of the Drury Lane Theater of London was assumed by a very eccentric and grotesque creature. It would be unfair to dismiss him as a mere charlatan; however empirical his proceedings, he was his own chief dupe. He was crazily vain, very ignorant, extravagant, disorderly, tawdry, and vulgar, but he was humane; he was ingenious after a fashion; he was enterprising beyond all reasonable bounds; he possessed much natural wit; and he was animated by an enthusiasm unquestionably genuine, for all its comical and crackbrained modes of expression. His name — it cannot yet be forgotten — was Louis Jullien.

"His first appearance in England was in 1838; in 1839 he was rendering some assistance at Drury Lane as a soloist at Concerts d'Hiver, performing now on his piccolo, imitating the notes of a bird in his own *Rossignol Waltz*, now on the clarichord, a new brass-valved instrument which he was the first to introduce. Then he became the conductor. He possessed a certain instinct for new effects and combinations of sound and delighted in orchestral uproar of a prodigious sort. How far he was really responsible for the compositions and compilations that bore his name may be questioned; for some little time he concealed his own connection with them, attributing them to a supposititious German musician, Roch Albert.

"He had a garden-roller dragged over sheets of iron to simulate the roar of artillery; pans of red fire were lighted

at intervals so that while the sense of hearing was assailed by the strangest clangor and hubbub, the faculties of eyes and of nose might be no less amazed by the flash and glare and the pungent fumes of nitrate of strontium."

The London newspapers of the 1840's were full of advertisements of Jullien's concerts. There was usually a tempting promise: "The program will include the *Nightingale Valse,* performed on the piccolo by M. Jullien. One of M. Jullien's most favored valses will be presented to each lady visiting the Dress Circle or Private Boxes." The multitudes who turned out for Jullien's concerts were seldom disappointed. There was always a big show if not much great music. The *Musical Examiner* of London gives a detailed report of a typical Jullien concert, in the issue of February 24, 1844:

"M. Jullien's last musical invention, entitled *A Grand Descriptive Fantasia selected from Roch Albert's opera of the Destruction of Pompeii,* was presented last week at the Covent Garden Theater. It is a compound of fiddling, red fire, bells, gunpowder, rattles, crackers, and chorus singing. The property man has evidently been instructed to spare no pains in searching for all the dormant thunder belonging to the establishment, and his industry was most productive. There is a low grumbling to indicate the brewing eruption; then a hymn on the principle of the tetrachord, and of course as discordant as the moans of the mountain itself; a fête of Terpsichore follows, and a jolly outbreak of Bacchanals. The grand coup takes place here — the joint production of the composer, carpenter, and fireworks-maker — and in the analytical language of the bill, it depicts 'the explosion of the crater, the falling of the temples, and the total destruction of the city.' The row made here was tremendous; and the clatter was pretty considerably augmented by the howls of three hundred chorus singers who were planted somewhere in the upper regions — no one could tell where. At one point the gas was alarmingly lowered to typify sudden darkness; in the next moment the strained calico over the orchestra became transparent with blood-red fire; and figures like gaunt specters of the Brocken were seen floating about in shadow. These, whom we at first took to be gnomes disembogued from the mountain, turned out to be the industrious functionaries who tended the pots of crimson fire and gave the maroons the hint to discharge. When the gunpowder supplies were exhausted, the fantasia was considered at an end, the fiddlers shut up their books, and the gas resumed its duty. The audience, having rubbed their eyes, then cheered vociferously. Of the music of M. Jullien — for he himself is said to be the great Roch Albert — little need be said: it was quite to the purpose and did not dishonor the thunder with which it was allied."

Not only men but beasts were impressed with Jullien's thunderous exhibitions. When he presented one of his "monster concerts" at the Surrey Zoological Gardens in London in June 1846, the booming of the four-pounders used by Jullien to accompany the national anthem perturbed the animals. The *Musical World* reported:

[228]

"The menagerie was all affright with the noise. The tropic tiger mistook it for the hurtling of his native elements and roared in unison thunder, dreaming of his youngling woods in Sumatra or Borneo. The radical hyena grinned ghastly at the uproar, expectant of dissolution. The bounding leopard leapt at his bars, hearing in thought the roar of musketry. The sovereign lion snuffed the noise and, growling defiance, walked calmly up and down his den. Only the bear was apathetic. Neither Rossini nor Jullien affected him."

Jullien returned to the Surrey Zoological Gardens in the summer of 1850. With a fine flair for publicity, he connected his own benefit performance with a thanksgiving on the escape of Queen Victoria from an attack which had been made upon her shortly before. The *Musical World* described the occasion:

"M. Jullien announced that in gratulation for her Majesty's escape, *God Save the Queen* would be played with the entire strength of his tremendous orchestra accompanied with a salvo or salute of twenty-one guns—eight, twelve, or twenty-four pounders. When the cannon commenced, echo alone for a while was heard, but after a few shots, the people began with vociferous throats to cheer; the wild beasts answered the people in feline, canine, and ursine roars, barks, and growls; the birds screamed and clapped their wings; and the monkeys left off showing their antics to mingle their shrill cries in the tumult; and all for Her Most Gracious Majesty's escape without their being aware of it. The earth reeled beneath the mighty hurly-burly, and the window-panes as remote as the Kensington Oval, conscious of the Jullienquake, burst their glassy sides."

Punch published a burlesque sketch of Jullien's show under the title, "Bombardment at the Surrey Zoological Gardens."

"Jullien is about to bombard the Surrey Zoological. He is to conduct a park of artillery on Friday. His baton, we suppose, will be a lighted fusée. He should be appointed Musical

Master (or rather Maestro) of the Ordnance Office. We subjoin part of his program:

"*Battle of Prague*, played with ten eight-pounders and six thousand muskets. The solos will be kindly undertaken on this occasion by Queen Elizabeth's pocket pistol. No less than ten thousand pounds of powder will be set off during the performance of the *Battle*.

"*The Hailstone Chorus*. The hailstones will be given with the aid of paving-stones, discharged from four hundred carts by an eminent Turnpike Road Commissioner.

"*The Lullaby Quadrilles*, with cracker accompaniments. Forty children-in-arms have been engaged to give the loudest effect to the forte passages. The eldest is only four months old.

"*Wilt Thou Love Me When My Hair Is Gone?* A new ballad sung by Miss Rowland, accompanied by M. Jullien on the railway whistle.

"*I'm Not the Fool You Take Me For!* Being an answer to the above, with an explosive finale of Roman candles and rockets. The prelude will be played on a pair of American revolvers."

In 1853 Jullien invaded America, appropriately enough under the auspices of Mr. Barnum. He staged his customary "monster concerts" at the Crystal Palace in New York. As a friendly gesture toward American musicians, Jullien included in one of his concerts two American compositions, a *Santa Claus* Symphony by the militant champion of American music, William Henry Fry, and some chamber music by George Frederick Bristow. Jullien made a speech in Frenchified English in which he declared that Fry possessed a "genius for orchestration unsurpassed by any composer of the day." His compliment for Bristow gives an illuminating glance at the colonial status of American music a hundred years ago: "Jullien pronounced Mr. Bristow a classic composer, declaring that he had successfully essayed the most difficult of all instrumental writing, that of the quartet."

Bristow accepted this dubious accolade as a great honor. As a token of gratitude, he crowned Jullien with a golden wreath "valued at eight hundred dollars." Jullien responded with a speech and "a French climax, an unutterable shrug, a shrug which expressed whole volumes of emotion."

Forty-two thousand people attended Jullien's concert at the Crystal Palace on June 15, 1854. The high point of the occasion was Jullien's *Fireman's Quadrille*. Exaggerated accounts made it appear that a real fire was staged in the hall and that real firemen poured real water from a real fire hose, that women fainted and had to be carried out, etc. In actual fact, the fire was synthetic, and the audience was warned by Barnum about the forthcoming conflagration.

Barnum and Jullien took advantage of the annual city parade at which New York fire companies with their red fire engines were the chief attractions and secured their co-operation for the *Fireman's Quadrille*. The New York *Daily Times* reported:

"Jullien's *Fireman's Quadrille*, composed for the occasion, terminated the second part of the concert, prior to which Mr. Barnum addressed the audience, to desire that they would not be alarmed at the frightful effects which would be introduced. Jullien has availed himself of the occasion of the annual parade. All the fire companies are out in their gala costumes; we hear the bands and, what is better, see them as they pass along in steady line. Presently the alarm bell is heard; bustle ensues; engines hurry to the scene of action; speaking trumpets discourse harsh vocalism to the runners; the fire is reached and all the excitement of a struggle with the mighty element is produced in its wildest mood.

"To produce the necessary effects, Mr. Jullien has had to invent a variety of instruments and machines to imitate the working of the engines, the falling of the house, the hissing of the water on the flames, etc. To heighten the illusion, red fire is burned outside the building; the firemen's bands, first heard in the distance, approach nearer, and then actually march across the orchestra."

The New York *Musical Times* reported the occasion as follows:

"The *Fireman's Quadrille* possesses all the well-known qualities of the author: brilliancy of style and a supreme mastery of orchestration. There are, besides, novelties of excellent effect consisting of two military bands mingling successively with the main orchestra. The platform orchestra suddenly ceases to play, and immediately a brass band is heard behind the amphitheater fronting the audience. The band draws nearer and nearer, descends to the platform and joins the orchestra. Some minutes later a second band of different character, reed and brass, is heard, also at a distance, and descends to the platform. Then an awful scene is preparing — the alarm bell sounds an ominous summons. Something like a blaze in the top of the building appears, and shortly after, the cupola is wrapped in flame! Fearful conflagration! The bell tolls deeply on, joining the general blast of the grand orchestra and bands, producing a terrific effect, thus crowning a composition called the *Fireman's Quadrille*. The piece was clamorously encored."

Along with his noisy pieces, Jullien included numerous solo numbers which could hardly be heard in the huge hall of the Crystal Palace. There were no microphones or other sound amplifiers then. The New York *Musical Times* complained that most of the music could not be heard at all:

"The soloist of the *Messiah* was standing out in front — the fiddle bows were moving, but the music didn't come! The crowd commenced moving also, and a confused noise echoed from side to side of the vast dome. Of M. Frazer's solo exactly two notes were heard. Madame Bonchelle then came forward and *probably* sang her solo, 'Rejoice Greatly, O Daughter of Zion,' nine notes of which were heard. Also Miss Brainerd *probably* sang that beautiful solo, 'I Know That My Redeemer Liveth.' The highest and lowest notes of the duet on two pianos by Mrs. Wallace were heard. M. Drouet's solo on the flute was also doubtless well played. We saw him with a flute at his mouth. Just before the *Fireman's Quadrille,* Mr. Barnum appeared and commenced speaking. The cry, 'Louder, louder!' arose from every part of the vast audience; and he was understood to say that although the Crystal Palace would be set on fire and tumble down about our heads, there was no occasion for alarm except for the firemen."

As Jullien bade farewell to America, there were dissenting voices in the press regarding his attitude toward American music. Fry and Bristow eulogized him, but there were other composers who had submitted their compositions to Jullien and who had not been performed. The newspapers published an attack on Jullien, describing him as "an Anglicized French Jew." It seemed that a member of Jullien's American band, a German musician named Knaebel had composed a choral work for eight male voices and a brass band, entitled *Bunker Hill.* Jullien had announced it for performance and then hastily canceled it, the reason being, so asserted Jullien's detractors, that Jullien did not want to offend the English, for his wife was British, and England was his second home.

The British press showed great interest in Jullien's American tour. The *Musical World* published an article, "Jullien's Farewell to America," in which it also commented on the attitude of American audiences toward the war that then raged in the Crimean peninsula:

"Last night Jullien took his farewell of America, and a 'Concert Monster' was given for his benefit at the Crystal Palace. After ten months of continuous labor, he resigns his baton and returns to Europe.

"A tremendous rush to the Crystal Palace commenced at six and continued incessantly until nine, by which time the amazing number of forty-two thousand persons had paid for admission. Every place in the building where standing room could be obtained was packed with human beings, and the entertainment was well received throughout.

[233]

"The program consisted of the usual variety, but included two new features: one, the Andante from a symphony by M. Jullien entitled *The Last Judgment,* and second, the war marches and national airs of the present belligerent nations in the Crimean War, *Partant pour la Syrie,* and the *Marseillaise, Rule Britannia* and *God Save the Queen,* the Muscovite hymn from Jullien's opera, *Pietro il Grande,* the *Song of the Cossacks,* and lastly the *Turkish War March.* The movement from the symphony was received with great applause, and the audience prepared for the national music.

"It was to be feared that something of jealousy might still have lingered in the American mind, that the recollection of *Rule Britannia* might have awakened old feelings of strife and discord and that the sympathies with the Russians, openly expressed by renegade Irishmen, might have found some echo in this immense assemblage of Americans. But such fears were at once dispelled by the reception given to *Rule Britannia,* and when the first notes of *God Save the Queen* were heard from the orchestra, the whole of this mighty mass rose as one man, the greater part standing uncovered during the performance and encoring the air with republican lungs quite as ardently as the most loyal assembly of Britons. The Russian hymns, notwithstanding their musical merit, were received in solemn silence while the *Turkish War March* was vociferously applauded."

Grandiose ideas always possessed Jullien's mind. He composed *A Hymn of Universal Harmony* with the intention of performing it "in all the uncivilized parts of the earth." He believed he could hear the harmony of the spheres. Once he put his fingers into his ears and declared that he heard within his cranium a perfect A-natural: *"Un la colossal donné par le globe terrestre en roulant dans l'espace!"* Then whistling a shrill D or E-flat or F, he would cry: *"C'est le la, le la veritable, le la des sphères! Voilà le diapason de l'éternité!"*

When the news of Mendelssohn's death was brought to him during a rehearsal, he struck his forehead with his fist and exclaimed: "Ah! This is what happens to all men of genius! I shall never compose any more!" The ultimate in his delusion of grandeur came when he decided to set the Lord's Prayer to music. "Just imagine," he said to Jules Rivière, who reports the incident, "the work will bear on its title page two of the greatest names in history:

"The Lord's Prayer
Words by
Jesus Christ
Music by
Jullien"

Jullien's successes in London began to wane as the public taste became surfeited with his type of musical showmanship. He returned to Paris only to find he was no longer famous. Jules Rivière tells the end of the Jullien saga:

"One afternoon during the Carnival when the boulevards were crowded with promenaders, Jullien, jumping into an open fiacre, told the driver to stop at the corner of the Rue Montmartre. And there he stood erect in the carriage delivering a long speech to the bystanders. 'I am Jullien,' he said, 'the great Jullien, and I am going to give a series of grand concerts in Paris.' After speaking for some time, he took his piccolo from his pocket and played variations upon it, proceeding thence to the Boulevard des Italiens, where he told the driver to stop again whilst he commenced another harangue which was followed by more piccolo playing. And the same crazy behavior was repeated near the Madeleine. Jullien was mad, and the next day he cut his throat in an alley leading out of the Rue de la Chaussé d'Antin, dying a couple of days later in the hospital."

Saved by a Music Dictionary

Leonard Lyons' column, *The Lyons Den*, reports the following truthful incident which occurred in August 1942:

"Nicolas Slonimsky is the composer-conductor who returned recently from a tour through South America. Last week he went to Concord, Mass., to meditate and read Thoreau. At the entrance of Sleepy Hollow Cemetery he asked an official for directions. The official instead asked him for his draft-registration card. When Slonimsky couldn't identify himself satisfactorily, he was taken to the police station. 'Take me to the public library and I'll prove who I am,' the conductor suggested. The police took him there. And on page 329 of David Ewen's book, *Living Musicians*, he found the proof — a sketch and biography of himself."

Dumb Piano

Moriz Rosenthal practiced on his dumb piano in a hotel during his tour of the southern states. A Negro maid asked him what the thing was. He explained that it was a magic piano that could be heard only by people who had not sinned within the past twenty-four hours. She hesitated for a moment, then precipitately fled from the room.

Beethoven versus Boston's Best

When Moriz Rosenthal gave a piano recital in Boston he included on the program one of Beethoven's last sonatas. His manager expressed doubts that such a lengthy work could have popular appeal. But Rosenthal insisted: "I assure you," he said, "that not more than ten people in Boston can compose better music."

Quantz in Excellent Spirits

The celebrated flutist Quantz who was, along with Bach, a musical friend of Frederick the Great, died in Potsdam shortly after completing the Allegro for his three hundreth flute concerto. Frederick the Great played it over and remarked: "This is a gay little piece. I am so glad Quantz left this world in such excellent spirits."

Trumpeter's Mortal Wounds

Weckerlin in his *Musiciana* relates many amusing anecdotes but none more droll than the text of a letter addressed by a French army trumpeter to Napoleon III:

"Sire, I have received under your beloved uncle two mortal wounds which for thirty-eight years have been my ornaments, one in the right buttock, and the other in Wagram. If these deserve the Legion of Honor, I thank you in advance."

His Majesty's Missing Flats

Joseph Weigl, an Austrian musician and contemporary of Haydn, wrote a string quartet for a concert at the palace of the Emperor Francis I. At a rehearsal, the Emperor — himself an amateur violinist — decided to take the first violin part himself. Majestically he ignored the flats in the key signature. Weigl, not knowing how to correct the imperial violinist, finally approached him and said with the utmost humility: "Would your Majesty grant my humble prayer for a most gracious B-flat?"

Modulating Birthdays

Reviewing the second edition of Grove's *Dictionary of Music and Musicians*, Philip Hale remarked that "in the making of dictionaries there is no such thing as plenary inspiration."

With or without plenary inspiration, dictionaries of musical biographies seldom agree with one another in the matter of dates. Indeed, sometimes a biographical article contains a chronological impossibility within itself. For instance, the second edition of Grove's Dictionary gives the dates of Mussorgsky's birth and death as 1835 and 1881, at the same time stating that Mussorgsky died on his forty-second birthday. That 1881 minus 1835 is not forty-two is sufficiently obvious; yet no one on the editorial staff noticed the error, and it was repeated in the third edition of the Dictionary. Mussorgsky was born in 1839, not 1835, and he died not on his forty-second birthday, but one week after it. In the meantime, the error went into general reference works, including the *Encyclopedia Britannica,* and there were several centennial concerts of Mussorgsky's music presented on the ninty-sixth anniversary of his birth, in 1935.

In the third edition of Grove's Dictionary, the date of Rameau's birth is given as October 23, 1683, but in the footnote to the same article, it is stated that Rameau was baptized on September 25 of the same year, that is, four weeks before his alleged date of birth! In corroboration of the October date, the article refers to the inscription on Rameau's monument in his native town of Dijon. As a matter of fact, only the year of Rameau's birth is indicated on his monument.

Weber's centennial was celebrated in Germany on the wrong date because of the error in all music dictionaries and in all published biographies of Weber. For some reason nobody tried to secure a copy of Weber's certificate of baptism, available to any inquirer, in the parochial registries of Weber's birthplace, the town of Eutin in North Germany. Weber was born not on December 18, 1786, but a month earlier, and was baptized on November 20, 1786.

The date of baptism is frequently given in music dictionaries instead of the actual date of birth. For instance, in the third edition of Baker's *Biographical Dictionary of Musicians,* the editor states that Puccini, in an autographed letter, gave him his date of birth as December 23, 1858. But this was actually the date of his baptism, solemnized a day after his birth. The records of the municipality of Lucca reveal that Puccini, *"una creatura di sesso maschile alla quale furono imposti i nomi di*

Giacomo, Antonio, Domenico, Michele, Seconda, Maria," was born in Lucca at 2:00 A.M. on the day of December 22, 1858.

In a great number of cases, the musicians themselves deliberately postdate their birthdays in order to make themselves younger. Thus we have the ludicrous example of movable dates from one to the next edition of a *Who's Who* or a similar reference work. For example, the Cleveland Orchestra program book of October 1929 gives the date of birth of an American composer-conductor as June 1, 1899. Five years later, in a biographical notice for the New York Philharmonic Symphony program book, the year of his birth is pushed to 1900. And in *America's Young Men* the date is June 1, 1901.

In its issue of March 13, 1944, *Life* Magazine ran a picture story on contemporary musicians and inconsiderately cited their dates of birth. Immediately, the editors received numerous letters pointing out that the dates were wrong and should be advanced into the future from two to ten years. Lotte Lehmann wrote: "As a woman, I must say that it was a bit disconcerting to see that you have made me several years older than I really am (which I feel is old enough!). . . . The only *beau geste* the editors can make to reinstate themselves as gentlemen and scholars is to blame the whole thing on the typesetter and say that he meant to print 1895!!!" The trouble with the date proffered by Lotte Lehmann is that it would make her a full-fledged opera star at the age of fifteen, for she, according to her autobiography, supported by ascertainable records, was engaged at the Hamburg Opera in 1910. The real date of her birth is February 27, 1888.

In its editorial postscript to these complaints, *Life* put the blame where it belongs:

"Revealing a musician's age is as delicate a matter as revealing a trick of breathing or of pedaling a sostenuto. *Life's* errors resulted not from editorial carelessness with official sources, but from a wholesale desire on the part of musicians to keep their ages a matter of uncertainty. *Life* feels this desire is understandable. But it doesn't feel that musicians should complain about the confusion they themselves create."

Perhaps the only way to handle the problem of birthdays is to follow the example of Whistler, who was confronted in Paris by a compatriot from Massachusetts. When queried whether he was born in Lowell, Mass., about sixty-seven years before, he replied: "I shall be born when and where I want, and I do not choose to be born at Lowell, and I refuse to be sixty-seven." His preferred birthplace was St. Petersburg, Russia.

A similar desire for a more glamorous birthplace prompted the American-born operetta composer, Louis Varney, to insist that he was born in Paris while in reality he was born in New Orleans on May 30, 1844; his birth is recorded in Book 7, Folio 375, of the New Orleans archives. His father was a director of the French Opera Company in New Orleans and married a native French woman. Louis Varney was taken to Paris at the age of seven and remained there all his life.

Child prodigies enjoy a special privilege of cutting down their ages. One might say that the chronological rate of their growth is retarded; they age slowly. This peculiar phenomenon is observable even within the covers of an official biography. For instance, an erstwhile child prodigy named Raoul Koczalski had a biography written by Bernhard Vogel. According to this biography, Koczalski made his first public appearance at the age of four in March 1888, having been born on January 3, 1884, but in later chapters of the same book, his date of birth is shifted without warning to 1885.

The most honest *ci-devant* child prodigy is Yehudi

Menuhin. He actually corrected his official birth date making himself nine months older. The New York *Times* of January 11, 1942, broke the story under the caption: "Menuhin Confesses about His Birthday Now That He Is over 25." The story ran as follows:

"Now that Yehudi Menuhin is twenty-five and has reached the status of a mature performer, he has confessed that, like many another prodigy, his age was given out as younger than he really was when he made his first appearance here. He was not eight when he gave that first recital on January 17, 1926. He was three months short of ten. He also wants to square the record. Many reference books going on the date originally given out, give his birth date as January 22, 1917. The correct date is April 22, 1916.

"The change in the month was made before the change in the year, Mr. Menuhin explained, for when his parents sent him to public school in San Francisco, they had to say he was older than he was to get him in, so they shifted the date to January. He hated the school and remained there one day, but the new date stuck. At the time of his debut, it was decided to keep the new date, but to alter the year."

The greatest of the great among men of music succumbed to the temptation of cutting a few years off their true ages. In old editions of music dictionaries the year of Beethoven's birth is often given as 1772 instead of the correct date, 1770. This is not a biographer's error. The date was given by Beethoven himself to his friends. Moreover, when Beethoven was confronted with the parish entry of his baptism giving the year 1770, he explained that it referred to his older brother, also named Ludwig, who had died in infancy. There was in fact an infant named Ludwig Maria born on April 1, 1769 who lived but six days.

By a curious coincidence, an explanation similar to Beethoven's was given by a young Brazilian conductor and composer, Eleazar de Carvalho, to account for the conflicting birth dates, 1912 and 1915, given in his biographical notices. Confirming the 1915 date, he said that it was true that an Eleazar de Carvalho was born in 1912, but it was his older brother who died in infancy. When he was born, his parents called him Eleazar Segundo.

Singers particularly are wont to doctor their birthdays in the direction of eternal youth. Thus, John Sims Reeves, the English singer, states in his autobiography that he was born on October 21, 1821. But documentary evidence reveals that he was born on September 26, 1818. The Welsh singer, David Ffrangcon-Davies, gave the year of his birth as 1856, but the official *Who Was Who* states that he was born in 1850.

Oscar Wilde once said: "No woman should ever be quite accurate about her age. It looks so calculating." The autobiographical notices by most female musicians amply corroborate this maxim. Thus, Mathilde Marchesi listed the year of her birth as 1826. But when she died in London in 1913, the family announcement in the obituary column of the London *Times* read: "Died in her ninety-second year," which would place her birth at 1822. Even the family didn't know that she was past her ninety-second birthday, for she was born, according to the registries of her native town, Frankfort, in Germany, on March 24, 1821. She died on November 18, 1913, and her age was therefore ninety-two years, seven months and twenty-four days.

The famous Canadian prima donna, Emma Lajeunesse, known as Albani, was born not in 1852, as given in most dictionaries, but in 1847. The correct date was established through the registries of a convent school which she attended in Canada as a child. Incidentally, there are strong indications that Albani was born not in Canada but in Plattsburg, New York.

The correct date of birth of the "greatest Carmen,"

Emma Calvé, was established from the registries of Décazeville, France, where she was born on August 15, 1858, and not on any later date given in various dictionaries. Still another Emma, Emma Thursby, had quite a number of years clipped off her age, to judge by the dictionaries. She was born in 1845, not in 1854 or 1857, as variously given.

An exception among operatic divas is the Shanghai-born Emma Eames. In her memoirs, she gives the correct year of her birth as 1865, even though several dictionaries make her two years younger.

Some birthdays are symbolic. Stephen Foster was born on the Fourth of July, and this fact somehow adds color to his position as a national composer of American songs. George M. Cohan, the composer of *Over There*, attached great significance to the fact that he, like Stephen Foster, was born on Independence Day. Unfortunately, research undertaken by his biographer, Ward Morehouse, unearthed his birth certificate, which proved that Cohan was born on July 3, 1878, not July 4.

Roy Harris, who is an American composer *par excellence*, was born in a log cabin in Lincoln County, Oklahoma, on February 12, 1898. The fact that he was born on Lincoln's Birthday in Lincoln County made a considerable impression on his mind. "The shadow of Abe Lincoln has hovered over my life from childhood," writes Roy Harris in the program notes for his Sixth Symphony, which parallels in its structure the paragraphs of the Gettysburg Address. "This was, I suppose, inevitable," continues Harris, "for the very simple reason that my birthday fell on the national holiday honoring Lincoln's birth, which meant that, on that day, school was dismissed."

Premature burials are of frequent occurrence in music dictionaries. Thus Moser's *Musiklexikon* lists Daniel

Gregory Mason — still fortunately among us — as having departed this life on March 15, 1930, and this was copied by other European dictionaries. The pianist Alexander Siloti lived a quarter of a century after 1919, when according to Grove, he was supposed to have died. And the English operetta composer, Sidney Jones, survived by thirty-two years the death date assigned to him by Riemann.

Often the victim of a premature musical obituary rises to refute the news. The prima donna of the first half of the nineteenth century, Angelica Catalani, protested against repeated attempts to drive her underground, in a letter published in the *Musical World* of November 8, 1844:

"Sir: What have I done to the German press that they have now for the fourth time killed me? Though at the age of sixty-four, I still retain my health. The French journals, misled by those of Germany, have twice announced my death, the English once. At first, the intelligence was more laughable than frightening to me, and I read with satisfaction the many praises with which my fancied decease was accompanied. The spring of my life and my efforts seemed once more strewn with the flowers which were to have covered my grave, but which, fortunately for me, does not contain my corpse. But I must confess, the repetition of the statements of my dissolution begins to alarm me. What base cruelty to continually announce to an old woman her death! I shall at last believe it myself and really die."

Angelica Catalani finally died in Paris on June 12, 1849, having outlived her obituary notices by five years.

When the editor of a music dictionary wrote to Brazil in 1940 to find out the exact date of death of the Brazilian composer, Gomes de Araujo, who was born in 1846, he unexpectedly received a reply from the ancient man himself, in English: "It is a fact that I was born on the fifth of August, 1846, but in spite of this being quite a

[244]

long existence, I should say that I am still healthy."
Gomes de Araujo died on September 8, 1942.

The story is told that when Gretchaninoff came to New York in 1939 and introduced himself to a music publisher, the latter looked at him in unconcealed aston∗ishment. "Gretchaninoff?" he exclaimed, "My God! I thought you were dead!" At the age of eighty-three, Gretchaninoff still continues to compose vigorously and prolifically.

The most spectacular case of premature burial is that of Amy Fay, the author of a book, *Music Study in Germany*. In the 1922 edition of this book, Oscar Sonneck, then head of the music division of the Library of Congress, wrote a preface in which he reflected upon the melancholy fact that most people described in the book were dead, "Miss Fay included, who died in 1921." But as it turned out, Miss Fay was very much alive at the time and had only moved to Watertown, Massachusetts. There she lived, and presumably collected royalties from the posthumous edition of her book. She died on February 28, 1928, a few months before Sonneck himself departed this life. One wondered whether Sonneck had ever discovered his error.

Lovers of chronological discrepancies and diverting incompatibilities will find much amusement in browsing over music dictionaries. There is for instance the following case of double personality exhibited in *A Dictionary of Modern Music and Musicians*, edited by the late A. Eaglefield Hull.

MALISHEFSKY, Vitold Josephovitch. Russ. compr. b. Moghilof-Podolsk, 8 Sept. 1873. Stud. under Rimsky-Korsakov. Now lives in Poland.

MALISZEWSKI, Witold. Polish compr. condr. b. Mohylow Podolski, 8 July, 1873. In 1898 began to study theory under Rimsky-Korsakov at Petrograd Cons.; at present lives in Warsaw.

In the same dictionary two different composers, Omer Letorey and Pierre Henri Ernest Letorey are combined into one with the result that this double composer is made into the author of operettas and the recipient of the Prix de Rome. Also in the same dictionary one finds that Gustav Mahler married Alma Mahler in 1904, while she married him in an adjoining entry two years earlier, in 1902. Prenatal 'cello recitals are credited in the dictionary to David Popper, who is said to have been born in Prague on June 18, 1876, and "traveled throughout Europe as 'cello virtuoso, 1868-73."

Eaglefield Hull, the editor of this dictionary, was a strange man. A musician of advanced ideas, he was careless in his methods. When he published a book, *Music, Classical, Romantic, and Modern,* he borrowed freely from various authors without the faintest credit line. The music journals on both sides of the Atlantic pounced on him viciously. The book was withdrawn from circulation by the publishers. Hull suffered a nervous breakdown, jumped under the train in a London railroad station, and died a few days later.

How Bach walked three hundred miles eleven or more years before he was born is told in an early edition of a popular music history, *How Music Grew:* "Bach, who must have been a prodigious walker, walked three hundred miles to hear Johann Buxtehude (1600-1674) play the organ." Bach was born in 1685, and it was not Johann but his son, Dietrich Buxtehude, whom Bach heard. The error was corrected in later editions of *How Music Grew.*

Finally there is the delectable tale of Mahler and the censors engagingly told by Burton Rascoe in his book, *Before I Forget:*

"Just before the war, Frederick Stock, the conductor of the Chicago Symphony Orchestra, had arranged with Gustav

[246]

Mahler, the Austrian composer, to stage in Chicago the world première of Mahler's so-called Symphony of a Thousand. Mahler mailed the score to Stock just before August 4, 1914. The score was seized in England and held there for the duration of the war in the belief that it was an elaborate cipher message to German spies."

A wonderful story, unfortunately vitiated by the fact that Mahler was long dead when World War I broke out and could not possibly have taken the time out to mail his score to Chicago. The world première of Mahler's Symphony was given under his direction in Munich, on September 12, 1910; the score was published and available to anyone. Yet the tale is certain to bob up in books of anecdotes about musicians. A good story like this will not be allowed to go to waste on account of a minor discrepancy of dates.

A Sad Short Story

Christian Kriens was a precocious boy in his native Amsterdam in Holland. He made his debut at the age of fourteen with his father's symphony orchestra in the quadruple capacity of pianist, violinist, conductor, and composer. He played Beethoven's violin concerto; then switching over to the piano, he performed the Emperor Concerto. He also conducted his own Second Symphony. In 1907 he decided to come to America. He was young and energetic. *Musical America* of November 19, 1910 published an interview with Kriens with these headlines:

"No Wealth, No Friends, No Influence, Yet Optimistic — Christian Kriens, Composer, Tells How He Made His Way Despite Handicaps — Advantages of America over Europe — Mr. Kriens Is Not Only Optimistic, He Is Enthusiastic, and His Enthusiasm Is Upheld by an Activity That Bids Well for His Own Future."

On December 17, 1934 the body of Christian Kriens

was found in his Hartford, Conn. apartment. He had shot himself dead. Eleven days before his death, he lost his position as music director of the local radio station. He left a note saying that he no longer hoped to earn a living with music.

V

RED, WHITE AND BLUE NOTES

Constitution Set to Music

The following story of the United States Constitution having been set to music by a Boston composer named Greeler must be accepted on faith, for no such composition has been discovered in the United States music libraries, and no such name appears in any book on American composers. The story of the harmonized Constitution was published in the *Musical World* of London in the issue of November 28, 1874:

"The authors of the Constitution of the Union thought more of reason than of rhyme, and their prose is not too well adapted to harmony, but the patriotic inspiration of Mr. Greeler, the Boston composer, overcomes every difficulty. He has made his score a genuine musical epopœia, and had it performed before a numerous public. The performance did not last less than six hours. The preamble of the Constitution forms a broad and majestic recitative, well sustained by altos and double basses. The first clause is written for a tenor; the other choruses are given to the bass, soprano, and baritone. The music of the clause treating of state's rights is written in a minor key for bass and tenor.

At the end of every clause, the recitative of the preamble is re-introduced and then repeated by the chorus. The constitutional amendments are treated as fugues and serve to introduce a formidable finale, in which the big drum and the gong play an important part. The general instrumentation is very scholarly, and the harmony surprising."

The Flamboyant Pioneer

Among forgotten pioneers of American music is Charles Jerome Hopkins. He was a colorful figure on the American scene in the last quarter of the nineteenth century. He was constantly agitating for the cause of American music, and was never shy of proclaiming himself as one of the great forces in American culture. One of his rightful claims, which may well be sustained by the impartial judgment of musical chronology, was that he had originated "musicianly and scientific *Kinder-Oper*." All previous attempts in this direction, according to Hopkins, were adaptations from adult operas. The work on which he based his claim was *Taffy and Old Munch*, which he wrote in the 1880's especially for children's voices, with very few solos and a reduced orchestra.

Hopkins liked to promote his enterprises with the support of scientific reasons. Thus when he organized his singing school, which he called "Young Philharmonics," he advanced the argument that "mortality is greatest among children, and the practice of singing is one of the best-known preventives of consumption." In a flowery report for the season 1886-1887, he appealed to the public for support:

"Three Free Singing and Opera Schools were maintained for eight months in armories and halls, with nearly 1,000 pupils — both sexes — taught by MR. HOPKINS IN PERSON. FIVE CONCERTS AND LITTLE OPERAS were given for the fund by selected pupils. Mr. Hopkins interviewed 359 PERSONS who declined to subscribe for tickets

— many of them requiring SIX to TEN VISITS before they could even be seen, involving certainly not less than TWELVE HUNDRED FRUITLESS CALLS on 171 PERSONS whose subscriptions, together with door sales, amounted to $1,028.15 with which to pay concert hall and theater rents, rehearsal, extras, gas, coal, printing, advertising, stationery, postage, children's carfares, doorkeepers, ushers, and messengers.

"FRIENDS ARE BESOUGHT not to withdraw their names but to renew as subscribers to our Concerts, which are far below their proper standard of dignity simply for want of an ORCHESTRA, and money is indispensable for that. All of which is respectfully submitted to his friends (and enemies) by their most obedient laboring man and servant, the 'unpractical,' 'visionary,' 'crank,' and 'musical fiend' of some newspapers."

The musical journals of the time frequently ran amusing items about the doings of Jerome Hopkins. Thus, *The Folio* of June 1871 published a story under the caption, "Why He Is Crazy":

"Mr. C. Jerome Hopkins furnishes us with the following reasons why he is considered crazy by some of his acquaintances:

" 'I believe an American can be a true artist. I don't drink whiskey, lager beer, or any intoxicating liquors. I never borrow money. I keep good company. I work continually for the advancement of art. I tell the truth. I owe no man. I use no profane language. I mind my own business. I have succeeded in establishing fine music schools in New York.' "

The New York *Musical Gazette* reported some eccentricities of Jerome Hopkins in 1872:

"Mr. C. Jerome Hopkins dresses in the costume of a North American Indian and carries a tomahawk and a scalping knife. It is rumored that he occasionally cuts up an unfortunate musician who doesn't happen to suit him and manufactures him into fugues. This accounts for the fact that he is obliged to play his fugues from memory; and also for the unearthly sound they have when he plays them. The wail of the victim is always to be heard."

As time went by and Hopkins grew more aggressive, the jocular banter gave way to snarling attacks. *Music and Drama* of December 13, 1882 came out with nothing less than an accusation of swindling:

"Our old friend, Jerome Hopkins, the author of *Samuel*, an opera-oratorio or oratorio-opera, is a sadly misjudged man. For years he has been spending his own fortune in drilling choirs and producing *Samuel*, and ungrateful people insinuate that he never had any fortune to spend. Wicked people indeed hint that he has been living and buying houses by the aid of money obtained from the patrons of *Samuel*. Jerome is a well-meaning man full of enthusiasm which unfortunately is misdirected."

In 1889 Hopkins went to England on a tour as lecturer, pianist, musical organizer, and self-appointed cultural plenipotentiary. True to type, he announced his appearances in flamboyant posters. In Maidstone he printed the following announcement:

"Dear Readers: Strange though it seems, the world really does move, and stranger still, even the Priests now condescend to permit it! Selah. Therefore, Music should not stand still but should advance together with Philosophy, Manufacture, Inventions, and Chemistry. Mr. Jerome Hopkins is the first American Operatic Oratorio Composer and Pianist who has ever ventured to invade England with NEW-WORLD Musical theories and practices. He comes from a 'wide-awake' country whose citizens know a vast deal about English music but of whose Music the dear English cousins know almost nothing. Believe it, this man will Interest, Entertain, and Amuse you, and will teach you something about America, if not about Music.

"If more than the expenses is subscribed, Jerome Hopkins has promised the Mayor to give Twenty-five Per Cent thereof to Any Charity His Worship may select. You will be delighted and Wonder-Struck if You Attend, and You Will Forever Regret it if you don't, for Jerome Hopkins must travel right on, on, ON. He has much to do and but a Short Life to do it in."

Hopkins also published a sixteen-page pamphlet in which he did his best to twist the British lion's tail. He listed "Johnny Bull's Ten Commandments," among which were the following: "Thou shalt not take the name of Old Fogies and consecrated Idiots in vain, for the Home Secretary will not hold him guiltless that taketh their names in vain." "Thou shalt not let thy right hand know what thy left does when thou playest upon the piano." While in London, Hopkins attempted to purchase a corpse at an undertaker's establishment.

He got into real trouble when he began pestering an English doctor of medicine, dunning him for the price of subscription to his concerts. *The Folio* of March 1890 reported the episode in a story, "Music versus Physic":

"Jerome Hopkins of New York, who has lately been giving concerts in London, has sued some of his genteel patrons for the amount of their subscription which they had forgotten to pay. Abong the latter was one Dr. Thomas Boor Crosby, the Lord Mayor's physician, whom Hopkins sued for three pounds and twelve shillings, but failed to recover.

The Doctor claims that he only allowed Hopkins to use his name after being importuned by the latter and received from him tickets which he understood to be complimentary. Upon losing the suit, Hopkins began carrying on a one-sided correspondence with the Doctor from all parts of England.

"Hopkins' favorite method of communication was by postal card and these Crosby has been finding for a year or so on his breakfast table. Sometimes the card would carry a simple message that the Doctor was a blackguard, thief, or perjurer. Another time Hopkins would draw a parallel between Crosby and the late Judas Iscariot. Anon a skull and crossbones would come to taunt the physician with his professional failures, or a card would arrive containing a sketch of a duck in the act of quacking."

Crosby stood it all until Hopkins began to write poetry to him. When he came down to breakfast one day, he found his servants laboring hard to suppress their grins. A postal card on the table read:

"With nobles and gentry Boor Crosby aspires
To pass as companion, for which he requires
His name in big print as a patron of music
For fiddling is surely much nicer than physic
But when for his honors pay day comes around
Quoth Sawbones: No guinea from me, I'll be bound!"

That was too much. Crosby wrote to Hopkins that he might have one week in which to apologize and promise to annoy him no more or there would be legal prosecution. Hopkins replied thus on a postal card: "Well, pay me what you owe me, you lying thief."

"The doctor applied for a warrant. Hopkins was brought to London and arraigned before Alderman Fowler at the Mansion House, and he was bound on his own recognizance to appear for trial at the Old Bailey. Dr. Crosby stated in his complaint: 'For a year now I have been getting these blackguard epistles, which make me the laughing stock of my servants and clerks. I allowed him to use my name as a patron at his urgent request. I purchased no tickets and owe him nothing, but I have been put to a large legal expense by his persecutions.'"

Jerome Hopkins was in his element in court, whether as an accuser, a defendant, or a witness. When he testified in a case concerning a will in New York in March 1887, he identified himself as editor of the Philharmonic Journal. He was then asked by an attorney if he was a music critic. By way of reply he inquired whether the attorney was a lawyer. The attorney then asked Hopkins if Mozart's *Turkish March* was really Turkish; to this Hopkins replied that it was as Turkish as Mrs. Thurber's opera was American, Mrs. Thurber being one of the principal promoters of opera in New York at the time. For once, the papers gave Hopkins hearty praise and reported that his repartee was greeted with "screams of laughter" in the courtroom.

Despite his aggressive vitality, Hopkins held little hope for the native American composer in the economic and social world of his day. In a melancholy letter published in the *Musical Courier* of February 1885, he listed the names of American musicians who killed themselves, or went to "a drunkard's grave":

Charles Hermann (six symphonies), a maniac and suicide.
Harry Sanderson (pianist), a drunkard's grave.
T. Hagen, a drunkard's grave.
E. Remack, a drunkard's grave.
William King (organist), a drunkard's grave.
A. H. Pease (pianist and composer), a drunkard's grave.
William Saer, early decline and consumption from disappointment.
Poor young Von Oeckelen, early decline and consumption from disappointment.
August Goeckel, early decline and consumption from disappointment.
U. C. Hill (founder of the New York Philharmonic), suicide.
Candido Berti (pianist), suicide.
H. N. Sawyer, suicide.

He concluded his letter by saying:

"I hope to live long enough to see a composer of operas, symphonies, and concertos here granted a chance to make a living, at least equal to that now enjoyed by a shoemaker or tailor, but to treat him as royally as if he were a tenor or ballet dancer would be beyond the wildest dreams of obediently yours, Jerome Hopkins."

In 1891 Hopkins filed his will at the Surrogate Court at Paterson, New Jersey, in which he wrote:

"I direct that my body shall be cremated or interred, whichever is cheapest. If interred, in winding sheet only, without coffin, on my own property at the bottom of the hill, the spot to be smoothed over and left unmarked."

Hopkins died on November 4, 1898. He bequeathed his musical manuscripts to Amy Fay. Few of his numerous compositions were ever published.

Miss Goldberg-Brillianti

American music journalists of yore were not believers in chivalry. They used frontier language when reviewing debut concerts of budding prima donnas. The *Musical Courier* of December 10, 1884 gives this succinct account of a singing lady's offering:

"A young (?) lady called Miss Amelia Goldberg-Brillianti, 'the American prima donna,' made her 'first appearance in America' at Steinway Hall. Let us hope that this may have been also her last appearance as she was so outrageously bad that even the not overeducated audience which had been drummed together began to smell a rat and made fun of the debutante."

Happy Birthday to You

Shortly before World War II, Western Union instituted a novel service of singing telegrams. A Western Union boy would deliver a message and sing for an astonished recipient a ditty suitable to the occasion. Most often it was *Happy Birthday to You*. The Western

Union people had a rude awakening when the Clayton F. Summy Company of Chicago sued them for infringement of copyright. Indeed, the tune, long regarded as of the folk-song variety, turned out to be the creation of two sisters, Patty and Mildred Hill, kindergarten teachers, authors of an album, *Song Stories for the Kindergarten*. The birthday melody was one of the "Song Stories," but it was called "Good Morning to All." The album was duly copyrighted by the Summy company in 1893, and the rights were still valid. The Western Union quickly changed their singing telegrams to an uncopyrighted tune, *For He's a Jolly Good Fellow*. Forewarned by this unpleasantness, the movies had to cut out the birthday song whenever it was used in the films until things were straightened out. Roy Harris, who used the tune in the Finale of his *Symphonic Dedication* to Howard Hanson on the occasion of the latter's fiftieth birthday, also got into trouble with the copyright owners despite the fact that his modern harmonization of the tune made it hardly recognizable. After the initial performance with the Boston Symphony Orchestra, the symphonic birthday greeting was silençed.

Samuel Osborn, U. S. A.

The unusual name of the American March King, John Philip Sousa, is responsible for the story that the name is an anagram, composed of the initials S. O., for Samuel Osborn, and U. S. A. The fact is that Sousa was born, providentially for a future author of famous American marches, in Washington, D. C., of a Portuguese father and a German mother, Sousa being a rather common Portuguese name. The March King himself never nurtured an inferiority complex about his being a composer of band music. He said he would much rather be "the composer of an inspirational march than of a manufactured symphony." When Soûsa conducted his march

Stars and Stripes Forever, at the Paris Exposition in 1900, a French woman told him: "Every time I hear *Stars and Stripes Forever*, it seems to me that I can see the American Eagle throwing arrows into the aurora borealis."

Rail-Splitter's Polka

Special music for presidential elections is now out of fashion, and presidential candidates are likely to pick up any popular song for campaign purposes. In the 1936 election Landon used Stephen Foster's song, *O Susanna*; Roosevelt had *Happy Days Are Here Again*. Alfred Smith in 1928 sang *Sidewalks of New York*. Truman likes the *Missouri Waltz*, and it has become his leitmotif in public appearances.

It was different in olden times. Then every candidate had several songs written specially for him with aggressive texts and rollicking if corny rhythms. There were many such for Lincoln's second term in 1864, as for instance, a campaign song, *Abraham the Great and General Grant and Troupe*. The words ran as follows:

"I think Uncle Abe's the man who another term can stand
The Rebs and Copperheads with their scorning

And in eighteen-sixty-five we'll elect him if alive
For he'll bring us all right in the morning.

"What a pity people can't let alone our General Grant
While he gathers all the Rebels 'neath his awning!
He'll give old Jeff the chance to have a 'swinging dance'
And we'll all 'see him home' in the morning."

Another interesting item connected with the 1864 campaign was the *Rail-splitter's Polka* dedicated to "The Republican Presidential Candidate Hon. A. Lincoln," and composed by one A. Neuman. The rail-splitting allusion was, of course, a sentimental reference to Lincoln's humble occupation in his youth. The capital letter R on the title page of the Polka was formed by crossing rails. The music of the Polka was the regular German variety, but there were some incisive grace notes suggesting the energetic rail-splitting with sparks flying off in all directions.

The Law on the Marimba

It was in the summer of 1947. A judge in Media, Pennsylvania, heard the complaint of neighbors against a woman who played the marimba hours on end, starting from early morning, which made the neighborhood virtually uninhabitable. The court ruled that though the marimba is not a public nuisance, it should not be employed more than three hours on any single day and not more than sixty consecutive minutes. The judge further commented: "The situation is similar to that employed in certain parts of the world where a person is compelled to remain in a certain position and to have drops of water fall continuously on his head."

They Laughed When I Sat Down at the Piano

Professional musicians are skeptical about the social advantages of a fellow who can wade through the first movement of the *Moonlight* Sonata, but the most famous musical advertisement has sold this idea to thousands of satisfied customers. It bears the intriguing motto: "They Laughed When I Sat Down at the Piano but When I Started To Play—!" A drawing represents a young man whirling the piano stool. "Can he really play?" a girl whispers. "Heavens, no," Arthur exclaims. "He never played a note in his life." The story continues: "To the amazement of all my friends, I strode confidently over to the piano and sat down. . . . Instantly a tense silence fell on the guests. I played the first few bars of Beethoven's immortal *Moonlight* Sonata. I heard gasps of amazement. My friends sat breathless — spellbound!" The rest of the story tells how the hero had mastered the difficult art of piano playing without a teacher in a matter of weeks and advised prospective pianists to obtain a copy of the free book, *Music Lessons in Your Own Home,* including a demonstration lesson.

The advertisement was conceived and executed by John Caples, vice-president of Batten, Barton, Durstine and Osborn, Inc., in 1925. It was run in a number of magazines such as *Physical Culture, Popular Science,*

Smart Set, the *Christian Endeavor World*, *The Girls'*
Companion, *Young People's Weekly*, etc. A sour note
was injected when a music teacher wrote in saying that
the *Moonlight* Sonata was beyond her own abilities to
play. As a result, the advertisement was revamped with
Liszt's *Liebestraum* instead of the *Moonlight* Sonata
as a prize number. But *Liebestraum* is even more difficult than the original selection! The advertisement is
still being run, with *Liebestraum* held up as a key to
social success and feminine adulation.

Uneasy Flying Trapeze

Although the acrobats in the famous trapeze song
are supposed to perform their act with the greatest of
ease, the tune was actually barred by the Ringling Bros.
and Barnum and Bailey Circus after an accident that
caused a broken arm for one of the trapeze fliers, Gus
Bell. It happened in 1940 when Mr. Bell, Mrs. Bell, and
another couple of married trapeze fliers were performing
in Canada. The band blared the trapeze song. It seems
that the rhythm of the song was bad; Gus Bell grabbed
his partner by his fingers and went sailing into the grand-
stand. He got off easily with only a broken arm, but the
accident put a jinx on the song and it was never played
again, at least not for the Bells. Gus Bell declared to
the New York *Times* reporter in April 1947 that uneasy
moments come too often to justify the lyrics. His prefer-
ence is for the *Anniversary Waltz*, the 1947 hit tune revamped by Al Jolson from the old waltz tune, the *Waves
of the Danube* by an obscure Rumanian bandmaster,
Ivanovici.

Irving Berlin's Amanuensis

Irving Berlin has never made a secret of the fact that
he cannot put notes on paper as any ordinary unsuccessful long-haired composer does in his daily routine.

[261]

Irving Berlin improvises his melodies on a piano especially constructed to suit his peculiar technique. For Irving Berlin can play in only one key, F-sharp, and his piano has a transposition gadget near the pedal which enables the composer to change the pitch of the only key he knows and adapt the tune to the pitch of his voice and vice versa.

A crisis came when, on a trip to the West Indies, his piano, which he had with him in his cabin, broke down. "I took it apart," declared Irving Berlin in an interview in November 1940, "and put it together again but had two pieces left over. I managed to play the instrument, but it was a little higher in pitch than usual." This mishap was not sufficient, however, to clog Irving Berlin's inspiration. He was back with three new songs.

Still Irving Berlin has had to have someone to put notes down on music paper. His first amanuensis was Henry Vollmer, who took down *Oh! How I Hate To Get Up in the Morning* and several other songs by Irving Berlin. In a letter to the New York *Times* in June 1942 Vollmer wrote: "I found it quite easy to put Mr. Berlin's melodies on paper (he did not at that time give dictation until the melody was complete) and the tunes went down on paper with very few corrections, just as a good business man might dictate a letter."

God Bless America

Popular songs are usually created on the spur of the moment and live out their ephemeral life in weeks, rarely months. But it sometimes happens that a song discarded or little noticed during the original production is revived at an opportune moment with spectacular success. This is the story of *God Bless America* by Irving Berlin. He wrote it in 1918 when he was a draft sergeant in training at Camp Upton, for a show entitled *Yip Yip Yaphank*. For some reason the song was withdrawn from production and remained in oblivion for twenty years. Then Kate Smith, the benignantly adipose radio star found herself in need of a partiotic song for Armistice Day of 1938. Irving Berlin suggested his old number, and Kate Smith sang it on the radio. It struck fire at once. When World War II came, *God Bless America* became the most performed national song next to the *Star-Spangled Banner*. People stood up when it was sung, and the song was heard wherever the American Army, Navy, and Air Force went on the far-flung fronts.

The same simplicity of the melodic outline that made the song famous, exposed it to the charges of plagiarism. Alfred H. Aarons, an octogenarian, sued Irving Berlin and Kate Smith for damages, asserting that certain portions of his own song, *America, My Home So Fair,* copyrighted in 1918, were used in *God Bless America.* Like many similar suits that involved other songs, this one too was dismissed by the court for insufficient evidence.

Mary Had a Little Lamb

Many composers have tried to write music in the style of someone else. Schumann inserted several Chopinesque bars in his *Carnaval* and entitled the section "Chopin." Perhaps the most thorough essay in this imitative art has been contributed by Edward Ballantine, in his Variations for Piano on the nursery rhyme, *Mary Had a Little Lamb,* written in the styles from Bach to Gershwin.

But these Variations must be seen as well as heard in order to be fully appreciated. For in the printed music, Ballantine gives a subtle and often ironic imitation of the composer's personal manner in indicating the tempo and expression marks. Brahms is represented by a "Lambsody No. 1" in which the theme is played *"energisch."* Richard Strauss, in the "tone poem, freely after Mother Goose, The Superlamb," sets the tempo as

"*Allegro eroico,*" later qualified as "*non meno eroico ma più erotico.*" The climax is marked "*ad libido.*" Ballantine's take-off on Puccini includes a vocal part, "*Maria aveva uno piccolo agnello,*" to be sung "*carusomente.*" Then comes Stravinsky in a "Sonata in less than one Movement," which includes such profoundly self-evident injunctions as "Play in strict time as I.S."; "*Chaque note a sa propre valeur*"; and "Raise r.h. quickly with l.h." George Gershwin is featured with "Lamb in Blue," and a footnote gives notice that "this concert variation on the foregoing Lamb Trot may be omitted."

The Strange Death of Louis Gottschalk

When Gottschalk, the dashing virtuoso pianist of the mid-nineteenth century, died in Rio de Janeiro on December 18, 1869, at the peak of his career and amid spectacular successes, rumors began to spread that his death was the result of a murderous attack. One story, popular for quite a while, was that the jealous husband of a woman who was found with Gottschalk in a hotel room in Rio, emasculated him in a ferocious attack with a knife, and that Gottschalk died several days later. This legend is discredited by the medical documentation pertaining to his case, which states that he died of pneumonia after eighteen days in the hospital. A more plausible story of the events that led to Gottschalk's death was reported by a Brazilian doctor, Severiano, who attended Gottschalk. His story is told in the June 1871 issue of the Boston musical publication, *The Folio:*

"Gottschalk sent Firmin, his agent, to Sao Paulo, which is a seat for young college men, to make arrangements for a concert. The college boys annoyed Firmin and tried similar tricks on Gottschalk, who ordered them from the room. That night, as he was leaving the concert hall, he was struck in the back with a sandbag. He was stunned but recovered and went to Rio de Janeiro. He complained afterward of an oppression in the chest, which was caused by the ligaments of the lungs from the blow of the sandbag. An abscess which had formed on his chest broke during his last concert and caused his prostration. A post-mortem examination disclosed a cancerous formation in one of his lungs. The details were hushed, and it is only by recent explanation of Firmin and the physician that correction of the mistaken rumors has been offered."

Juke Boxes and Chaucer

The plebeian juke boxes seem to have patrician ancestry. The word "juke" has been traced to the old English vocable, "Iowken," which is found in Chaucer's *Troilus and Criseyde*, meaning "to rest" or "sleep." The same word is used in the southern states in America in the form of "jouke." Local inns in the South were called "jouke joints," and music boxes installed in these establishments became known as "jook" boxes, which were soon changed to "juke" boxes. The manufacturers of these contraptions prefer to call juke boxes by the more dignified name of Automatic Coin Machines. In 1945 there were a quarter of a million juke boxes in the United States. The average intake of a juke box at a nickel a song is sixteen dollars weekly, the annual total aggregating about 232 million dollars.

Ugly Jazz

When in August 1946 the National Association of Teachers of Speech was asked to name the ten ugliest words in the English language, "jazz" figured among them. The remaining nine were: phlegmatic, crunch, flatulent, cacophony, treachery, sap, plutocrat, gripe, plump.

Commercial Folklore

The singing commercials, those familiar little radio jingles that advertise a breakfast food, a soap, or a deodorant, are unanimously regarded as a nuisance, but they are now part and parcel of musical Americana. In fact, several of these singing commercials have become song hits in their own right. The most ingratiating singing commercial is *Chiquita Banana*. The theme of the song can be traced to a memorandum that the vice-president of a fruit company sent to the vice-president of an advertising agency:

"The banana is most readily assimilated when the starches have been converted to a soluble sugar. Green-tipped and all-yellow bananas will best attain ripeness if kept at a temperature of from 68 to 72 degrees Fahrenheit. Refrigeration tends to retard the ripening."

The agency set to work, and in no time turned out a torrid tune with words that stressed the fact that the banana comes from the very tropical equator and should not be put in the refrigerator. The banana song was performed for the first time on a radio broadcast in November 1944, with an Irish vocalist, Patty Clayton. But the singer who put the song across was Elsa Miranda, a Latin stenographer. She was billed as "Chiquita Banana" in a radio show in April 1945. Her radio voice proved perfect for a tropical tune and both she and the tune became popular overnight. The crew of a navy destroyer voted Elsa Miranda as "the girl they would most like to get into a refrigerator with." *Variety* said that it was "the first instance of a commercial made into a pop tune." The lyrics were later rewritten to promote the conservation of food in wartime. *Chiquita Banana* was translated into five languages; it became a big juke-box and disc-jockey hit, and it was featured along with other commercials in a symphonic concoction called *Jingles All the Way*. For n usic historians, it is necessary to add that *Chiquita Banana* was not the first banana song to become a popular success. The first, of course, was that tantalizing ditty of the 1920's, *Yes, We Have No Bananas*.

Hardly less popular than Chiquita Banana is the soft drink radio jingle, *Pepsi-Cola Hits the Spot*. It originated in 1940. The complete text of the jingle was this:

> "Nickel, nickel, too de-dee-da-da-da
> Nickel, nickel, too do-dee-da-da-da!
> Pepsi-Cola hits the spot!
> Twelve full ounces, that's a lot,
> Twice as much for a nickel too!
> Pepsi-Cola is the drink for you!
> Nickel, nickel, nickel, nickel
> Trickle, trickle, trickle, trickle
> Nickel, nickel, nickel, nickel!"

With the outbreak of World War II, the price of Pepsi-Cola went up to seven cents, and the lyrics were revised to read: "Twice as much and better, too."

The music of singing commercials sticks to the most elementary harmonies. Virtually all jingles are in major — sales could not possibly be promoted in mournful minor keys. The basic components of a radio jingle are usually the three notes of the major triad. The Pepsi-Cola jingle, Dentyne Chewing Gum, and Campbell Soup ("Mm good, Mm good") are all derived from the major triad. The form of a sequence, with a simple phrase repeated one degree higher or lower, is also favored. Delight and ebullience of spirits are expressed by an upward leap of an octave. It appears in the Pepsi-Cola jingle on the words, "twice as much." The octave is also featured in *Rinso White*, which is, strictly speaking, not a tune but merely an intervallic exclamation. There is a story about three radio employees who were bragging of their respective salaries. A trumpet player boasted that he received thirty dollars for tooting a couple of notes in a radio show. Another declared he got fifty dollars for a roll on the drums. But the softest job of all was claimed by the fellow whose duty was to pinch the lady performer of *Rinso White* at the exact moment when she hit the high note.

The most successful composers of singing commercials are Alan Bradley Kent and Austen Herbert Croom-Johnson, working as a team. They are responsible for nearly ninety per cent of radio jingles now in use. Among their productions are the Pepsi-Cola song, the Mission Bell Wine jingle, *Listen to the Handy Flit Gun,* and the milk song, *MoooOO to YouUUUU.* They dislike deodorants and never went beyond the first line of a commercial: "Under-arming can be charming."

Arranging radio commercials is big business, too. The foremost arranger of commercials is Mack Shopnick, who advertises himself in *Variety* as "The World's Most Famous Unknown Orchestra Leader." His arrangements are heard at least fifty thousand times every week. These arrangements are scored for different numbers of instruments and voices, from a male quartet with a guitar to a sizable instrumental and choral group. In the trade jargon, the ratio between instruments and voices is determined by percentages. For instance, *Mama, Mama, Won't You Larvex Me* is a sixty-forty commercial because it is sixty per cent instrumental and forty per cent vocal. Whistles, foghorns, and bird noises are added to the instrumentation if required by the nature of the product.

The length of a singing commercial varies from fifteen

seconds to one whole minute. It is, of course, of great importance to fit a radio jingle precisely into the allotted time, not a second long, not a second short.

Special effects add to the impressiveness of radio commercials. The cavernous sound of B.O. is produced by what is known as silent singing. A girl vocalist forms the sounds "beee-ohhh" with her lips while an electrical device pipes in a foghorn blast through her vocal chords. The theme itself consists of two notes, F and B-flat, a fifth lower, in the low register supposedly suggestive of the dread body odor.

Unquestionably the most popular radio commercial is the silent one sponsored by a mattress manufacturer of Louisville, Kentucky. It sponsors eleven hours of silence on the local radio station between 7:00 P.M. and 6:00 A.M. daily, when the radio audience is urged to enjoy a restful night on the advertiser's mattress.

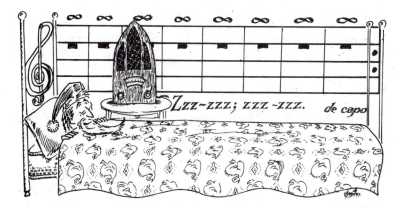

Mairzyology

Baby double talk struck Tin Pan Alley in 1944 and lasted long enough to drive the adult population to mild neurosis. The amazing aspect of this particular craze was that its creator, or at least its catalyst, was a four-year-old child, Nelia Drake, daughter of the song writer, Milton Drake. She came from kindergarten one day and announced: "Cowzy tweet and sowzy tweet and liddle sharsky doisters." This gave Milton Drake an idea, which he explained in an interview with the Boston *Sunday Advertiser* of February 6, 1944, under the appropriate caption, "Mairzy Doats and Dozy Doats, but We'll Justay Kanasprin."

"Kids slur their words," he said. "They talk from sound, not spelling. That's how we got *Mairzy Doats.*" The song conveys the obvious truth that Mares Eat Oats, and Does Eat Oats.

Mairzy Doats was first heard on the radio January 10, 1944, and thereafter sold at the rate of thirty thousand copies daily for several weeks. As Milton Drake put it, in a language system he calls Mairzyology:

> "Kiddech ants ong
> Far the rite sit
> Milyink oppees old."

Translated and decoded, the jingle means: "Kiddy chants song, Father writes it, Million copies sold."

Music with a Moustache

Singing barbers and their vocalizing patrons of the 1900's were humble in the appreciation of their art. They certainly could never dream that their singing would one day come to be regarded as an American folk art and that the renaissance of barber shop singing would be solemnly promoted at the World's Fair in the greatest city on earth, with the sponsorship of the Mayor.

Yet this is exactly what happened. As part of the festivities at the New York World's Fair of 1940, a National Championship for Barber Shop Quartets was held in New York on July 22-26, 1940, under sponsorship of the

Society for the Preservation and Encouragement of Barber Shop Quartet Singing in America. Mayor La Guardia, as president of New York Chapter No. 1 of the Society, addressed an open letter "To All Harmonizers," in which he welcomed the contestants with these words: "You will find that harmony will be the password that will open our doors and our hearts to you."

The booklet issued in connection with the National Championship for Barber Shop Quartets includes this statement on barber shop singing:

"Barber shop harmony is recognized by scholars as an authentic form of American folk music, particularly in its emphasis on improvisation. It is a musical and social activity in which practically anyone can take part, yet capable of highly impressive and exciting performance by experts. To a public rather weary of the noisy effects of modern jazz and swing, barber shop harmony comes as a welcome relief. In its quiet and unobtrusive fashion, it exerts an equal fascination with far more of human interest and permanent appeal. It is the most democratic of art forms, bringing together men of all kinds, from every walk of life, on the common ground of instinctive harmony."

The Society for the Preservation and Encouragement of Barber Shop Quartet Singing in America, or SPEBSQSA, was organized on April 11, 1938, by Owen C. Cash, an oil man of Tulsa, Oklahoma. Cash communicates the following historical note regarding the birth of the Society, which he characterizes as "a fast growing, democratic, down-to-earth, charming organization."

"For a year or more I had been collecting the words to all the old barber shop favorites. I decided to have a meeting of twelve men that I knew in Tulsa who, on occasions, had been caught in the throes of a barber shop chord. Much to my surprise on the meeting night, thirty-five men instead of twelve showed up. Each man originally notified had brought two or three cronies I did not know. All the old favorites were harmonized, and it was impossible to get the brothers to take time off to eat the Dutch lunch that had been prepared. Someone inquired, 'When are we meeting again?' Another of the brothers suggested, 'We can't get together before tomorrow night.' Actually, we had a meeting in less than a week and seventy-five brothers showed up. Attendance doubled for the next three or four meetings, the newspapers wrote a story or two about it which was picked up by the A.P. and U.P. wire services, and within two months chapters were formed all the way from Hollywood, Bing Crosby, president, to New York, Mayor La Guardia, president."

The basic requirement of good barber shop singing is that the four voices of the quartet should blend to perfection. In other words, no member should be too far superior to any other member. Thus singers whose individual excellence is dubious may form a perfectly good barber shop quartet. The great secret of the perfect blend is the constant exercise of quadruple counterpoint. This means, of course, that the four voices, two tenors, a baritone and a bass constantly criss-cross so that every member has a chance at the melody, and at the same time the listeners cannot tell who sings what note. The method is similar to the scoring of the opening theme of the last movement of Tchaikovsky's *Pathétique* Symphony. Symphony-goers imagine that they hear the first violins passionately squeezing the melodious tune but a look at the score will convince them of their auditory illusion. The first violins carry only the notes Nos. 2, 4, and 6, and the second violins furnish the notes Nos. 1, 3, and 5 of the melody.

Barber shop quartets bear appropriately nostalgic names, such as Bartlesville Barflies, Flat Foot Four, Chord Busters, Melody Maulers, Frog Hollow Four, and Chromatic Canaries. There are even lady barber shop singers, of which two teams have distinguished themselves, the Barberettes of Peoria, Illinois, and the Charmerettes of Jackson, Michigan.

[272]

The bible of the SPEBSQSA is *Barber Shop Ballads* by Sigmund Spaeth, a collection of favorites of the sentimental era of American music. But later songs, even Broadway hits, may be included in a barber shop songfest. Only one air was banned for a time. It was the famous *Sweet Adeline,* which the SPEBSQSA felt was associated with immoderate drinking.

Henry Armstrong, the composer of *Sweet Adeline,* now a retired postal clerk, was greatly chagrined at the indictment of his song as a hymn of the drunks, and protested to the SPEBSQSA. The Society reconsidered the case and decided in favor of the composer's contention that the song was basically a love ballad. It was reclassified "sweet" and permitted for use at any barber-shop gathering, even in the dry states.

The history of *Sweet Adeline* is told in satisfying detail in the *New Yorker* of February 25, 1939. Additional sidelights are found in the interview with the composer published in the *Boston Traveler* of October 4, 1945. In this interview Armstrong stated that he was about seventeen years old when he dreamed up the tune. His lyricist was Richard Gerard, who had a line that he wanted to use in the song: "For you I pine." But he could not find a suitable rhyme. As the composer and the lyric writer were walking down a New York street, they saw a concert hall announcement, "Farewell Appearance of Adelina Patti." The possible rhyme, "Adeline-pine," struck them at once, and the song was born as we know it now.

Shakespeare on Boogie-Woogie

Shakespeare's prophetic soul anticipated even boogie-woogie. "How sour sweet music is when time is broke and no proportion kept."

From Ragtime to Re-Bop

In his best-seller, *The Hucksters,* Frederick Wakeman

[273]

tossess off such phrases as *"One O'clock Jump* ended with a millennial dissonance"; "the girl at the microphone finished her slow torchy interpretation of the song, and the orchestra segued into a hot wild jivey chorus."

Wakeman's novel was published in 1946, but the jive talk is already out of date. The latest thing is Re-bop, or according to some authorities, Be-bop. The essence of Re-bop or Be-bop is velocity, some of it reaching twenty notes a second, not in glissando but clearly articulated. One of the most eminent Be-bopists, Dizzie Gillespie, explains that the accents in Be-bop tend to fall on the upbeat while in swing it falls more on the downbeat. "Coupling this with its legato characteristic, you might get a phrase like ooBAHoo-BAHooBAH, while in swing it would be OO-bah, OO-bah, OO-bah."

According to the same authority, Re-bop, or Be-bop, comes from a two-note Be-bop tag that ends a musical phrase in popular band playing. The technique of Be-bop is particularly suitable to the modulatory style. It is *de rigueur* that the harmony should change very frequently, preferably several times within a single bar. This separates it from the harmonic scheme of boogie-woogie which is akin to the classical chaconne and requires a rigid formula of chord progressions, with a bass determining the course of both harmony and melody.

To quote *In the Groove* of December 1947:

"Be-bop isn't a new kind of music; it's just a new approach to improvising or writing jazz, with a broader harmonic basis and so many melodic and rhythmic subtleties all wrapped up in so much technical fluency that at first it dazzles and bewilders you."

Rudi Blesh writes on "Anatomy of Be-bop" in the New York *Herald Tribune* of December 14, 1947:

"Be-bop is a fantastic music that produces a peculiar nervous excitement. This excitement, deriving far more from

[274]

manner than from matter, tends after repeated objective hearings to recede, leaving operative only an unnerving effect. Phrased in incoherently broken rhythms, successive and disparate instrumental solos are projected against short 'modern' chordal sequences.

"Original Be-bop compositions eschew melodic development and, almost, any melody at all. The melody of non-Be-bop compositions is deliberately disintegrated, a tendency that began in earlier swing music. Musically speaking, some form of development must be substituted for the melodic if an art form is to result. Seeming *non-sequiturs* can be artfully combined to express an integrated idea, and this method, a psychological one, is common in modern music and literature. But the irrelevant parts of Be-bop are exactly what they seem; they add up to no such unity. Completely eclectic, drawing from African and Caribbean sources as well as from whole-tone impressionist harmony and dissonant Stravinsky harmony, Be-bop offers no coherent development of idea. A capricious and neurotically rhapsodic sequence of effects for their own sake, it comes perilously close to complete nonsense as a musical expression."

Going back in time, we find that boogie-woogie was born on December 23, 1938 when a concert of popular music was presented in Carnegie Hall, New York, featuring such classics as *Beat Me, Daddy, Eight to the Bar*. Before the advent of boogie-woogie, a major development in popular music was swing, which originated about 1935. The word "jive" arose at about the same time, as a corruption of jibe, meaning "to harmonize." According to Cab Calloway's *Hepster's Dictionary* (hepster being, of course, a hep cat, i.e., a swing musician); to jive means "to kid along, to blarney, stuff and things, also lingo or speech."

Jazz is the generic term that embraces swing, jive, and boogie-woogie. The origin of the word jazz is obscure. Its alleged derivation from the French *jaser* (to chat idly) is based on an unfounded surmise. But at least we know when and where jazz appeared for the first time.

On October 27, 1916, *Variety* added to the list of new musical phenomena, the "so-called jazz band." The qualifying epithet "so-called" indicates that jazz was a new word then. The spelling alternated between jas, jass, and jazz, which is another proof of the newness of the thing. The first jazz band played in New York in February 1917. After World War I, jazz made its way into Europe. On November 17, 1918, an American jazz band played for the first time at the Casino de Paris.

The impact of jazz and swing on the peaceful population was tremendous. The monstrousness of new music was denounced in the newspapers and in the pulpit. The headlines in the New York *Times* of May 30, 1938 announced to the horrified public: SWING BANDS PUT 23,400 IN FRENZY. . . . JITTERBUGS CAVORT AS 25 ORCHESTRAS BLARE IN CARNIVAL. Another headline read: PASTOR SCORES SWING AS DEBASING YOUTH. DECLARES IT SHOWS AN OBVIOUS DEGENERACY IN OUR CULTURE AND FROTHINESS OF AGE.

Sufferers from the iniquities of jazz and swing went to court for protection, but the modern judges were not always with them, as is suggested by the headlines in the New York *Times* story of June 30, 1938: 2 A.M. SWING MUSIC UPHELD BY COURT. RESIDENTS LOSE PLEA TO CURB 15-PIECE BAND. CAN'T SLEEP, THEY ASSERT. BUT MAGISTRATE RULES THAT LIVELY STRAINS DO NOT DISTURB THE PEACE.

William Allen White bemoaned the new dance music in an editorial for his Emporia *Gazette*:

"Fifty-five years ago and more, the writer hereof earned his first dollar playing for dances in Butler county, a young boy in his middle teens. We make no boasts but our outfit consisting of a blind fiddler, a competent cornetist, and this deponent at the cabinet organ or piano, as the case happened to be — used to go out in the country to farm dances. . . . In those prehistoric days, dance music was tuneful, something you could whistle. . . . And with a buxom armful of gently protesting but finally surrendering corn-fed, Walnut Valley gal in your arms, to the slow and formal threnody of the waltz, a fellow kind of felt he was of some importance.

"Now these details of the dance romantic . . . were as different from the dance we saw last night and the music was as different from that which squawked and shrieked and roared and bellowed in syncopated savagery, as if the two — the music and the dance of the old days — had been threaded and heard upon another planet."

Foreigners, particularly foreign musicians, love jazz. When George H. Mendelssohn, great-great-grandson of the composer, arrived in New York in 1941, he declared in an interview with the New York *Times* that he liked jazz very much. And Stravinsky was quoted in *Time* as saying in January, 1941: "I love swings. It is to the Harlem I go. It is so sympathetic to watch the Negro boys and girls dancing and to watch them eating the long, what is it you call them, frankfurters, no — hot dogs — in the long rolls. It is so sympathetic. I love all kinds of swings."

The manufacturers of swing music proved their adapability to the urgency of the times when they created Defense Swing. The New York *Times* of July 29, 1941, described the new step as follows:

"It is a swing dance of the fox-trot type, with no suggestion of the jitterbug. . . . It starts with a military action, with the young man moving toward his partner with a shooting gesture of his hands. The young woman throws up her hands in a momentary defense movement, and they start to dance."

Tempers really blew up when the swingsters invaded classical music and proceeded to jazzify Bach. On October 24, 1938. A. L. Dennis, president of the Bach Society of New Jersey, addressed a letter to the Federal Communications Commission, expressing his distress at hearing a jazz version of Bach's Toccata in D minor, in which "the beautiful fugue effects were destroyed by the savage slurring of the saxophone and the jungled discords of the clarinet." He proposed that "any radio station that violates the canon of decency by permitting the syncopating of classics, particularly Bach's music, be penalized by having its license suspended."

Naturally, no legal action could be taken against the mangling of Bach by unscrupulous jivesters. In fact, jazzification and sentimentalization of classics made a tremendous forward step in the 1940's. Tchaikovsky's Piano Concerto became *Tonight We Love*. Rachmaninoff's Second Piano Concerto furnished the theme for *Full Moon and Empty Arms*. A commentary on the trend was the appearance of a song entitled *Everybody's Making Money But Tchaikovsky*. Movies featuring lives of celebrated composers, hideously distorted, with mutilated and reorchestrated masterpieces by these composers, unexpectedly proved a big box-office attraction. In the wake of a Chopin movie called *A Song To Remember*, a popular song was made from Chopin's Polonaise in A-flat major, Op. 53 featured in the picture. The song, *Till the End of Time*, sold nearly a million and a half copies of sheet music, more than a million recordings, and was played for nineteen consecutive weeks on "The Hit Parade."

But there is nothing new under the sun. Popular songs were made from classical symphonies long before the advent of jazz. The second subject of the first movement of Tchaikovsky's Sixth Symphony was used in 1910, in the London revue, *Harp of Love*, with the following words:

> "When on this harp these notes are played, are played,
> True love shall come to man and maid, and maid."

Rachmaninoff's celebrated Prelude in C-sharp minor was converted into a ragtime number during World War I, and published under the name *Russian Rag*.

It all began with ragtime, which was the greatest bugbear of musical society in the dying days of the old century. An editorial entitled, "Degenerate Music," and published in the *Musical Courier* of September 13, 1899, commented:

"A wave of vulgar, filthy, and suggestive music has inundated the land. The pabulum of theater and summer hotel orchestras is 'coon music.' Nothing but ragtime prevails, and the cake-walk with its obscene posturings, its lewd gestures. . . . One reads with amazement and disgust of the historical and aristocratic names joining in this sex dance. Our children, our young men and women, are continually exposed to the contiguity, to the monotonous attrition of this vulgarizing music. It is artistically and morally depressing, and should be suppressed by press and pulpit. The 'coon song' must go."

In its issue of May 22, 1901, the *Musical Courier* carried a dispatch from Denver under the caption, "Ragtime Banished." It quoted the resolution adopted by the American Federation of Musicians pledging that its members "shall henceforth make every effort to suppress and discourage the playing and publishing of such musical trash by substituting the works of recognized and competent composers, thereby teaching the general public to appreciate a wholesome, decent, and intellectual class of music."

But even "recognized and competent composers" were often suspect of being contaminated by the pernicious rhythms of "coon songs." When the famous prima donna Nordica sang as an encore a song by Ethelbert Nevin, *Mighty Lak' a Rose*, at her Chicago recital, the music critic of the Chicago *Tribune* was nonplussed: "Five German lieder were sung and a 'coon song' was given as encore. To cavil at the taste that permits the giving of a 'coon song' as an encore to a group of German lieder

[279]

were to question Madame Nordica's sense of the fitness of things, and that no one would care to do."

Nordica tried to clarify matters by defending Nevin's status as a composer and at the same time condemning the new popular music. "No concert singer of any eminence sings popular music, and popular music in this country for several years has been the 'coon song" and the ragtime, and these are never sung at concerts in which artists of any standing whatever participate," she declared. "This particular song of Ethelbert Nevin's belongs to the best class of latter-day American composition, and is so distinct from 'coon song' or ragtime as to make it a surprise that anyone should identify it with such popular music."

But another American diva courageously accepted ragtime as a national art. The *Boston Herald* published an interview with her in its issue of November 16, 1901, with the headline: NEVADA LIKES RAGTIME. THE PRIMA DONNA ARRIVES HOME AND HOPES THEY WILL NOT SQUELCH THE NEW FAD.

There were individual voices in the press rising in favor of the maligned new rhythms and predicting a fruitful development of ragtime. Rupert Hughes philosophized in the *Musical Record* of Boston for April 1, 1899:

"If ragtime were called *tempo di raga* or *rague-temps*, it might win honors more speedily. If the word could be allied to the harmonic *ragas* of the East Indians, it would be more acceptable. What the derivation of ragtime is I haven't the faintest idea. The Negroes call their clog-dancing 'ragging' and the dance a 'rag.' There is a Spanish verb *raer* (to scrape), and a French naval term, *ragué* (scraped), both doubtless from the Latin *rado*.

"Ragtime will find its way gradually into the works of some great genius and will thereafter be canonized, and the day will come when the decadents of the next, the twentieth, century will revolt against it and will call it 'a hidebound, sapless, scholastic form, dead as its contemporaries, canon and fugue.' Meanwhile, it is young and unhackneyed, and throbbing with life. And it is racial.

Miss Myrta L. Mason, assistant librarian of the music department of the Library of Congress, published a scholarly letter in the *Musical Courier* of May 30, 1900, in which she suggested that ragtime may indeed be related to the *ragas* of India:

"If a bit that I have gleaned in the study of Hindustani music be of any assistance, I cheerfully quote the matter that seems to refer to the subject of ragtime:

Sal, or *Rag*, is a mode in music. There are six in number, expressing music, song, tune, anger, passion, love.

"This is but one link in the chain of musical matters, but if all will give of their knowledge in any way related to this word, there may at some time come conclusions based upon thorough understanding of the misuse of a perfected thing. Ragtime, as used today, appeals only to the baser instincts. Such ends come from originally high standards when abased."

By 1905 ragtime was definitely a part of the language. Learned societies were ready to discuss ragtime as an objective phenomenon. The monthly *Journal* of the International Music Society devoted considerable space to the analysis of ragtime in its issue of June 1905:

"Ragtime is briefly 'Bad Time,' and its rhythmic eccentricities were recently compared to the gait of a hurried mule amongst anthills. The comparison suggests the shocks in unexpected places which the cultured musician receives on listening to music in this immeasurably measureless measure, the musical language of the unutterably absurd.

"Its origin is in the peculiar verbal accentuation. The average eastener will say: 'I reckon *thar's* a *con*siderable and *extra*ordinary diffe*rence* between your circum*stances* and our *re*quirements.' This perverse shifting of the accent is largely due to a desire on the part of the speaker to make an immediate impression, and the mannerism has become a

[281]

habit. It is, of course, a bad form of exaggeration, and one of its results is seen in the variety of the American popular song. Ragtime is the outcome of rag-speech, a speech which preaches the gospel of force, which casts tradition, balance, beauty, elegance, and refinement to the winds, and which believes that more effect can be made by punching certain syllables into the brain of the listener. It becomes modified when allied with music, and is then largely content with shifting the strong accent from the first beat to the second beat of the bar. There is a cross-rhythm, with a kind of halting contrapuntal ornamentation in the accompaniment which sometimes brings a stress onto the fourth beat of the bar. . . . The phrases being no longer presented with regular and recurrent pulsations, give rise to a sense of disorder, which, combined with the emotional expression of the music, suggests an irresponsibility and a sensation of careless jollity agreeable to the tired or vacuous brain."

The morality of ragtime was a burning question as late as 1916. In January of that year Ivan Narodny wrote a letter to the *Evening Sun* saying that the rhythm of ragtime

"suggests the odor of the saloon, the smell of backyards and subways. Its style is decadent. It is music meant for the tired and materially bored minds. It is essentially obvious, vulgar, and yet shockingly strong for the reason that it ends fortissimo."

And the *Musical Courier* of February 1, 1917 quotes an unnamed authority to the effect that "ragtime is tonal drunkenness."

The chronology of popular American music can be tabulated in this way:

Ragtime	1899-1916
Jazz	1916-1935
Swing	1935-1938
Boogie-woogie	1938-1947
Re-bop	1947- ?

Of course, there has been overlapping of styles. Swing did not succeed jazz; it has modified the manner of jazz playing. Boogie-woogie is merely a peculiar technique adapted to legitimate jazz numbers. Re-bop signalizes the adoption of dissonant harmony and comes closest to the association of serious modern music with popular dance music. Through all these avatars, jazz has remained the generic name for popular rhythms, and jazz is likely to go down in music history as the dominant style of popular music in this century.

VI

THE CARNIVAL OF ANIMALS

Parental Ivories

A circus gag popular in the 1890's involved an elephant pianist. The master of ceremonies would announce that his trained elephant would play several tunes on the piano with his trunk. An upright piano was placed in the ring. The elephant walked slowly toward it, opened the lid and then recoiled in horror. The London *Million* related:

"His eye dilated with rage and fear. He lifted his trunk in the air, and with a wild scream of terror rushed out of the arena. After a flurry of excitement, the proprietor entered the ring and announced that, much to his regret, the performance had to be canceled. The fact was, he said, that the elephant had recognized in the keyboard of the piano a portion of the tusks of his long-lost mother who had fallen a prey to the ivory-hunters of Africa."

[284]

Animal Orchestra

When Philip II went to Brussels on a royal errand in 1549, he was greeted by an animal orchestra composed of villagers in the costumes of a bear, a wolf, or a sheep. In the orchestra were also included twenty live cats placed in twenty small boxes. Their tails extended through holes in the boxes and were attached to the organ keys. When a musician played the organ, the tails were pulled in appropriate harmony, and the cats emitted their contrapuntal meows. Without any knowledge of the royal precedent, a musician wrote, four centuries later, a piece entitled *Anatomy of Melancholy*, also requiring the services of a live cat similarly caged. But, mindful of the Society for Prevention of Cruelty to Animals, he never put the piece into actual performance.

Catano

Musical instruments employing live cats have been reported off and on in the musical journals. The description of one such instrument, appropriately named Catano, is found in the *Gazetta Musicale di Milano* for the year 1892:

"Catano consists of a wooden case with rows of narrow compartments into each of which is put a cat. The lower tones are produced by full grown animals and the highest by kittens. The heads are fastened in loopholes, and their tails are operated by a species of keyboard at the end of the case like that of a concert grand. When a key is put down, a cat's tail is pulled, and he begins to caterwaul loudly or otherwise according to the force with which the key is manipulated. To produce a common (cat) chord three keys in close position are struck and held down firmly unless a staccato effect is desired, in which case the opposite touch is applied. Anyone who has studied music can easily play the Catano, but for the purposes of accompaniment, especially in sacred music, the Catano is not considered particularly useful or appropriate."

The Cat Opera

Stories about cats used in musical compositions are reported from time to time ever since Scarlatti's cat walked across the keys of his harpsichord and gave him the inspiration for his *Katzenfuge*. But it was an American who first developed the idea of a cat concert with a whole orchestra of meowing cats participating in the harmony. At least so reports the estimable *Folio* in its issue of December 1869, under the heading, "Cat Opera or the First Opera Bouffe":

"In 1829 Curtis from Cincinnati decided to have a grand Philharmonic concert in which cats should take a prominent part. Experimenting on a few cats, he tried pinching their ears, sticking pins into them to develop the music. But the most certain way was to apply the back of a case knife across the tail which never failed to elicit a note. Curtis employed Johnson, who could build organs and perhaps make one to accompany the cats' voices. He ordered six dozen cats, and accommodations were prepared for them in boxes.

"Johnson continued building the organ, and an adaptation of the extra blade keys to the cats' tails. He arranged the singers in narrow boxes which guarded against clawing by having four holes in the bottom through which the legs protruded. The tails were enclosed in tubes provided with longitudinal slats, across which the blade keys worked. These keys were connected with those of the organ, so that the keys and their appropriate voices should be in unison. In about a month, Curtis had a complete choir ranging from the kitten of two months to the venerable toms. At the completion of the organ, there were a few rehearsals, and then posters announcing the performance were plastered in various places:

CURTIS CAT HARMONICON!
GRAND VOCAL
and
INSTRUMENTAL CONCERT!
FORTY-EIGHT CATS!

"The house was crowded by the boatmen. The curtain

rose and disclosed to view the Cat Harmonicon — two rows of cat-heads, two dozen each glared with their lustrous green and yellow eyes at the audience. Little ruffles were around their necks, miniature music stands with books and candles were in front of them.

"The first number was *Auld Lang Syne*, which Johnson began. The cats were excited to fury by the uproarious audience and the severe pounding of their tails.

"They forgot all lessons, paid no attention to time, tune, rhythm, or reason, but squealed, mewed, yelled, spat, and phizzed in the madness of pain and terror, drowning the sound of the organ in the unearthly tornado of caterwauling. Never was an audience so completely enchanted. Yells of laughter burst from the men. They stamped with all their might and the platform came down. Curtis freed his cats. They darted in every direction, adding to the confusion. There was a cry of 'Fire!' The engine came and poured a fresh deluge of water through the window drenching the crowd immediately. Peace was restored and everyone came tumbling pell-mell down the stairs."

More Cats

The most fantastic of all cat stories is found in the *Musical Courier* of August 16, 1893. It begins with strange noises emanating from a ramshackle house on the East Side in New York. One day a cat was seen coming down from the upper floor of the building, and at another time a dozen or more cats came rushing from the front door. The cats were all black, and the colored porter who was sweeping the halls of the building sounded an alarm. A reporter was sent by the New York *Journal* to investigate. The *Musical Courier* reports the rest of the story:

"Waiting till dark when the noises were said to be heard, the reporter cautiously entered the suspected house. Going up the rickety stairs he finally reached the top and settled down to await events. Soon he heard a low and mournful wail. Gradually it increased till the air was vibrated in a manner that made his hair stand on end. There really seemed to be some tune involved, something that sounded like *Home, Sweet Home.* Then it drifted into Wagner, and symphonies of a wild and weird nature made long trips in the atmosphere.

"It must be mortal; no one from the next world would ever come here to play Wagner in a garret. Finally a ray of light became distinguishable, evidently from a keyhole at the end of the hall. The scribe determined to knock. Advancing, he rapped loudly thrice — the strange melody ceased; another tap on the door, and from within a voice exclaimed:

" 'Who vas dose?'

" 'Open the door!'

" 'Vat you vant?'

"The reporter hazarded a shot and said he wanted to see the machine. This time the door was cautiously opened and a queer figure demanded:

" 'Who told you I got a machine?'

"After some parleying, the reporter was admitted. The room was of fairly good size, with low ceiling, windows heavily curtained; it was lighted by tallow candles. Suddenly a row of lights, like phosphorus, became visible at the other end of the room. 'That's my machine,' said the inventor, as he pointed to it. Crossing the floor, he drew back an immense portière and it was then the reporter beheld the strangest sight his eyes had ever looked upon.

The old man, with white flowing hair and clad in the costume of a century ago, almost patriarchal in mien except for a cruel look about his deep-set eyes and ashy face, sat grinding out tunes from an organ made of cats.

"After rendering several selections from Beethoven, the inventor left his infernal machine and, rummaging around in a corner, brought out a jug of beer and some cheese. He turned a pint or so of milk into a little trough running through the organ for the cats. He said he never let the cats out of the organ after he got them in. He had done so once, but they all seemed to have a grudge against him and had nearly torn off all his clothes by a general assault. His arrangement was very simple: a large case like a church organ; in this, a row of stalls or boxes; in each box a pin sticking up through the bottom connecting with a keyboard, so that when the cats were in their compartments and he wanted a tune, all he had to do was to touch the keys. It had taken him a long time to get the scale of cats, but he had finally succeeded. At the time of the reporter's visit he was trying further to get some of the more advanced cats to sing in concert outside the organ."

Sharkey and the Radio

Trained seals have their troubles with copyrighted tunes just as crooners do. At the Southern Sportsman Show broadcast from New Orleans on March 6, 1941, a trained seal named Sharkey was to perform on a set of horns the tune *Where the River Shannon Flows*. There was a feud at the time between the radio networks and the American Society of Composers, Authors, and Publishers, and the ASCAP lawyers would not permit the seal to perform on the air. Unfortunately, this was the only tune that Sharkey knew how to play. The performance had to be canceled. It is not known whether Sharkey was given his fee: a couple of small fish, which trained seals receive as a reward for a musical performance.

Monkey in Four Hands

An unidentified newspaper clipping circa 1888 reports this incredible story. A music teacher in Kentucky taught a monkey to play the piano. The monkey developed such virtuosity that he could not only play piano duets in four hands with the aid of his four paws, but also learned to turn the pages with his tail. The dispatch said that the human pupils of the Kentucky professor could not even remotely emulate the monkey pianist.

Love Song in B-flat

The Curator of Reptiles of the Brookfield Zoo in Chicago was frustrated in his effort to induce the male alligator to mate. As a desperate measure, he hired a quartet of four French horns to play B-flat in unison, which is the nearest approximation of the alligator's mating call. The musicians blew hard and long, but nothing happened. The alligator remained as sleazily frigid as ever.

Seventy-seventh Member of the Symphony

Singing birds have for a long time held a place of honor in program music. Beethoven used ersatz birds, flute for the nightingale, oboe for the quail, and clarinet for the cuckoo. Respighi realistically introduced a phonograph recording of a real nightingale in the symphonic poem, *Pines of Rome*. Wagner and many other composers have invariably selected the flute for their bird parts. But in the summer of 1947 a live mocking-bird spontaneously joined the National Symphony Orchestra of Washington, D. C. It perched on a lamp post or a flagpole atop the bandstand, and whenever there was a vocal soloist, the bird joined her in brilliant trills. And it became positively ecstatic during the performance of Prokofiev's symphonic fairy tale, *Peter and the Wolf,* in which the bird is represented by the flute. The National Symphony Orchestra officially elected the mocking-bird as a seventy-seventh member, on an amateur basis, of course.

Opera Horse

The most famous operatic animal was Anna, the white mare, who died at the Pegasus Club, Rockleigh, New Jersey, on March 22, 1940, at the advanced age of thirty-nine. Anna was the horse that pulled the chariot of Rhadames in the scene of his triumphant entrance as conqueror in the Metropolitan presentation of *Aïda*. The legend had it that Anna had a high standard of musical appreciation, and that once when the tenor got off pitch, she emitted a couple of critical neighs. Anna appeared with Caruso, Gigli, and other famous singers. She also had a Hollywood career and was Rudolph Valentino's horse in that celebrated silent movie, *The Sheik*.

Symphony at an Animal Farm

After a performance in London of Prokofiev's Fifth Symphony, a caustic reviewer pointed out that the symphony was finished at the Soviet summer estate for composers, which accommodates 66 cows, 8,000 chickens, 135 pigs, and 20 composers.

Porco-Forte

Spike Jones, the most original orchestrator in Tinpanland, has included three live pigs in one of his band arrangements. So states the authoritative *In the Groove*. But Spike had a predecessor. The *Musical World* of November 14, 1839, reports the creation of a new instrument, the Porco-Forte:

"The Porco-Forte is the name of a new musical instrument said to have been invented in Cincinnati, of course. It is a long box, divided into compartments, one for each note, for as many octaves as may be wished. Into each division a pig is placed, and the tails of the porkers run through holes in the side of the box, arranged like keys of a piano. The tails are pinched by a sort of spring and lever machinery, and the effort is said to be delightful. If the pigs are well selected, they will wear about three years without tuning."

His Master's Voice

The picture of a fox-terrier attentively listening to the voice from the loudspeaker of an old-fashioned phonograph is familiar to everyone. The terrier was a real dog. His name was Nipper, and he belonged to Francis Barraud, the artist who painted the picture. The story goes that the dog posed for the picture naturally, being attracted by the talking machine and making a stance before the horn. Barraud sold the painting to the Gramophone Company of London for their trademark, and in 1901 the picture was passed to the Victor Company, which was an affiliate of the Gramophone Company. Nipper has appeared in Victor advertisements ever since.

Cows, Pigs, and Jazz

It seems that farm animals prefer jazz. Experiments conducted at milking time in New Zealand dairy farms in the summer 1947 prove that cows increase production when jazz records are played. The cows fidgeted and squirmed in their stalls at the sound of Mozart and Beethoven, and their milk production went down.

Pigs, too, thrive when popular music is played. In July 1947, 2,500 pigs were exposed to radio jazz at a New Jersey farm. They put on fat much faster. Their metabolism was especially pepped up when Bing Crosby's recordings were broadcast over the farm loudspeaker system.

British farm animals possess superior taste. The British Broadcasting Corporation received a letter from a radio fan in Surrey who wrote: "We find that our cows give their highest milk yields to the strains of eighteenth-century music, such as Haydn's quartets. Swing produces a definite kick-the-bucket tendency."

VII

VERSE AND WORSE

Catgut

Oliver Herford, the poet, puts the subject of catgut into some doggerel:

"The politest musician that ever was seen
Was Montague Meyerbeer Mendelssohn Green.
So extremely polite he would take off his hat
Whenever he happened to meet with a cat.

" 'It's not that I'm partial to cats,' he'd explain;
'Their music to me is unspeakable pain.
There's nothing that causes my flesh so to crawl
As when they perform a G-flat caterwaul.

" 'Yet I cannot help feeling in spite of their din
When I hear at a concert the first violin
Interpret some exquisite thing of my own
If it were not for the catgut I'd never be known.

" 'And so, when I bow as you see to a cat,
It isn't to her that I take off my hat;
But to fugues and sonatas that possibly hide
Uncomposed in her — well, in her tuneful inside!' "

Perturbed Spirits

Punch, in its issue of November 1918, published a
poetic spirit message from the unhappy composers of
certain celebrated piano pieces:

"O that Melody in F
How I wish that I were deaf!
Once I thought it rather fine,
Said the ghost of Rubinstein.

"Cease your dolorous self-pity,
For your cheap and tawdry ditty,
'Twas for groundlings only made,
Quick responded Chopin's shade.

"But it is the worst of crimes
When each day a dozen times
My C minor Prelude's mangled
And its lovely chords are jangled.

"Thus the ghosts with futile wailing
Went on impotently railing
While the player, quite at ease,
Pounded the unhappy keys."

Prodigious!

Prodigies here and prodigies there
Prodigies, prodigies everywhere.
Neat little nimble prodigy girls
Short frock, stockings, and corkscrew curls.
Pert little priggish prodigy boys
Long hair, knickers, and lots of noise.
Prodigy concerts at half-past eight,
Prodigies stay up far too late.
Prodigies taking by storm the town
Sketching an octave up and down,
Swelling fugues with a massive bass,
Fingers all in their proper place.
Firework fantasies, oh, so smart!
Chopin, Schubert, and old Mozart.
Some with Beethoven making free,
Wagner as easy as ABC.

Prodigy A deserves a medal
For skill in the use of the softer pedal
Prodigy B should have a prize
For her manner of using her hazel eyes.
Prodigies playing quick or slow,
Piano, Forte, FORTISSIMO
Little females and tiny males,
All of them thumping out their scales.
Little fellows in socks and shorts,
Beating their Broadwood pianofortes.
Little maidens in frill and frock,
Scraping away like one o'clock.
Little and clever — but why proceed?
Basta, basta! agreed, agreed!
Prodigies are such an awful bore
We've enough and too many and don't want more."

(Punch, 1893).

The Ass and the Flute

O'er a green field of grass
It just now came to pass
There did stray a young ass
  Accidentally.
And in this ass's way
I have also to say

There a little flute lay,
    Accidentally.
Well, the flute he espied,
He smelled it and pried,
And into it sighed,
    Accidentally.
Now the air in the flute
Did not pass through it mute,
Although breathed by a brute,
    Accidentally.
Without compass or chart
Without canons of art,
Thus an ass played his part,
    Accidentally.

(Boston *Musical Gazette*, July 1847)

Wagner But Loud

Wagner was definitely too loud for our grandparents.
Even the mellifluous *Lohengrin* caused acute inflamma-
tion of eardrums among the listeners of the Tory 1880's.
The following poem appeared in the July 1884 issue of
the *Musical Herald:*

"Yes, I was at the festival
    I tell you what, my boys,
That Wagner beats the rest of 'em
    For piling up the noise.

"I heard them all in 'Low and Green' —
    One of Old Wag's best plays.
You never saw such mixing up,
    They sang all kinds of ways.

"First, Elsa struck out on a tune
    That seemed a decent song;
But then the brasses tripped her up
    And made it end all wrong.

"The baritone came in just then
    With one tremendous howl;
But all the fiddles put him out
    And it was called a 'foul.'

[297]

"And then the tenor sailed in next
    And 'held the forte' awhile
But soon the drum rolls drowned *him* out —
    It would have made you smile.

"Of course things couldn't go on so,
    The leader interfered.
He shook his stick and made them stop,
    And then the people cheered.

"I sat there for three mortal hours
    Waiting to hear a song,
But all I heard was drums and horns
    And one loud hotel gong.

"I wouldn't sit through that again
    If I could get in free;
For though the music may be good
    It's much too rich for me."

The Music Columnist

How many years I have gone on
And gained a lasting fame
By grinding out a little pun
On each composer's name.

I spoke of slipping on my 'Bach,'
Of being 'Moz 'eart broken,'
And I could 'Handel' any joke
Which Haydn't best be spoken.

And when the puns were broken up
I tried another way;
With Wagner and a boiler shop
I made my columns gay.

So I will duet nevermore
And trio with great pain
To strike a higher path in art
Nor sink solo again.

(*Musical Herald*, February 1885)

Musical Names

The following poem published in the *Musical Standard* of January 15, 1870, contains, hidden among common English words, the names of Beethoven, Heller, Haydn, Gluck, Handel, Cramer, Arne, Hummel, and Clementi:

"I love the BEE THO' VENomous his sting
Trust that arranger, HE'LL ERadicate all faults.
While the sun shines make your HAY DNieper river,
    toll away.
With glee he sanG: 'LUCKy I am!'
Aim higH AND ELevate all musical taste.
No master can CRAM ERudition into a backward pupil.
Near thee, deAR NEar thee, there lurk I,
Where bees HUM MELodious airs close by!
Is it a miraCLE MEN TIre of monotonous chants?'"

Epigram on the Perfect Fourth

"A perfect fourth? cries Tom. Whoe'er gave birth
To such a riddle, should stick a fiddle
On his numbskull ring until he sing
A scale of perfect fourths from end to end.
Was ever such a noddy? Why, almost everybody
Knows that not e'en one thing perfect is on earth —
How then can we expect to find a perfect fourth?"

(*Musical World*, 1863)

Short Music Histories

The following limericks are found in the *Musical Herald* of 1888:

"An ancient musician named Gluck
The manner Italian forsuck;
    He fought with Piccinni
    Gave way to Rossini
You'll find all his views in a buck."

"Another composer, named Haydn
The field of Sonata would waydn;
    He wrote the *Creation*

[299]

Which made a sensation
And this was the work which he dayd'n."

"A German composer named Brahms
Caused in music the greatest of quahms;
His themes so complex
Some people would vex
From symphonies down to the psahms."

"There was a composer named Liszt
Who from writing could never desizst;
He made Polonaises
Quite worthy of praises,
And now that he's gone, he is miszt."

"There was a composer named Auber
Who seldom was somber or sauber.
Yet he held aloof
From the opera bouffe,
But he lived past life's golden Octauber."

"The noble composer named Franz
Did his best German songs to enhanz;
He settled in Halle
Way down in a Valle
As old age began to advanz."

"A German composer named Groun
When Frederick came to the Croun
Composed a motette
Which, don't you forgette,
Was rather too good to put doun."

"That eminent Frenchman, Halévy
Ne'er fought in the army or nevy.
Yet musical work
He never would shork;
He always ate turkey with grevy."

"There was a composer named Spohr
Whose works were a hundred or mohr.
His great work *Jessonda*
Long time was a wonda,
But now his successes are o'hr."

"And lastly we speak about Weber
Who wrote without trouble or leber
    He ne'er was pedantic
    But always romantic
And Meyerbeer oft was his neber."

The following polylimerick appeared in the January 1884 issue of the *Musical Herald*.

"Though full of great musical lore
Old Bach is a terrible bore
    A fugue without a tune
    He thought was a boon
So he wrote seventeen thousand or more."

"I don't think that ever I swore so
As when I first heard a Liszt *Morceau*
    Chromatic suspensions
    And other dissensions
Are what people say they adore so."

"When a tune is with sugar o'erladen
Just the thing for a boarding-school maiden
    With sweet viols and flute
    Then beyond all dispute
It's some composition by Haydn."

"When all of the brasses are sturdy
When the tune's like an old hurdy-gurdy
    When the cornet's turned loose
    And the drum plays the deuce
It's all operatic — by Verdi."

The following are from the *Musical World*, 1863:

"There was a composer called Balfe
Who wrote much and so well that if halfe
    What he wrote was his own
    He would stand quite alone
That prolific composer called Balfe."

"There was an old 'fiddle' called Joachim
Who resolving in wedlock to yoke him
    Came across Miss Schneeweiss

When he in a trice
Transmuted her into Frau Joachim."

"*Il y avait un jeune vieux Rossini*
Dont le règne ne s'ra jamais fini
Le monde verra renaître
Sans cesse le maître
En fêtera le bambin Rossini."

"*Es war ein Altmeister von Meyerbeer.*
Wär's irgendwo ein Theater leer,
Er würd es erfüllen
Mit Leute und Stillen,
Sie alle zu hören von Meyerbeer."

Off Pitch

"On the beautiful slopes of Lugano
Dwelt a girl with a gorgeous soprano;
But the tragical thing
Was she never could sing
In the key that was played on the piano."

"There was a young man of Rangoon
Who thought he could play the bassoon.
There was always a hitch
When he fell from the pitch
For he never would keep to the tune."

"There was a young man named DeL&
Who played the bass horn in the b&.
He made such a blast
That as he went past
He blew all the fruit off a st&."

"There was a young miss of Missouri
Whose teacher got into a fury
Because she preferred
Of all music she'd heard
R. Wagner's *Tannhäuser* potpourri."

"There was a young man in Bombay
Who tried on the cornet to play.
High C he could reach
But it broke with a screech
And the neighbors they all moved away."

"A fellow once played clarinet
  In a manner which made people fret
    Till some suffering souls
    Poured glue in the holes
  And said, 'Stop it, and don't you forget.' "

"There was an esthetic young fellow
  Who played on the violoncello
    When he drew his long bow
    O'er the bass string, Oh!
  It seemed like a bullock's loud bellow."

"There was a young woman from Rio
  Who tried to play Handel's Trio.
    Her skill was so scanty
    She played it Andante
  Instead of Allegro con brio."

"There was a young woman named Hatch
  Who was fond of the music of Batch.
    It isn't as fussy
    As that of Debussy —
  Sit down, I'll play you a snatch."

Instrumental Nostalgia

"The oboe player has a long, pale cheek
  His lips are thin, his visage lank and weak
  His hair is curly; on his sad, pale face
  'Merit unrecognized' you clearly trace;
  Crafty and sly, he loves a quiet beer,
  His instrument above all things to him is dear.

[303]

"The player on the clarinet has some pretense, you see.
He is conscious of his merits and full of melody.
His temper is hasty, his heart is kind and warm,
He has a secret passion which does not do him harm.
You may always know the lodging of his reedy instrument;
Because the neighbors all hang out a notice: Rooms to rent.

"The horn player in his heart of hearts
Loves the long convoluted bell-mouthed horn;
Yet often he is doomed to play the cornet parts,
An instrument he holds in deepest scorn.
He blames the young composers of the day.
He thinks that none of them can treat him right;
He shuts his eyes when other brasses play,
And cannot hear a trombone in his sight.
He is stoutly built, somewhat inclined to be fat
And plays at ten-pins in an old soft hat.

"He blows for parleys and flags of truce.
Such is the trumpet's martial use,
No man in the band is so proud as he
When he blows the double levee.

You seem retiring, bassoon, and shy.
Yet there is a twinkle in your eye;
Your eyes are bright, your looks are gay
When you have a solo bar to play.
You play it with skill, and play it with care
And look so nice with your thin gray hair.

"O blower on the straight long flute!
You are eloquent even when you are mute!
Your hair is groomed, your eyes are mild.
You love your candy like a small child.

"The trombonist when playing looks savage and severe;
He loves the works of Wagner and the scores of Meyerbeer;
He loves the drums and trumpets; his head is always bent;
He has lots of execution and little sentiment.

(*Music*, March 1882)

[304]

Ode to an Old Fiddle

From the *Musical World* of London (1834);

THE POOR FIDDLER'S ODE TO HIS OLD FIDDLE

Torn
Worn
Oppressed I mourn
B a d
S a d
Three-quarters mad
Money gone
Credit none
Duns at door
Half a score
Wife in lain
T w i n s a g a i n
Others ailing
Nurse a railing
Billy hooping
Betsy crouping
Besides poor Joe
With fester'd toe.
Come, then, my Fiddle,
Come, my time-worn friend,
With gay and brilliant sounds
Some sweet tho' transient solace lend,
Thy polished neck in close embrace
I clasp, whilst joy illumines my face.
When o'er thy strings I draw my bow,
My drooping spirit pants to rise;
A lively strain I touch — and, lo!
I seem to mount above the skies.
There on Fancy's wing I soar
Heedless of the duns at door;
Oblivious all, I feel my woes no more;
But skip o'er the strings,
As my old Fiddle sings,
"Cheerily oh! merrily go!
"PRESTO! good master,
"You very well know
"I will find Music,
"If you will find bow,
"From E, up in alto, to G, down below."
Fatigued, I pause to change the time
For some *Adagio*, solemn and sublime.
With graceful action moves the sinuous arm;
My heart, responsive to the soothing charm,
Throbs equably; whilst every health-corroding care
Lies prostrate, vanquished by the soft mellifluous air.
More and more plaintive grown, my eyes with tears o'erflow,
And Resignation mild soon smooths my wrinkled brow.
Reedy Hautboy may squeak, wailing Flauto may squall,
The Serpent may grunt, and the Trombone may bawl;
But, by Poll,* my old Fiddle's the prince of them all.
Could e'en Dryden return, thy praise to rehearse,
His Ode to Cecilia would seem rugged verse.
Now to thy case, in flannel warm to lie,
Till call'd again to pipe thy master's eye.

* Apollo.